MARKS OF WAR

This is a graceful and meticulously researched book ... on the psychological effects of war trauma. The richness of its material is exceptional ... [Raftery's] work spans the lifetimes of the men described in his book – from youth, through military service, on to what is often a psychologically troubled old age. In this book, we discover the lives of flesh and blood men, not clinical abstractions.

Professor Allan Young, Anthropology Department, McGill University

* * * * *

This work is an original, reflective and nuanced analysis of the long-term impact of war. It sheds considerable light on the diverse ways in which war experiences have shaped the lives of those men who returned from the Second World War. It is an excellent study, of considerable insight, and an exemplary piece of scholarship.

Associate Professor Joy Damousi, Department of History, University of Melbourne

* * * * *

Accounts of the effects of war on the minds of men have been the domain of both considerable scientific study and some of the greatest works of literature. This book represents a bridge, capturing the humanistic elements of the suffering and memories of Australian veterans of the New Guinea campaign in World War Two. It integrates the narratives of men's lives and horror with the growing and changing knowledge about the nature of post-traumatic stress. For any person wishing to understand the impact and scars of war, this book is an important contribution.

Professor Sandy McFarlane, Department of Psychiatry, University of Adelaide

John Raftery has been a practising psychologist since 1975.
He has had a long-term interest in the impact of traumatic events. For over ten years he has been researching the effects of war service on veterans and their families in Australia.
This book is based on research he conducted for his PhD thesis
at the University of Adelaide.

Marks of War

War Neurosis and the Legacy of Kokoda

John Raftery

LYTHRUM PRESS

ADELAIDE

First published by
Lythrum Press
128 Hindley Street
Adelaide
South Australia 5000

April 2003

Typeset in 10/13 Galliard
Designed and produced by Michael Deves
Cover artwork by Julianne Pulford
Printed and bound by Hyde Park Press

National Library of Australia
Cataloguing-in-Publication entry

Raftery, John, 1941-
Marks of war: war neurosis and the legacy of Kokoda

Bibliography
Includes index
ISBN 0 9579960 2 0

1. Veterans - Mental health - Australia. 2. World War, 1939-1945 - Psychological aspects. 3. World War, 1939-1945 - Veterans - Australia. 4. Post-traumatic stress disorder - Patients - Interviews. 5. Veterans - Australia - Interviews. I. Title.

362.2042208697

Contents

Acknowledgements

I am deeply indebted to a remarkable band of men and women: the veterans, their partners and families who allowed me to enter their world in my fumbling attempts to understand their experience. I was very much encouraged by the support of veterans' associations, particularly those of the 2/27th and 39th Battalions.

Apart from veterans and their families, a number of other people have supported me in what has been a long and sometimes difficult journey.

I owe special thanks to my partner, Judith, who has witnessed my many struggles with this book, has always believed in me, and been my most constructive critic and editor. Although they passed away before they knew of my research and achievements, I was sustained by the memory of my father, Bill, whose story of World War One was mostly lost, and my mother, Zita, who probably knew more than she shared. My brother and sisters have wondered what I was doing but have always encouraged me.

I completed the original research and the thesis on which this book is based within the Department of Public Health at the University of Adelaide, with the support of a Post Graduate Scholarship. My work was informed by the wisdom and guidance of my supervisors Dr Neville Hicks and Professor Ian John, and I acknowledge them both for strongly supporting a piece of research that did not fit neatly into the academic mould.

I want to acknowledge the support of many friends and colleagues, particularly those in the Australasian Society for Traumatic Stress Studies, who have encouraged me and offered constructive feedback on my work. I also acknowledge the assistance of the RSL and the Department of Veterans' Affairs.

Illustrations from the Australian War Memorial collection are identified by 'AWM' and the negative number.

To William George Raftery,
who survived the Great and Terrible War,

and

to my sons Simon and David,
whom I hope will never be involved in such mayhem.

AWM 013845

Foreword

To those who have been exposed to the horror of war, and especially the front-line soldier, the cessation of hostilities brings an indescribable feeling of relief, along with a sense of disbelief that he has survived while some of his comrades have not. Many of the survivors have been wounded, some more than once. To show signs of weakness under extreme stress is to admit to fear, and so feelings are suppressed. Most traumatic experiences are rarely talked about.

Some ten years ago John Raftery commenced an in-depth study of veterans who had experienced traumatic incidents during their war years. His purpose was to record these experiences and their effects, and he interviewed many veterans and their families. The result is a book that must surely be of importance and interest to all people working with veterans of war, and with the effects of trauma in general. There are so few books that relate to this area that this is a valuable addition, and hopefully it will encourage other professionals to devote time to this work.

Initially there was some tentativeness about the interviews – people were hesitant to discuss their feelings and experiences. This was slowly dispelled as John established relationships with the people, and returned on many occasions for further talks and clarification. His gentle and patient understanding of how the interviewees felt helped them to relax and share their confidences with him. John has gained credibility, and the people involved have trusted him with their innermost thoughts and feelings; this confidence was strengthened by the way in which John recorded his work. Interviewees' confidentiality has been respected at all stages over the years.

This work has given a 'voice' to the experiences and feelings of many veterans, their wives and children. This voice has the capacity to bring awareness and understanding – and hopefully peace of mind – to many other families who have been in this situation.

As an original member of the 2/27th Australian Infantry Battalion who served in all the Battalion's campaigns, including the Western Desert, Syria, Kokoda Track, Gona, Ramu, Markham Valley and Borneo, I feel privileged to commend this book to those who wish to have a deeper understanding of the problems faced by returning veterans and their families over the years, regardless of where or when the conflict took place.

R.G. Baldwin
SX 2905

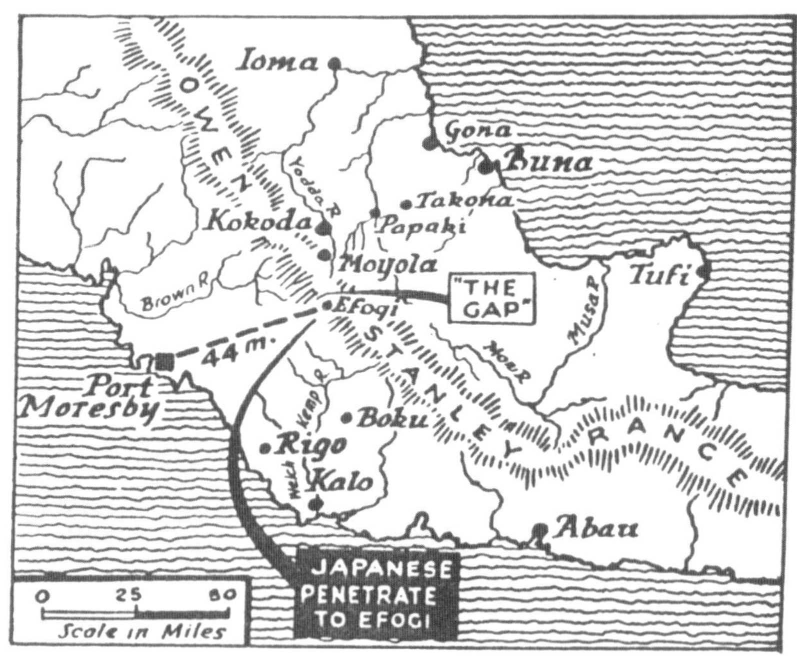

A contemporary newspaper map of the Kokoda campaign.
Sun, *11 September 1942*

Preface

Marked Men

It is just over sixty years since 1942, the most critical year for Australia in World War Two, the year of the Kokoda campaign. When Japan attacked Pearl Harbor on 7 December 1941, the war became a more direct threat to Australia than it had been to that point. Fighting in the Malayan campaign, which began when the Japanese invaded Kota Bharu on the night of 6/7 December 1941 and lasted a short but fiercely fought two months, Australians were among the first to experience the brutality of battle and imprisonment under the Japanese. Following the fall of Singapore on 15 February 1942 the majority of the 22,000 Australian men and women who became POWs were taken prisoner by the Japanese, and more followed on the islands of the Indonesian archipelago and Papua and New Guinea. In Java, for example, most of the 2/3rd Machine Gun Battalion, which had distinguished itself in the Middle East, was captured by the advancing Japanese when the unit was diverted to Java without its armoury. On 18 February, three days after the fall of Singapore, Darwin, on mainland Australia, was bombed. In the following weeks the Japanese invaded the Dutch East Indies (now Indonesia), and by March 1942 were taking over East New Britain and had landed on mainland New Guinea.

Throughout this book 'New Guinea' will be used to refer to the whole of the Papua and New Guinea regions. Port Moresby and Milne Bay, two of the major sites for Australian troops, were on the southern or Papuan side of the mainland. The main outer islands of Bougainville and East and West New Britain will be referred to as separate regions. Papua New Guinea, which includes the mainland and outer islands, including New Ireland, Bougainville and East New Britain as well as the smaller islands, was not incorporated as a nation until 1976.

In January 1942 the Japanese invaded Rabaul, a northern island of New Guinea, and routed the 2/22nd Battalion and part of the New Guinea Volunteer Rifles. At least 158 of the survivors of that invasion were tied to coconut palms and bayoneted on the beach at Tol Plantation.[1] Survivors of the invasion were among the 1,035 Australian prisoners aboard the Japanese prisoner transport *Montevideo Maru* which was torpedoed by the USS *Sturgeon* heading out of Rabaul on 1 July 1942.

At the fall of Singapore most of the AIF was still deployed in the Middle East or on its way home, and militia units including the 39th and 53rd Battalions, mainly comprising young men with no battle experience, inadequate weaponry and limited training, were sent to stem the Japanese tide. They were later joined by units from the AIF including the 21st Brigade. For hundreds of young Australian men in these units this was the beginning of a critical chapter in their life story.

Some of these men were still in service on 2 September 1945 when General Sir Thomas Blamey co-signed the Instrument of Surrender of the Japanese on board the USS *Missouri* in Tokyo Bay on behalf of the Australian government, less than a month after the first atomic bombs destroyed Hiroshima and Nagasaki. The surrender marked the end of the 1,364 days of World War Two in the Pacific.[2]

On that day, Australian troops who were deployed or imprisoned throughout the south-west Pacific area, in places like Borneo, Papua, New Guinea, Bougainville, Solomon Islands and the various prison camps in South East Asia and Japan, began their repatriation. Many troops had already returned because of illness, wounds, mental breakdown or because they had completed their five years of service. A few remained after the surrender in peacekeeping roles in occupied territories where Japanese troops were being repatriated. This book is about one group of those Australian troops, the soldiers who survived the now-famous battles along the Kokoda Trail and the north coast of New Guinea.[3]

How did the stress of battle shape the lives of the men of Kokoda? The title of this book, *Marks of War*, was inspired by a poem written by Stirling Ashenden, 2/27th Battalion, a survivor of the New Guinea campaigns in World War Two, who wrote of how the war left its mark on every household.[4] 'Marked' is an appropriate description of the impact on the body and soul of the harrowing experiences of battle. The marks that the veterans bore in later life were not always of shame, nor were they signs of enduring pain. Some men wore them with pride because the marks set them aside from ordinary men. They had endured hardships and threat and many were wounded; they had looked death in the eye and survived. But some were marked for life by experiences that were seared into their psyche. These men were badly scarred inside and spent much of their lives searching for healing. Others bore their scars stoically and silently, choosing to get on with their lives, do their civil duty and hide their marks of war.

The experience of war provides a rich and complex site in which to explore the merging of personal histories and the history of ideas relating to stressful experience. The lives of a particular group of World War Two veterans is the starting point of this work, which is based on an intensive study of the lives of 65 men who fought on the Kokoda Trail and in other associated battles in 1942. The original study was submitted as a doctoral thesis. Rather than follow the path of many previous researchers, who have mostly studied combatants with measures of pathology and psychiatric diagnosis, I chose to rely primarily on personal narratives to construct their life stories. In telling their stories I have gone beyond the individual narrative to explore the larger history in which these veterans were participants. This book weaves a tapestry of the life stories of these men into the broader landscape of the history of war neurosis and ideas about war-related stress. These social constructions influenced the way men dealt with their marks of war.

This has allowed me to step outside the current dominant practice and theoretical paradigm in which the personal experience of the distress arising out of trauma is construed as a psychiatric illness. I can thus provide a more comprehensive account of the long-term effects of war through the more personalised world of the life story. This is a significant contribution to scholarship since the public discourse surrounding the two World Wars has carefully suppressed any serious exploration of the negative effects of war.[5]

My study of the lives of veterans was framed against my own experience. My father, William George Raftery, was born in 1894 and died in 1982, and survived over three years in the battlefield in World War One. He was an ordinary bloke who went away and 'did his bit', did not receive a commission and was issued with service medals when he returned. Men like him made no great fuss but got on with their lives and 'put those years behind them' when they came home. Apart from a few who wrote about their experiences, they said little about what had happened or how the war had affected them.[6]

William sailed for Egypt on 2 May 1916 and returned to Australia via Southampton on 12 May 1919. His pay book records 1,199 days of service. He spent time away from the front in London, Scotland, Ireland and parts of France. William and his brother Jack, who had left Australia in 1915, each had 3/– per day deducted from their pay and sent back to their mother Mary in Tarcowie in the upper north of South Australia. Jack and William met up early on in their service in Egypt. It was army policy that an older brother could 'claim' a younger brother so that they would be in the same unit. Jack had been with the 9th Light Horse in Egypt but transferred to a trench mortar unit that was sent to France. From France he 'claimed' William, but they were never to meet up; because of a rebellious Aussie streak in my father he was sent to the front line sooner than he expected.

> I was only in Egypt about four weeks and they were calling for volunteers for France. Brother Jack, who had already been in Egypt five months, volunteered. Jack, like a lot more of course, thought there would be no war in Egypt.
>
> We left there for Salisbury Plains [in England] to train for artillery. After about a week I failed to salute an English officer. I had a little felt hat I got in France and was wearing this in camp. He asked me if I was civvy or soldier. Muggins me again said 'civvy'. He said 'I'll make you a soldier' and I was put on the next lot for France. Jack could still have claimed me but as it was tough in France we thought it was better to separate and so I went to a camp in Le Havre and trained as a gunner, 4th Division Artillery.[7]

As a gunner, my father contributed to shelling those on the other side of the line, which seemed to achieve little both politically or strategically. He just did what he had to do. After nearly three years of service he returned to Australia to take up his life again in Bullyacre, a small settlement in the mid north of South Australia, and left behind the memories of Amiens, the Somme and Ypres ('a real hot spot').

William was a kind and gentle man, not someone whom you would expect to deliberately kill another human being, but he had participated in some of the worst

William George Raftery
Third Light Horse and 12th Australian Field Artillery Brigade, 1916–1919

slaughter of this century. I do not know if he ever talked to his mother or father about his experiences when he came home in 1919. The photograph of the handsome young soldier of 1916 was always on the wall of our home, but we were never told stories about his war unless we asked. He did not boast and he did not complain about any treatment he received. Very occasionally he would tell amusing stories about the Pommies and their lack of courage, or about officers like General Birdwood who were too far above their station for the unpretentious boys from the bush.[8]

We had no unit history on the family shelves and I cannot recall any other veteran coming to visit to talk about old times. Towards the end of his life, however, after some prompting, William talked a little about the terrible conditions in France and Belgium in 1917 and 1918, and about coming home to a small farming community in 1919. Pressed a little further for some of his life story, he revealed some cameos of his experience of conflict and why he persisted under extreme conditions.

> I was in 47 Battery of the 12th Australian Field Artillery Brigade. Our guns were 18 pounders ... We used to get a two-page leaflet with any jokes etc. and cartoons. One I still remember was the Aussies sitting down bareback picking chats [body lice] from their shirts. It was headed 'A chat by the wayside'. Believe it or not we used to run our nails along the seams of our singlets and kill the lice, turn them inside out for a while and then back again. That's dinkum.

In the artillery my father was somewhat removed from the trauma of the trenches but he had one personal encounter with an enemy soldier after a barrage:

> In the artillery you fired from 300 to 1,000 yards so you just didn't know what damage [you had done] from where you were. But from communications (and land line when it was working) you found out if you were on or off target. When you moved forward after a hop-over and saw the dead you either said 'poor bugger' or a silent prayer. There was only one [German] that I knew I could have killed who was mortally wounded and begged me by actions to shoot him, but I couldn't come at that. Anyhow he soon died.

He spoke of men falling off the duckboards and perishing in the frozen mud during one of the worst winters on record in France. He described how he would wake up with icicles hanging from his nostrils after sleeping out with only a greatcoat and a groundsheet. He did not dwell on the fear and horror of being involved in artillery barrages with 18 pounders, nor on the mutilated bodies that he no doubt had to retrieve as an ambulance driver. Like so many other veterans, he died without ever telling the whole story of his war and how it might have affected him. He was just another young man who did not want to attract the worst of labels, that of coward, and did not want to appear to shirk his duty to his country: 'I was no hero. You just did things rather than show the white feather.' This was typical of the understatement that masked the mayhem and bloodshed of the Fields of Flanders.[9]

There was another side to his story. After my father died I discovered things about his life that had never been revealed in his stories. His change from a gunner to a driver in January 1918, for example was never explained. He never fulfilled his promise to elaborate: 'Some day when I feel in the mood [I will tell you] how I changed from gunner to driver [horses] again, and then cook's cart driver – which wasn't as good as it sounds'. There was also a long period in hospital. I discovered from his army records that between October 1917 and January 1918 he had spent 103 days in the Australian General Hospital in Le Havre, a military convalescent hospital.

A few post cards and letters indicated that he did have a personal life away from the front. As with all soldiers, his service had not always been in the heat of battle, and he must have spent a lot of time in the villages of France and Belgium. After he died I found letters from two French women, indicating that he had had contact with French families and may even have been billeted with some. There is also a suggestion of intimacy with one of these women. This was Blanche, who wrote to 'her dearest friend' while he was awaiting embarkation in England in December 1918, regretting she had not seen him before he had left, hoping he had not forgotten her, and saying how good he had been to her and her friends. She thanked him for the little gift he had left and vowed 'I shall always be thinking of you, I can't forget you, you always so good for us and plenty respect', signing off with 'Goodbye Little Aussie. Your B xx.' Later she had sent him a photograph with a further message of her lasting friendship.

Thérèse de Ferron from Paris was more subdued in April 1920 in a reply to a letter William had written from Tarcowie, where he had settled. She would be 'delighted to hear from him again … here we do not forget what you have done'. Her 'poor country was recovering slowly' and she thought that the Allies had not always been just towards France in their interpretation of the peace treaty. After the war he had never told us about these women. As a psychologist and researcher I had expected that I might discover in his records some hint of the strain of battle and a traumatic past. Instead I found another life of tenderness and romance amid the mud and blood.

For most of his post-war life my father was generally fit and healthy, working full-time well beyond the normal retiring age. But he smoked heavily and in his later years he developed chronic emphysema. His ageing body also caused him pain. I remember many mornings towards the end of his life when he moved very stiffly after a night disturbed by fibrositis. Perhaps this was the result of sleeping out in that terrible winter of France in 1917. Or was it unresolved traumatic experience or guilt that was stored in the body? The only professionals he consulted were the local country physician about various ailments later in life, and a hearing specialist for his deafness. He avoided hospital as far as possible and refused to have an operation for a hernia, which bothered him for much of his later life. The only other time he was admitted to hospital was when he broke a leg in a work accident. If he did have disturbing memories of parts of those war years he kept them well hidden, and most of what he experienced died with him.

My father was one of the thousands of men who came home from World War

One who never told the whole of their story nor were encouraged to make sense of that potentially disturbing part of their lives. Their children can only make assumptions from a few personal anecdotes or historical accounts that generally do not provide a complete narrative. I discovered through the writing of this book that there are many children of veterans who captured only a small part of their father's story.

My father's death serendipitously brought me a step closer to a formal study of the effects of war. In October 1982 I made a rush trip from Papua New Guinea to be with my father before he died. On my flight back to South Australia, I fortuitously found a copy of Bert Facey's *A Fortunate Life* in the Sydney airport bookshop. I read it avidly. Some of Facey's experiences paralleled those of my father. They were born in the same year, both served in the Great War, and both settled back into rural life in later years. Facey landed on the beach at Gallipoli in 1915 and was eventually repatriated after he was crushed by a shell blast. The interesting feature of his account is that he devoted the same number of pages to his army career of about one year, as he did to his 61 years after discharge. Most of his text depicts his life of hardship and survival before the war. Gallipoli is described in detail, but if there was any re-experiencing in later life of that sorry landing or the grief he felt about the death of his brother there, or the dead of Shrapnel Gully, he made no reference to it. He did mention the strain of battle, which produced 'a lot of nerve cases', but this was not part of his own experience of recovery from injury, getting married, finding work, and resettling into civilian life.

My reading of Facey's work at the time prepared me to become intensely involved in the life story as a genre. In listening to narratives of war service and trying to piece together my father's story, I was scraping away at a large part of Australian psychological history that had been sealed over. This concealment may have been a way of protecting a traumatised self but it was not just an individual act. It was part of a larger national act of submerging experiences of violence. This history has generally been closed to wives and children, who were not allowed into the inner world of veterans at any time, even in the reminiscence of later years. Within my father's life context there was no space to explore the other formative happenings away from the ugliness of the front line.

I settled back in Australia in 1983, significantly affected by my own experience of serious illness and a number of dramatic events in Papua New Guinea. I had to reinvent my life and this was greatly influenced by my formal study of the effects of traumatic experience. I set out on a long journey that brought together the strands of my own life: New Guinea, a father who had told only part of his story, and an academic and professional interest in traumatic stress.

I make no apologies for the complexity of the book. It is not simply a retelling of war stories. It is a serious examination of the reality of battle experience and its long-term effects, and of how ideas about mental health can shape how we as a society produce our narratives of stressful events.

Marks of War documents a significant part of the landscape of Australia's psychological history. It tells the story of the effects of front-line service on men's inner lives, explores the medical ideas that were used to deal with those who could not cope with the strain of battle, or the ghosts of post-war life, and describes the social context that limited the degree to which men could make sense of their memories of war.

Writing about men whom I grew to respect was not easy. I had to find a balance between revealing their frailties while at the same time acknowledging their bravery and pride in serving their country. This is a complex story because I am portraying lives against a backdrop of the medical ideas that were used to frame any failings. The book is set out so that the reader can dip into its two strands – veterans' lives and the history of ideas about what is commonly known as war neurosis – at any point. It begins with an introduction on war and Australia's traumatic past, followed by two chapters addressing the history of the application of psycho-medical practice in World War One and World War Two. These chapters provide a backdrop to a detailed portrayal in Chapter Four of the experience of battle and hardship in New Guinea in 1942 and early 1943. Chapter Five explores how the survivors of those battles and the contemporary media constructed their war memories. That chapter provides a bridge to the detailed account of the post-war lives of the survivors. The lives of the most damaged men are set within the context of the psychiatric rehabilitation system that was established to cater for them.

I conclude with reflection on a century of war and the dilemmas that confront members of the healing professions who support organised violence as a way of resolving disputes.

CHAPTER 1

Australia, War, and a Traumatic Past

War has been part of the social fabric of all nations and societies over time and represents one of the greatest threats to global health. We have witnessed a century in which we had two wars that we thought would 'end all wars', but the end of the century has seen war and conflict continue unabated. As well as resulting in the death of civilians and combatants, war destroys the social infrastructure essential to normal health, creates disease and introduces foreign diseases, and causes long term physical and psychological damage. Cumulatively it is the greatest contributor to trauma and social dislocation and brings into sharp relief the short and long-term threats to the health of society from catastrophic events.

Tony McMichael, an eminent scholar in the field of population and global health, draws on a Biblical analogy to portray the scourge:

> Human life expectancy, in the space of a mere century or so, has become much longer that ever before ... We have partially reined in two of the four Biblical Horsemen of the Apocalypse: Famine and Pestilence ... The other two horsemen, War and Conquest, still roam menacingly on their red and white steeds. Warfare continues.[1]

Since European settlement, Australia has been spared the scourge of a major war on its soil, unlike all other inhabited continents and the majority of countries, including the United States.[2] Nonetheless, war has formed a central part of the history and emergence of Australia's national identity. In these wars over one million Australian men and women have served overseas from a country that has never had more than 19 million people at any one time.

In the First World War, 60,284 (18.2 per cent) of the approximately 331,781 Australian personnel serving overseas lost their lives. On the Western Front alone, between April 1916 and August 1918, 46,000 Australians died and over 320,000 non-fatal casualties were recorded.[3] In World War Two more than 10 per cent of the population enlisted, and of the 696,660 men and women who served outside of Australia, 28,565 were imprisoned. The total dying in World War Two from battle or other causes was 39,429.[4] The stark reality of these physical casualties can be seen in the average daily rates of death, particularly in World War One, where 41 Australian soldiers died for each day of the war. This meant that a young soldier had a one-in-five chance of dying as a member of the Australian Imperial Forces. In World War Two the actual battle deaths amounted to 13 per day for each day of the war, and an average of 18 men and women died each day from all causes.

One of the achievements of the twentieth century is sound epidemiological evidence that traumatic events can have a serious and lasting effect on mental health. However, relatively little is known about the effect of the trauma of war on Australian troops and even less about its effect on civilians. Other tragic but lesser events have been the focus of research and have attracted more research attention than major wars.[5] Dramatic events such as a mass shooting in Melbourne, the Granville train crash in NSW,[6] and the Ash Wednesday bushfires have resulted in event-impact research.[7] Daily tragedies such as industrial accidents, road crashes (more than 2,000 killed and 24,000 seriously injured annually) and suicide (approximately 2,500 per year) all contribute to the collective traumatic memory and have become the subject of extensive research.

Relatively little is known about the psychological impact on Australians who returned from the two world wars, but some evidence is found in historical studies of war. For example Gammage (1980), provided a detailed account of the experiences of World War One soldiers at Gallipoli and on the Western Front, and documented the appallingly stressful conditions as well as some of the mental effects of such strain. He noted particularly that 'the hardest adjustments were those of the mind', and described the efforts many men made to 'blot out the gruesome sights and the waste of a horrible past'. One of Gammage's informants noted that several old hands were observed cracking up as the occupation at Gallipoli set in. Another said 'one's nerves get very nervy ... having been on a continuous strain of looking, watching and listening'.[8]

Thomson (1994) explored the interface between the historical construction of World War One by C.E.W. Bean and the personal narratives of surviving veterans. Some of his informants testified to nervous problems both during wartime and after the war. One informant developed a 'nervous disorder' in France and broke down again in later life. This type of breakdown had to be managed against the expectation of being a noble ANZAC warrior.[9] Adam-Smith (1992) unearthed fleeting references to psychological strain during captivity and in the homecoming of prisoners of war.[10] The carnage of war in itself is potentially a major contributor to psychological distress of secondary victims such as families, as well as combatants. The grief of Australian families at home has been documented by Damousi (1999).[11]

Hidden psychological problems of World War Two soldiers were uncovered in a study by John Barrett in his survey of 3,200 Australian veterans. His respondents volunteered numerous accounts describing stress in post-war life, from their own and other veterans' experience. Their stress was often masked by drunkenness, suicide, difficulties in relationships and anti-social behaviour, some of which resulted in imprisonment. The most commonly reported aberrant behaviour, excessive use of alcohol, began in military service and continued in a dysfunctional way after discharge. Of his whole sample, 11 per cent of Barrett's informants reported some kind of psychological problem for themselves and 30 per cent spoke of others having such problems.[12]

Garton (1996) established that Australian veterans from both major wars had significant mental health problems following discharge. These problems, which Garton incorporated under the rubric of shell shock, were extended into post-war life in a number of ways, particularly in a quest for compensation. Garton produces evidence to suggest that there was a significant problem that was carefully hidden from public scrutiny and contained within official confidential records. In an earlier work on the social history of insanity in New South Wales, 1880–1940, he described the post-war psychological problems of 'shell-shocked' World War One veterans.[13]

Other historical works, including battalion histories (Brune 1991, Barter 1994), point to evidence of ongoing effects of war strain, but references to this are tangential to their main story. Recent military and battalion histories make only passing mention of the reality of the effects of strain on individuals.[14] Johnston examined wartime strain and devoted three chapters to breakdown in the front line, but did not pursue this into post-war life.[15] Another biographical study of middle-class Melbourne people, by Janet McCalman, found that not all veterans returning to civilian life found post-war life easy to manage; they had limited access to counselling, and managed to survive the war 'only to break down once there was time and space for it'.[16] The official accounts of the medical history of World War Two, which will be discussed later at greater length, lack a thorough treatment of mental health issues.[17] The officially sanctioned histories of the 2/27th and 39th battalions, like most similar works, provide detailed lists of those killed and wounded and accounts of heroic feats, but record no information on mental strain or psychological casualties.[18]

Serious fictional writing about war emerged in both World War One and World War Two, the former probably being the most interesting. In these writings there is very limited reference to war strain and its effects. Some examples about World War One are Bert Bishop's *The Hell, the Humour and the Heartbreak: A Private's View of World War 1* (1991) and W.H. Downing's *To the Last Ridge* (1998). Two significant pieces of fiction with reference to strain are Leonard Mann, *Flesh in Armour* (1985), and Martin Boyd, *When Blackbirds Sing* (1972). A review of some relevant literature is found in *The Shock of Battle*, published by the English Department of the Defence Force Academy in 1989. Of the few novels focused on World War Two, Hungerford's *The Ridge and the River* (1992) is based on action in Bougainville where a central character broke down under the strain.

Post-war effects

In psycho-medical literature there is a body of international research on the post-war effects of World War Two combat and imprisonment, but comparatively little on Australian veterans. The unifying rubric of recent research is the condition of post-traumatic stress disorder. Underpinning this construction is the notion of toxic shock, which presumes that a traumatic event where there is no physical injury can result in or cause psychological damage.[19] This type of event threatens not only physical well-being, but the core of the inner psyche itself, and has reverberating effects over time.[20] The various revisions of the diagnosis of post-traumatic stress since 1980 have endorsed the view that the psychological effects of traumatic events endure over time. There is debate about this and the debate, as will be explained later, has it origins in the nineteenth century.[21]

An identifiable suite of non-Australian studies has established that long-term effects of war experience are both significant and observable. A wide range of studies – such as those of Hastings, Wright and Gluk (1943); Gillespie (1945); Kelley (1945); Grinker (1943); Grinker and Spiegel (1945); Muliner (1945); Swank and Marchant (1946); Appel (1946); Guttman (1946); Teicher (1946); and Kardiner and Spiegel (1947) – have established a link between war and negative post-war effects. A number of studies undertaken two to three decades after the end of World War Two confirmed the long-term effects of exposure – Archibald and Tuddenham (1965); Nefzger (1970); Beebe (1975); Askevold (1976) – and after 1980 – Zeiss and Dickman (1989); Speed et al. (1989); Goldstein (1987); Wilson (1989); Miller et al. (1989); Op den Velde et al. (1990); Hovens et al. (1992), (1993) and (1994); and Crocq et al. (1993). Spiro, Schnurr and Aldwin found from a study of 1,210 World War Two veterans in the Normative Aging Study that there was a significant link between military service and psychological ageing, and that combat exposure was 'particularly toxic'.[22] Recently, a number of British researchers and practitioners – Davies (1997), Hunt (1997), Orner et al. (1997) – also revisited the British World War Two population in smaller studies.

Further light has been shed on the long-term effects of war by a series of longitudinal studies that had been initiated well before World War Two. This small but significant body of research, utilising existing rich longitudinal data sets, re-examined links between World War Two experience and life outcomes. The Grant Study of 269 Harvard undergraduates begun in 1938 is one such study. George Vaillant, one of the researchers in that study, wrote the most comprehensive monograph on the Study in 1976, but did not address trauma. He returned with others to review the sample in 1995 to examine the effects of war service.[23] Of the original Grant cohort, 19 died in World War Two and 152 served overseas. These men were studied 'intensively' and interviewed before and after World War Two and between the ages of 47 and 57. The 1995 interviews included information on war service. Surviving members of the cohort were physically examined every five years and surveyed by mailed questionnaire every two years. Within the acknowledged limitations – for example that Harvard undergraduates excluded men of lower socioeconomic status – the data confirm that traumatic experience can have enduring effects, whether these are defined in terms of PTSD, or other morbidity measures such as neuroticism and major depressive disorder.

Another significant body of research originated with cohorts of Californian children in the 1920s (Oakland Growth Study, the Berkeley Guidance Study and the Terman Study of gifted children at Stanford). Systematic observations, testing and interviews at regular intervals documented a generation assessing the effects of

World War Two over their life span. Glen Elder, of the Center for Population Studies in University of North Carolina, and a number of collaborators, including Bessel van der Kolk, re-assessed the survivors in these cohorts in the late 1980s. They established that military service and combat exposure could have developmental as well as detrimental effects on individuals as long as four decades after the precipitating event.[24]

As the World War Two population moves into the later stages of life there has been some renewed interest in the enduring effect of earlier stressful events. In a review of studies of ageing veterans and Holocaust survivors, Kahana reinforced the findings of Elder et al. and concluded that:

> Memories of trauma continue to intrude into the lives of these older adults, thereby testifying to the long-term duration of PTSD symptoms subsequent to war stress. At the same time these data underscore the remarkable resiliency among long term survivors of extreme stress.[25]

No such extensive research has been conducted in Australia, but the available evidence supports a view that many Australian veterans did struggle after they returned home. Dent, Tennant and Goulston (1987) compared the mental health of 170 surviving Australian ex-prisoners of the Japanese with 172 veterans who served in the Pacific in World War Two and found some evidence of depression in the sample but did not establish a diagnosis of PTSD. Kidson, Douglas and Holwill (1993) found a relatively high incidence of PTSD among World War Two veterans receiving psychiatric treatment in a Department of Veterans' Affairs hospital.[26] Macleod (1991, 1994) and Parr (1995) documented similar effects among New Zealand World War Two veterans.

Medicalising war stress

The effects of the strain of war have been examined largely within a medical framework. Terminology and medical labelling is significant in any discussion of this medicalisation. The history of how this medical labelling came about will be explored in detail in the two following chapters, but I will briefly address some features here. Australian military labels were borrowed from the British Army. The labels for war stress were the same as those assigned to the mental disorders of peacetime – anxiety state, depression, hysteria, neurasthenia, traumatic neurosis and psychosis – and none of these labels mentioned the war.[27] These civil terms such as hysteria and neurosis have deep social and cultural roots. The primary basis of classification was neurosis, which was an invention of the eighteenth century, made popular in the nineteenth century, to account for symptoms where there was no observable neuro-physiological lesion.

Well before the beginning of World War Two, shell shock and traumatic neurosis (neurosis attributed to trauma-induced neurobiological lesion) were no longer considered useful concepts to explain the psychological casualty, but this rejection opened up a much more complex philosophical and medical discourse. If the condition could no longer be attributed to a simple pathogen such as explosive shock, a coherent explanation had to be found in the way the individual responded to an event. This is why psycho-dynamic explanations had such appeal. These explanations, broadly grouped under the rubric of neuroses, eventually became acceptable to military authorities for a number of reasons, not the least of which was economic.

Shell shock was the only term with a reference to war, but it was rejected during World War One in favour of standard psychiatric labels of disease. The significance of this shift was two-fold. In the first place, it left the way open for dynamic explanation of how a psychic shock could produce disturbance. Secondly, the new labelling suggested that emotional and mental distress was not related to dreadful things soldiers may have seen, done or had done to them in conflict. This shifted attention not only away from the possibility of automatic compensation, but also deflected it from the destructiveness of war as a source of ill health. The rejection of the term shell shock early placed the emphasis on the weakness of the individual rather than the nature of war.

Another feature of the constructions of the mental disorders of war was the tension between psychological and neuro-physiological explanations of dysfunction, and whether the traumatic experience actually caused a neurological lesion and produced a kind of psychic wound. This question highlights the tension between mechanistic and psychological interpretations in the construction of illness. Different generations have proposed answers to these puzzles and the two major wars of this century became testing grounds for these answers. During World War One functional disorder and neurosis assumed dominance.[28] The 'disorder' was construed to be fundamentally psychological in origin, and this explanation continued to hold sway throughout World War Two. Such a construction left open the possibility that the inadequate constitution of the soldier could account for any breakdowns.

Uncovering the story

My search for an understanding of the post-war lives of World War Two veterans centres on those who experienced an intense period of combat in New Guinea in 1942. To uncover the story I made extensive contact with veterans and their organisations, by attending reunions, small gatherings, funerals and ceremonies. I analysed battalion association newsletters, formed close ties with several key informants, and read extensively in military and medical history. The central part of my work was interviewing and surveying veterans. I also interviewed secondary witnesses, such as family members.[29]

The majority of veterans were re-interviewed several times. The accounts of 65 veterans were finally used in the study. Most of the informants had enlisted in the 2/27th Battalion, a unit formed in South Australia. The rest came from the 39th and 53rd Militia Battalions, and a few from two other units (2/14th and 2/16th) in the 21st Brigade. The stories of nine deceased men were put together posthumously from medical and other records and interviews with family members. The common experience of all these informants was the period of intense engagement against the Japanese army between February and December 1942. Other survivors were interviewed but were not included if they did not fulfil the exposure requirement or were considered to be unreliable informants.

Of the 56 informants still alive at the beginning of my research, 17 died before its completion. This was not an unexpected outcome, given the age of the participants, but in retrospect it proved somewhat fortuitous in that it provided an opportunity to comment on the completion of their life span, and in some cases to gather information on their last days. Where possible and ethical, information was sensitively obtained from relatives as to the manner of the veteran's death, and whether there was evidence of war-related disturbance in their last days. The sample is thus sufficiently representative, and the subjects' combat exposure sufficiently similar, for me to make meaningful observations about the effects of war strain and post-war experience.

Veterans' accounts of combat and post-war life were rounded out by interviewing other front-line personnel such as former regimental medical officers, medical aides and chaplains who had served in New Guinea. In addition, group interviews were conducted with some members of the 2/27th and ex-39th Battalions. I also examined in detail Murdoch Sound Archive transcripts of veterans from the 53rd/55th, 39th and 2/27th Battalions. These transcripts, although not covering the whole of life, provided confirmatory information on conditions and experiences in New Guinea and provided some insight into life after war.

From the original survey pool of 65 participants, 23 men were approached for additional information in the form of two short questionnaires – a Memory Questionnaire, an adaptation of the Impact of Events Scale,[30] and a Belief Questionnaire, which sought their views about war, memory practices and ways of managing memories. These two questionnaires were not used as clinical instruments, but to elicit more qualitative information on the way men construed and reacted to their war memories.

This excavation of lives was careful and painstaking. Although I was interested in psychological and social outcomes, this was not a clinical examination of the mental status of these men. My intention was to compose life stories, not examine symptoms and arrive at a diagnosis. This life story approach was informed by a view that:

> Listening to people talk in their own terms about what had been significant in their lives seemed to us far more valuable than studying preconceived psychometric scales or contrived experiments.[31]

I encouraged veterans to talk about the phases in their lives – their childhood, growing up, pre-war experience, entry into war and war experience. They could also describe their homecoming and re-settling, as well as features of their mid-life, their career, marriage, family and life events. I also uncovered an interior life that was accessed through accounts of dreams, feelings, and any difficulties they might have experienced.[32]

I was aware of the potential to disturb veterans by uncovering war memories, so I approached them cautiously and sensitively. This was also a reason for not undertaking a blanket survey of association members. Experience confirmed my sense of caution, and I cite two examples of this. One is the case of a survivor of the first Japanese assault on Kokoda and the battle for Gona. He completed a questionnaire in which he described in some detail the experience of escaping from Kokoda carrying a wounded mate. He had 'trained himself to forget' but was sure he would 'have a bad night after all this recall'.

A second example is a veteran, aged 83, who agreed to an interview after reading the study description and signing a consent form. In the interview he recounted his New Guinea experiences, about which he still felt bitter, and the difficulties of getting himself re-established after discharge. Part of his post-war story was about his wife's fatal illness and the three years he nursed her before she died. At the end of the interview he stated that it had been good to talk, and agreed to look at a questionnaire that would allow him more time to reflect on his life events. In a follow-up telephone conversation a few days later he was more subdued and thought it had not been a good idea to take part. The remembering had 'taken him back too far' and 'some things were best left in the memory'. I did not pressure him to complete the questionnaire.

Another consideration in recording life stories is the veracity of the story. In fact, experience suggested that some stories needed to be treated with caution. One veteran initiated the contact and arrived at my home for an interview. His skill as a raconteur was seductive, and initial indications were that he was revealing a classic trauma story. In his version he was a good soldier serving in a crack commando unit in Syria and New Guinea, and the trauma of New Guinea had pushed him over the edge to become a 'nerve case'. While in New Guinea he claimed he had endured horrific experiences in combat, had witnessed torture and atrocity, and eventually broke down. He was discharged medically unfit, and spent the rest of his life in and out of hospital with various diagnoses, including depression. Examination of his medical file and interviews with family members revealed that he had fabricated many of his stories, and had constructed a trauma narrative that justified his distress and compensation. This experience reinforced the need for caution in the ready acceptance of a dramatic story and warranted the gathering of broad-based information from which to formulate a version of the life story of a veteran.

A protective reticence applied to spouses as well as veterans. In July 1999 I was invited to speak at a meeting of Legacy women. There I met a widow whose husband had been a member of the battalion that I had been following up. She agreed to be interviewed, and I anticipated this meeting as another opportunity to tap into a rich memory store. When I arrived at her address she was not at home. When I telephoned later she said she no longer wanted to talk. My contact had stirred up a past she had managed to submerge: 'I had buried that with my husband. I don't want to bring that up again. He never spoke about it like most of the men. I can't bear to think about it. The past is the past. I don't need it.'[33] This woman was rightly upset, and confirmed the need for great sensitivity and respect for the right to be silent. She obviously had a deep pool of hurt, the details of which I would never know.

* * * * *

The stage is now set to explore the three major features of this book. The first is the set of ideas and practices that influenced the way war stress was talked about and managed during and after World War One and World War Two. The second is the description of the experiences of men during battle in New Guinea. The third and most extensive feature is the post-war lives of these veterans.

CHAPTER 2

Moral and Mental Disorders: The Neurotic Soldier in World War One

> It is probable that a 'moral' condition – not yet hysteria – constrained not a few men, whose descent into the limbo of a fully-developed neurosis began with a conscious, or semi-conscious failure to act as his soldier's 'conscience' dictated he should.
>
> The sum total of medical observation on the 'mental' phenomena of the war, and the consensus of informed medical opinion based on it, appear strongly to favour a conviction that the moral and mental disorders of behaviour met with in war are not *sui generis* but in their essential pathogeny and nature are identical with those met with in peace.[1]

This story of how men withstood the strain of war begins in World War One. The mental damage to veterans has been very effectively sealed away from any serious public critique, but the treatment of the psychological casualties of that war, particularly in the post-war period, provided a platform for the ideas that became entrenched in World War Two. In discussing this, I will touch briefly on the psychiatric services available during World War One, and the ideas that informed practice both during combat and later.

Medical ideas of mental illness in the nineteenth and early twentieth centuries dictated the way the army dealt with soldiers affected by the stress of battle in World War One. The physicians and neurologists of the nineteenth century had grappled with problematic patients, mostly women, who presented with pains and various symptoms, but had no identifiable lesion. The debates about traumatic injury centred on 'Railway Spine' in passengers injured on the 'Iron Rails', and on the hysteria and neurasthenia of young women who were deemed to be excited by modern life. Hysteria has a complicated history and is linked, at least conceptually, with the notion of neurosis, and preceded neurosis as a formal diagnosis.[2] As well as being a medical construction of a problematic condition, hysteria had the added element of mimesis, in that the symptomatology reflected the experience that produced the condition. For example, a soldier who had been unable to shout a warning to his comrade would later not be able to speak.

In the nineteenth century, a time when psychiatry and neurology were struggling for academic and professional recognition, little interest had been taken in the psychological casualties during war time.[3] Consequently, there was little preparation for battle casualties in the First War. This was not the first time large numbers of psychological casualties had emerged from battle. In the American Civil War (1861–1865), in which over 600,000 Americans died on American soil, there was no provision for such casualties, even though there is some evidence of long term psychological damage to soldiers. If those who were disturbed did survive, their difficulties were hidden away in primitive civil institutions for the insane.[4] Binneveld (1997) noted recently that 'for psychiatry the conflict proved to be of no significance. The psychologically wounded soldier passed into oblivion'.[5] It is claimed that Silas Weir Mitchell, who actually served in the American Civil War as a Union surgeon, treated soldiers who were diagnosed with neurasthenia and hyperasthesia using his Rest Cure, but it is more likely that his interest in the diagnosis and treatment developed later.[6]

A form of organised military psychiatric service in war does appear to have been in place during the Russo-Japanese War (1904–1905). In that conflict psychiatric casualties were extensive, and the Russian army medical department and the Red Cross Society of Russia established the 'first forward psychiatric clearing hospital equipped with its own specialists'. At that time, however, there was no specific term for this type of casualty. Ellis (1984) maintains that Honigman used *Kriegsneurosen* (war neurosis) in 1907 as the first specific war-related term, but this term did not become entrenched in British literature.[7]

German and some British medical authorities expected that World War One would purge the world of the weaknesses brought on by the modern living conditions of the industrial urbanised world.[8] The course of the war in Europe soon proved this idea wrong. World War One became a major source of mental breakdown. The war thus became the first serious testing ground for the ideas about mental illness that had emerged from the nineteenth century. During and immediately after World War One the key medical stakeholders repeated the view that war presented nothing new to medical science. The major contribution of war was to confirm that the nervously wounded soldier was a threat to the manpower and morale of the war machine and needed to be weeded out or treated efficiently. Mental breakdown was considered a disease capable of infecting others, and following the war efforts were made to stop any contagion spreading, with a decision that any form of neurosis related to war service was not to be considered a pensionable war injury.

In World War One the Australian Medical Service had no responsibility for psychological casualties among its own troops until they were repatriated to Australia. Casualties in the field were managed by the British Army Medical Services, in which Australian doctors served. However, 1914 marked the introduction of psychic wounds into Australian war history, and it was the first war in which post-war mental health problems were acknowledged in legislative and administrative provisions for the repatriated soldier. As early as the Gallipoli campaign, where 'there was already evidence of abnormal behaviour caused by war strain, although the aetiology of shell shock was largely undeveloped', these ideas were put to the test.[9] As in Britain at the outbreak of the 1914–18 war, there was no commonly agreed body of knowledge on the effects of battle exposure.

More than 300,000 young Australian men like my father went to the battlefields to fight for the empire with no thought for the mental consequences; all too soon they found themselves at places like Gallipoli, and the Western Front, where they were placed under terrible strain. The kind of conditions men encountered in these campaigns, where almost 60,000 Australians were killed, is brought to life in a letter sent home from ANZAC Cove in June 1915:

> My Dear Mother,
>
> I am taking this opportunity of writing home to you, as one of our AMC men is catching a boat to leave for Australia tomorrow morning …
>
> Well mother, we could not say too much in letters about what goes on here as they would be torn up. We went to Egypt under sealed orders and went to an island called Timnos, and stopped there for ten days. We steamed away to the war, and were told we might have to land under fire. In the morning before daylight we heard the big guns firing, and a little while after we could hear and see them.
>
> Everyone was ordered on deck, and we saw boats being lowered off the other boats in the harbour, then we got orders to disembark and land. We could see and hear rifle, machine gun and shrapnel fire; it was splashing all around us, and when we got a little closer, it simply rained bullets and shrapnel. We were fairly lucky, only a few in our boat-load got hit landing, but one boat load was towed in together (about 150 men and only 29 landed safely out of them). When we landed, we could see our boys, bayonets out and after the Turks, and we had to follow. Our mates were dropping down all around us, but we could not do anything for them. We had to push forward and we did it. We had to stop there for a week, with very little water and tucker, as when we landed we threw our packs away …
>
> We camped in a rest camp a couple of miles from the point for a few days, and then we got orders to move. Marched a couple of miles, then had to dig trenches. Just as we finished we had orders to go forward – no-one knew how far. We had five minutes to leave the place, and advanced under shrapnel, very heavy, for 300 yards. It was nothing to see a section get wiped right out with one shell, but we had to go straight on, as to stop meant death; there was no cover at all. So we went forward. About 700 left the camp (with our reinforcements) and when we arrived at the firing line, half of them were wounded.
>
> Went straight on for about 400 yards under fire just like rain, and had to lie on level ground and dig trenches. Hundreds got shot trying to dig in, but we held on till dark when we were reinforced. The moans and groans of the wounded were awful to listen to, but we could do nothing until stretcher bearers came and got them away; those that could walk had to chance getting shot again, getting back to the trenches where the doctors were. The field we had advanced over was strewn with dead Turks, and hundreds of our own men. You could not describe it on paper – it was an awful sight … Our Battalion mustered only 140, with 1st, 2nd, 3rd reinforcements. It was awful, you could not really imagine it.

> The first few days we were very nervous and the AMC [medical corps] was kept very busy. The beach was crowded with wounded and dead soldiers; even after a week on the beach there was a lot of casualties ...
>
> You can be sure now dear mother, that I will return home safe and sound to you, and all that I love at home ...
>
> Your loving son, Jack [10]

There is no record of what happened to this young man, though there is a suggestion in his letter that he and his mates suffered from their 'awful' experiences. His story was repeated thousands of times in the lives of other men from 1916 to 1918. Historian C.E.W. Bean described in graphic detail the conditions that might have led to such psychological 'injury',[11] as, to some extent, did the medical historian A.G. Butler.[12] Young men were involved in a massive war of attrition, often confronted with incidents that crawled into the mind and lodged there. They saw close friends mown down or blown up alongside them; they were bombarded with shells or were caught in enfilading fire; they accepted the questionable decisions by high command; and they made fatal charges.

Those who broke down or became dysfunctional under such conditions were labelled with terms like neurosis, hysteria or psychosis. There was an array of other disease categories including conditions such as Disordered Action of the Heart (DAH), sometimes referred to as Effort Syndrome, which accounted for 'war weary' soldiers who showed no clinical evidence of organic disease.[13]

This was the war that prompted Freud to describe war neurosis as a 'traumatic neurosis, whose occurrence has been made possible by a conflict in the ego'. Freud thought that such neuroses would disappear during peacetime, but he did acknowledge the horror that was just emerging in 1916, and the collusion of the medical expert in the enterprise:

> We cannot but feel that no event has ever destroyed so much that is precious in the common possessions of humanity, confused so many of the clearest intelligences, or so thoroughly debased what is highest ... Science has herself lost her passionless impartiality; her deeply embittered servants seek for weapons from her with which to contribute towards the struggle with the enemy. Anthropologists feel driven to declare him [the enemy] inferior and degenerate, psychiatrists issue a diagnosis of his disease of mind and spirit.[14]

Traumatic neurosis initially had little place in the war. As the battles continued, 'shell shock' as a 'wound' lost credibility as the number of cases of breakdown with no 'commotional shock' grew. New and innovative labels and treatments had to be found when men did not respond to enforced rest, good food, and reassurance. The official medical historian, A.G. Butler observed:

> It is equally certain that a great many men who sought refuge under the Geneva Cross from the intolerable strains and shocks of warfare, were suffering from exhaustion, a breakdown of the power of resistance, physical and 'moral', and not, as in Colonel Campbell's Gallipoli cases, from the culmination of some grave, long-standing disorder of personality, inherited or otherwise.[15]

AWM E00941

The horrific conditions experienced by troops on the Western Front are apparent from these images. Above, Australian 9.2 inch howitzer in action at Ypres; below, exhausted soldiers of the 9th Field Ambulance in Belgium.

The view emerged that shell shock should have been more appropriately called 'battle shock', and the 'ultimate psychopathic picture' contained a large proportion of men who were not chronic, long term pathological cases. Consequently, casualties were labelled as suffering from mental conflict, anxiety states, moral, mental and perhaps physical shock, stupor, confusion and amnesia, and psycho-neuroses.

Australian casualties were reported early in the conflict. Major A.W. Campbell observed psychiatric casualties evacuated from battlefields of the Dardanelles to No. 2 Australian General Hospital (AGH) in Cairo in 1916.[16] These cases of 'neuroses and psychoses contributed to modern war casualty lists more heavily than we had previously supposed', and represent a problem hitherto unrecognised by authorities. Campbell classified the casualties broadly as:

- neuroses, including hysterical type reactions
- neurasthenia (including trench spine)
- psychoses (which Butler interpreted as a type of anxiety neurosis).

Casualties were also observed at Gallipoli; there were some 1,640 cases of neurosis, psychosis, and delinquent conduct treated in hospital, which represented 2.1 per cent of all disease admissions in 1915. Butler conceded that there was a psychic element in many illnesses and wounds that never appeared as psychiatric casualties.[17]

The term psychosis was applied to men who had experienced prolonged periods of strain and eventually broke down, as well as to those who were clearly 'insane'. Campbell argued that these cases, 'taken as a whole did not differ from those seen in civil practice'.[18] Another category of men was suffering from some battle-induced condition, but there was 'no end to these so-called functional affections of the motor apparatus and common sensibility'. For Campbell, admission to hospital was the end of the line, and these men were virtually 'useless for further fighting service'. In most cases patients, who exhibited restlessness, nervous demeanour, easy excitation, and disturbing dreams, reported some type of harrowing incident or extreme battle condition preceding their problems. However, extreme battle conditions were not considered a primary causative factor in the aetiology of the 'disease'. Rather, the reason for breakdown could be found in prior disposition and experience, which in some had shown up in training. Despite their experience of commotional shock, fatigue and mental strain, Campbell insisted on 'the importance of disposition', saying that 'time after time, on going into the family and personal histories of such cases, we found evidence of neuropathic and psychopathic tendency, and this was the fundamental cause of their downfall'. These men 'were not malingerers', but nevertheless were sources of 'psychic contagion' and a danger in the ward.[19]

The debate about whether the origin of a breakdown was to be found in the weakness of the individual or the intensity of battle conditions was not resolved. Butler tended towards a view that at Gallipoli the 'cause' of the injury was the battle conditions as much as a 'neurotic disposition'. As the war progressed, the significance of the shock of exploding shells gained some credence, but in the final analysis there was shift towards a belief that the incidence of breakdown was greatly influenced by the psychological disposition of the individual soldiers, which was itself influenced by the strength of morale in the unit.

In the context of war, Butler considered psychiatric casualties to be primarily 'moral and mental disorders'. He also pointed out that the medical profession had been unprepared for the mental casualties of World War One. There was no common body of expert opinion, there was little scientific basis for the measures that were taken, and the field was fragmented by a 'deep divide in opinions'. Butler decried the inadequacies of the medical knowledge available at the beginning of the war, particularly the classifications available for 'mental disease'. Breakdown under strain was as much a moral failure as it was a mental breakdown. Consequently, he argued that most of the mental disorders could be prevented through the 'promotion of moral health', and the answer was to acquire – through 'training, discipline and habituation' – mental attitudes that could withstand strain. Breakdown was accounted for in terms of a previous record of instability or dubious habits that were only detected after men had enlisted and were under pressure.[20]

Butler also considered a soldier's reaction to strain from a Freudian perspective. Freud believed that soldiers who were of better stock would not break down; their superior ego strength would protect them. Men in the ranks (from the lower classes) would be less likely to possess such strength. Butler reinforced this view.

> The old ego protects itself from the danger to life by flight into traumatic neurosis in defending itself against the new ego, which it recognises as threatening to life. The National Army was the condition, and fruitful soil, for the appearance of war neuroses; they could not appear in professional soldiers or mercenaries.[21]

There is no evidence that Australian psychiatric casualties reached the epidemic proportions documented in the British, Canadian and German forces, but men did return to Australia damaged and in need of rehabilitation. To deal with this problem, a conference was convened in June 1918 to decide how the Commonwealth would manage the 'neurasthenic soldier'. This prestigious gathering, presided over by the Surgeon-General G. Cuscaden, included Eric Sinclair, Principal Medical Officer of the 2nd Military District, A.H. Sturdee, Principal Medical Officer of the 3rd Military District, and several other experts. The meeting decided that the term neurasthenia would cover most conditions, including ordinary neurasthenia and hysteria, as well as toxic 'shell shock', Disordered Action of the Heart, and virtually any other disturbance, including certifiable insanity.

The final resolutions effectively were:

- There would be no 'boat leave' for psychiatric patients when they arrived.
- Men suffering from shell shock and true neurasthenia, the borderline insane, and curable inebriates, should be retained either until they were cured or were ready for referral for repatriation.
- Members from the 3rd Military District would be sent straight to MacLeod Hospital [an Australian General Hospital] where they would be segregated.

The number of pensions allocated to returned World War One soldiers indicated that there was a significant problem. By 1930 there were 12,844 veterans receiving pensions on psychiatric grounds. Given that these would have been granted only after close scrutiny, and many cases would have been rejected as not related to war service, this is a significant number.[22] By 1939 4,891 cases of war neurosis had been treated in repatriation facilities. In this case, war neurosis included shell shock, epilepsy, neurasthenia and alcoholism. There was some evidence of a slightly elevated prevalence of suicide among veterans.[23]

A.G. Butler also noted that around the time of World War One psychiatric facilities were primitive, and this view was reinforced by informed observers in Australia.[24] The parlous state of ideas and treatment is illustrated in the South Australian experience, where in 1914 Parkside Lunatic Asylum inmates were being diagnosed under such categories as mania, melancholia, alternating insanity, stupor, dementia, dementia praecox, delusional insanity, general paralysis, idiocy and imbecility, moral insanity, confusional insanity, and volitional insanity. Almost all of the 235 inmates in 1918 were from the lower social classes, the largest category being labourers (21 per cent) and domestics (29 per cent). A small number (16 per cent) were veterans, but in only two of these cases was war experience considered the principal contributor to the first onset of illness.[25]

As psychological casualties emerged from the AIF a number of medical men with experience of the British Army system tried to warn Australian authorities of the need for effective psychiatric rehabilitation. For example, J.W. Springthorpe, who had been in charge of the Australian war neurosis cases in the Australian Auxiliary Hospital in England between 1916 and 1918, had diagnosed and treated functional nervous disorders in the civil arena as well. In treating the 'neurasthenic or functionally diseased patient', he had rubbed shoulders with key British identities such as Hurst, Myers, Rivers, Collie and Fearnsides. Like Butler, he considered that in World War One the medical profession was almost entirely unprepared for the high psychiatric casualty rates among the British (15 per cent of 170,000 pensions), French (14,000 in one hospital alone), and Canadian troops (12 per cent of casualties in Quebec alone).

Springthorpe (1919) argued that in World War One many soldiers were found to be mentally and organically unfit to cope with mental strain. War had shown the overpowering part that emotion and suggestion played, rather than commotion or concussion in battle. Treatment had to be preceded by a process of sorting out the malingerers and those with organic brain concussion, so that treatment of the 'true neurasthenics, psychasthenics, neuromimetics and hysterics' could proceed. Suggestion and persuasion were key elements in this treatment. He argued that if the condition was induced by suggestion in the first place, men should be cured through suggestion and firm counselling, supplemented by finding them employment. Suggestion, persuasion and manipulation, applied after careful groundwork with the patient, could cure a condition where other more elaborate treatments such as electricity, massage, fixation, diathermy, radiant heat, baths and orthopaedic devices had failed. These physical treatments only encouraged patients to focus on their symptoms, and were thus comparatively negative. Re-education, where 'you attempt to rebuild the person mentally', was a more positive approach to rehabilitation, and required an atmosphere of cheerfulness, optimism, and understanding. A modified form of psychoanalysis, rather than the more intensive Freudian analysis, should be used in the initial stage to uncover the dynamics of the internal strife a soldier was experiencing. This was the only concession to Freud, as later interpretations of the neuroses of war completely rejected his original 'perverted' notion of the sexual basis of neuroses, and shunted Freud and his theories into obscurity.[26]

In 1916 W. Ernest Jones, Inspector General of the Insane in Victoria, also warned the Australian medical community about the likely return of neurotic soldiers.[27] He predicted that these men could have 'little-understood nervous and mental affections', and present 'unusual cases of hysteria, neurasthenia, phobias and obsessions of various kinds'. They might display loss of memory and/or speech, blindness, mutism, or stammering.

Jones illustrated his views with the case of a 20-year-old soldier who had been repatriated to Australia after being buried alive by an artillery shell at Gallipoli in July 1915. He was admitted to hospital because he was unable to speak and had occasional impulsive outbreaks and moody periods, but no evident organic lesion. While in transit back from Malta the soldier had been confined to a padded cell for a period after he had become violent and attacked other patients, and during the journey home he had attempted to throw himself overboard. Jones cited this as an example of the 'nervous and mental affection, not only where a definite wound has been received, but in many cases where nothing of the sort appears'.[28] During convalescence in Australia Jones saw the mute man a number of times; however, the key to his recovery was not the wiles of a psychotherapist, but a snake encountered on a picnic from the convalescent home. The excitement of killing the snake caused the soldier to shout, triggering a full recovery of speech. Jones cited the British Army medical specialists Mott and Sarbo to support his view that many such cases were functional disorders, since there was no organic damage to the nervous system.[29]

The theory of individual vulnerability to stress began to develop around this time. An editorial in a 1916 issue of the *Medical Journal of Australia*, in which Jones's article appeared, warned that there would be functional disorders from war and that they should be treated seriously. However 'a soldier with an unstable nervous system is indeed likely to exhibit some strange manifestations of an hysterical and neurasthenic nature'. The author also stated that 'the affection is not new: it has only become more frequent under the conditions of modern warfare'.[30]

Other contributions in the form of reviews of overseas publications on shell shock appeared in the *Medical Journal of Australia* in March 1919. The first was of Andre Leri's *Commotion and Shock of War*, in which the reviewer pointed out the need to distinguish between two similar conditions, one of which was clearly neurotic in origin, the other caused by organic lesion. A second review was of John McCurdy's *War Neuroses*, which highlighted the similarity between civil and military disorders. McCurdy argued that the neuroses of war essentially arose out of conflict between duty and the instinct for self-preservation, rather than the sexual instinct that explained civil neuroses. A neurosis appeared when mental mechanisms could no longer contain the effects of fatigue, explosions and other distressing occurrences, which 'are the spring releasing the accumulated morbid mental forces'.[31]

In April 1919 W.R. Regnell, who had worked at Seale Hayne, one of the main British military hospitals for the treatment of neurotic conditions, presented a paper to the South Australian meeting of the British Medical Association.[32] Regnell warned of the possibility of 'large numbers of neurotic casualties', and wanted authorities to avoid the mistake of awarding pensions for this disability. He believed that disorders like neurasthenia, psychasthenia and hysteria were largely functional and would worsen if compensated, but they could also be successfully treated if addressed at the right time with the right approach. Psychasthenics, for example, were unable to adapt themselves to reality and could best be cured through persuasion and psychotherapy. Regnell claimed that this form of psychotherapy was similar to that prescribed by Dejerine, Janet and Dubois, not that prescribed by Freud, Jones or Jung. This version of psychotherapy broadly consisted of an assessment (which could include dream analysis and word association) of the underlying sub-conscious mental conflict producing the symptoms, to provide a basis for treatment. The underlying complexes, the best example of which was love, were a 'direct stream of consciousness', which 'coloured a young man's thinking'. A number of other dynamic mechanisms such as repression were part of the internal dynamic, but the primary focus in therapy was on rooting out the underlying deep inner complexes, rather than dealing with any remnants of the war. Unless there was a definite injury, hysterical conditions were always functional, and since they were produced by suggestion they could be removed by 'pure persuasion'. 'The seat of the disorder is not in the arm or in the leg, but in the mind'. Other forms of treatment, such as electricity, drugs, massage and hypnotism, tended to focus on symptoms and were generally not recommended. Echoing his British and Australian counterparts, Regnell advocated firmness and authority in dealing with war neurotics.[33]

At the same conference a Dr Hayward, who had also worked in London during the war, reminded his audience that the 'neuroses described had been in evidence from time immemorial'. In these functional cases the severity of the condition bore no relationship to the original causality, such as mine explosions. Improvement of patients was strongly influenced by the personality of the medical officer in charge of the ward. Hayward thought that if the functional nature of these neuroses had been acknowledged earlier, society might have been spared the sight of the 'many mental wrecks in their midst'. Recovery could not be expected if these men were 'coddled' with support, such as pensions. He did not blame the soldier, arguing that he should not be discharged until given proper treatment and retraining.[34]

Treatment options were borrowed from British practice such as that at Maudsley Hospital and Seale Hayne. The root of the problem was amnesia, where the 'subconscious mind was worrying over the shock which originally produced the trouble'. The work of uncovering these memories through psychoanalysis and hypnoanalysis could be achieved only by experts. In another paper, Withington reported that 95 per cent of soldiers could be hypnotised, but agreed that such practice needed to be kept out of the hands of charlatans. Hypnosis, which increased suggestibility, and therefore facilitated persuasion, was highly recommended. Noble pointed out that in the various Red Cross institutions, and at No. 23 Auxiliary Hospital in New South Wales, those suffering from mental diseases and alcoholism were segregated from those affected with war neuroses. He advocated a very regimented treatment, in which a well-trained team would not have their efforts 'thwarted by outside interference from family members'. Nursing staff who even 'unconsciously suggested contra-therapy' would be weeded out. This treatment team would use psychoanalysis, suggestion, hypnotism, and physical treatments.[35]

In 1920 Godfrey reported on 400 men who were admitted to the No. 5 Australian General Hospital in Melbourne, with conditions of nervousness, hyperasthesia to light and noises, insomnia, night terrors, a feeling of falling through space when asleep, and impaired memory. Men also displayed tachycardia, tremors, stammering, aphonia, paraesthesia and anaesthesia, blindness, functional paralysis, deafness or visceral disorders. They were not 'shell-shocked', but were 'suffering from emotional traumata, and the term anxiety hysteria appeared to be appropriate'.[36]

The prominent Brisbane academic and clinical psychologist Elton Mayo was one innovative therapist in the post-war era who received little recognition. Towards the end of World War One his lectures on psychology at the University of Queensland sparked the interest of Dr Thomas Matthewson, who specialised in functional and nervous diseases at the Sick Children's Hospital in New South Wales. They developed a professional relationship, and Matthewson asked Mayo to assess some of his problematic patients. One case was a young officer who had returned from World War One distressed and been diagnosed with shell shock. He had been treated by a number of doctors without success, but one session with Mayo won his confidence and he continued treatment with significant improvement. Mayo used a number of techniques, such as Jung's association test and hypnosis, to tease out a soldier's experiences and repressed memories. He treated a number of psycho-neurotics and continued to advise Matthewson, even arranging for him to be appointed resident medical officer at the Russell Lea hospital for shell-shocked veterans in New South Wales. Mayo developed a dynamic psychological theory on war neuroses, and argued that effective 'cure' required abreaction and purposive re-education. His work with veterans effectively ceased, however, when he left for the United States in 1922 and embarked on a distinguished career in industrial psychology.[37]

The public discussion and debate about the needs of mentally damaged soldiers of World War One was very restrained, but at least provided evidence that it was of some concern. With the exception of the newspaper *Smith's Weekly*, a constant thorn in the side of the government, there was little outcry from outside authorities and groups on the treatment of psychologically damaged returned men. After a flurry of activity at the end of the war, any concern for the returned man gradually dissipated as post-war reconstruction got under way.

A pension was a key factor in successful psychiatric rehabilitation. A pension could give some security, but medical experts argued against them on the grounds that monetary reward would take away any incentive to recover. At the beginning of the war, pensions were allocated through a Pensions Board and granted from Patriotic Funds, which were in turn funded by public subscription. Pensions were taken over as a government responsibility in amendments to the *Pensions Act and Australian Soldier's Repatriation Act* of 18 January 1917, introduced by Senator Edward Miller. The Australian War Pensions Scheme was implemented in August 1918, and the government, having accepted responsibility for repatriation and compensation, established the Repatriation Department in 1918 to provide separate rehabilitation facilities for ex-servicemen.[38] The government could not ignore the needs of almost 300,000 men who might have posed a threat at the ballot box to the government of the day. Bodies like the RSSAILA, a powerful veteran lobby group established in 1916, persuaded the government to change its mind on entitlement for psychological injury.[39]

Despite this popular support for pensions, medical authorities did not encourage the allocation of pensions on psychiatric grounds. Butler, for example, stringently opposed granting pensions on such grounds, arguing that the 'nervous soldier' should not be released to contaminate the community, and if a soldier was not adequately treated before discharge, he would be a 'drain on the life blood of the nation'.

The same psychiatric labels used in war-time were used to classify men when they presented for post-war treatment and compensation. These labels included:

- simple exhaustion
- neurasthenia
- hysteria
- confusional states
- medical conditions – miscellaneous.

More serious psychotic conditions included idiocy, imbecility, feeble-mindedness, moral imbecility, mania, melancholia, maniacal-depression, insanity, mental stupor, delusional insanity, psychasthenia, acute delirium, infective disease insanity, general paralysis of the insane, confusional insanity, insanity due to alcohol, dementia praecox, and dementia primary or secondary.

Army authorities were reluctant to discharge mentally wounded men. There were two main reasons for retaining men in service until they were 'cured'. The first was to ensure that soldiers would not contaminate society after demobilisation. The second was to reduce the likelihood of a pension being granted on psychiatric grounds in civil life. It was argued that releasing untreated men could even exacerbate the original condition, and facilitate the development of an actual neurosis from a potential neurosis. The best prophylaxis for these men was the same as that recommended for the development of a strong fighting force – *esprit de corps*, discipline, and organisation. On Butler's estimation, 'the proportion of pensions for this type of disorder greatly exceeds the total sum of the disorder actually seen in the war', which could only be explained either through some form of latent neurosis or malingering. According to Butler, malingering was fostered in the economic depression of the 1930s.[40]

Until April 1918 responsibility for all care for veterans other than those still being treated in military hospitals lay with the mental institutions in each state. Initially, shell-shocked patients were isolated during their voyage home, and on embarkation were housed in specially designated sections of the hospitals in Sydney and Melbourne. Those who had not been cured within 12 months were sent back to their respective state lunacy departments. At this time all mentally disturbed citizens were subject to state statutes that determined how they were treated and housed.[41]

The facilities of the army and the Repatriation Department were obviously inadequate for the damaged soldier, not just because of scarce resources but also because of a lack of finance and the low status of mental illness. In the larger states of New South Wales and Victoria, separate non-government institutions were established. In New South Wales, for example, Sir James Joynton Smith, who financed the journal *Smith's Weekly*, converted his mansion in Coogee to a 40-bed hospital for those suffering from war strain.[42]

The Australian Red Cross (ARC) Home Hospitals and Convalescent Department established a network of post-hospital convalescence and rehabilitation facilities in New South Wales for 'mental and nerve cases'. The ARC built convalescent homes, hostels for the permanently incapacitated, and separate facilities for those suffering from severe shell shock and other psychological conditions.[43] Authorities were keen for local expertise to be utilised, such as the knowledge of the asylum-trained female nurses at Broughton Hall Military Hospital for Neurasthenics in New South Wales. There was also a strong recommendation to provide employment and vocational training as an integral part of treatment.[44]

The generous conditions in the ARC facilities contrasted starkly with the poor conditions in state asylums. Numbers in the ARC homes increased dramatically after 1917, as more damaged men returned from the front. Numbers increased again after the Armistice was declared in 1918, partly because of the release of many men who had been retained in hospital to make them fit for return to service or to 'cure' them before entry to society. In 1917 the first Nerve and Shell Shock Home was established to cater for those cases too severe for the convalescent home and not bad enough for acute facilities. Nerve cases constituted the second most prevalent 'disease' category requiring long-term rehabilitation, second only to tuberculosis. These men were the 'shell shock and neurasthenic cases in which severe relapses frequently take place'.[45]

Clinical services in ARC institutions included psychological assessment and treatment with psychoanalysis, hypnotism, relaxation, re-education, reassurance, suggestion, persuasion, electric massage and medications. When sufficient progress had been made the patients would be transferred to one of the country homes, where they would be in the open air with 'physical occupation and mental rest in the healthy highlands'. These well-organised farms provided outdoor activities such as dairying, poultry farming, vegetable growing and woodcutting. However, this idyllic existence could not last forever; sooner or later the patient had to re-enter the real world. However, the 'nerve cases' were:

> cruelly handicapped in not being able to obtain light employment when they leave our nerve hospitals. A patient is discharged after many months of careful treatment and supervision, ready and eager to become a useful citizen once more. What confronts him? Days and weeks of fruitless search for suitable work – then he gives up in despair. In several cases he has been known to take his life, in others he becomes really mental from worry and the prospect of a hopeless future for his wife and children. Another may be compelled to take on heavy manual labour for which he is physically and mentally unable. This means relapse and he is soon back in the nerve hospital depressed and discouraged having lost hope and self-confidence. Above all, they needed a helping hand that they might regain step by step their old confidence. Occupation of mind and body is their only salvation'.[46]

The demand for ARC services reached a peak at the end of 1919, and by the end of 1923 most of the homes had been closed or scaled down. Patients – who were still suffering from paralysis, loss of voice, shakiness, heart pounding, headaches, weakness, sleeplessness, and a host of other functional nervous disorders – were transferred to the Prince of Wales Hospital. A minority of men were unfit for 'responsible employment', but a few of the 'almost hopeless cases' who were readmitted did not require treatment for as long a period as in their first admission. The residual nerve cases were absorbed into the existing system, especially Callan Park Mental Hospital.[47] As the homes declined, the ARC transferred their effort towards hospital visitation and support.[48]

Within this context it is not surprising that right up until 1939 the medical approach to the psychologically damaged soldier was still characterised by a view that the ongoing psychological problems of the veteran were of his own doing and should not be attributed to war. Butler fundamentally considered the 'so-called war neurosis' to be a 'disability of conduct that comes more properly within the field of *morale*'. Following his review of more serious cases of disturbed men repatriated to Australia, which revealed 'no excess of major psychoses', he concluded that:

> The consensus of opinion in medical officers of the Repatriation Department strongly favours the view generally held, that the war *per se* cannot be regarded as a 'cause' of those various morbid states – diseases – that make up the content of major psychiatry.[49]

This view set the scene for the treatment of soldiers in the war to follow in 1939. In this sense the shell shock story of the Australian soldier was essentially no different from that of his British counterpart. He did not present anything new to medical science and his maladies were classified according to the medical classification system of the day, with no new diagnoses emerging. Shell shock, although persisting as a popular term, was eliminated from the official nomenclature, and replaced with terms representing functional or neurotic conditions. The locus of the problem was thus shifted from the pathogen of war to the pathological pre-trauma history and susceptibility of the soldier. Memory of traumatic experience was taken seriously by a small number of specialists, but lengthy psychotherapy was discouraged. All that the soldier really needed was some firm but kindly authority, thorough assessment of the problem, a healthy environment, and short-term psychotherapy consisting of explanation and persuasion.

Fundamentally, the focus was on individual pathology, and a soldier's disorders of war were primarily psychogenic in origin, not physical. The men who could not cope with the heat of battle were examined and classified according to the existing medically defined pathologies. Soldiers with no physical wound to justify their withdrawal were a danger to morale and efficiency and, although this was not openly stated, ran the risk of being called 'scrimshankers' (shirkers), as they were in the British Army. The post-war story of British soldiers has never been explored in detail, but some sense of the post-war struggle is embedded in classic stories such as that of Robert Graves, who admitted in *Goodbye to All That* that he had experienced mental distress after World War One, despite getting on with life.[50]

The response to the mentally damaged soldiers of World War One reflected some of the activity in the civil arena post-war. Movements like the Mental Hygiene Movement, in which causes for mental illness were found in hereditary and constitutional factors, fitted well with the interpretations on war-related breakdown. Many wartime experts, such as Springthorpe, Ellery, Dawson, Noble, Bostock, and Maudsley, were also leaders in the eugenics movement. They were influenced by European ideas on 'neurotic illness', and treatments like hypnosis and psychotherapy. The shell-shocked soldiers of World War One, who had no organic injury, fitted neatly within this framework.[51]

* * * * *

In this part of the Australian story, shell shock, or war neurosis, was not seen to be a major problem, and there was no evidence of an epidemic of casualties. The adopted psychiatric labels had the effect of shifting the emphasis away from the toxicity of war to the weakness of the individual. Any diagnosis that implied some organic lesion, such as shell shock, was rejected. Breakdowns were mental and moral disorders and a threat to the stability of the modern army. Even though men did return home in a damaged state and needed intensive care, the army medical authorities generally believed that if these men 'got on with life' and got a good job, such problems would go away and they would not be a drain on civilian resources.

Spanning the wars: the contribution of Paul Dane

In the treatment of World War Two veterans in Australia, long-term psychotherapy was the least preferred option, and was certainly not encouraged. Very few Australian psychiatrists either advocated or practised analytical psychotherapy with war neurosis cases. One exception was an 'irritable' Irishman called Paul Greig Dane, a symbol of rebellion in the treatment of casualties of war. His life spanned the two major wars, and he honed his psychoanalytic skills on both World War One and World War Two soldiers.

Dane was born in 1880 and worked as a psychiatrist until his death in 1950. He stood out because he was one of the few to develop and articulate a comprehensive theory to underpin his practice, and was probably the first in Australia to employ hypnosis and abreaction. Dane completed his MD at the University of Melbourne in 1909 and started his practice in Ballarat, where he also became an officer in the Sixth Field Ambulance. An exposure to the 'magic hand of the genius' of Freud came in the form of a lecture by Havelock Ellis in Sydney in 1911. When World War One was declared in 1914 he volunteered at the age of 34 and served as a medical officer in Egypt and at Gallipoli. He continued his work with veterans after discharge both in private practice and in the repatriation system. An interest in neurology and the problems of 'shell-shocked' soldiers led to disenchantment with electrical stimulation, and he was converted to psychotherapy under the influence of J.W. Springthorpe and C. Godfrey.[52]

Dane published his views in a number of articles. While he was a neurologist in the Caulfield (Victoria) Repatriation Hospital in the 1920s, he observed a 'steady stream' of neurotic soldiers. He argued strongly that wrong treatment was worse than no treatment at all, and that time 'does not work a cure'. Some of the treatments of the day, such as drugs, gland tabloids [*sic*], massage, baths and trips to the country, only served to encourage the soldier to fixate on his condition, and to enrich the 'quack'.[53] In his early work Dane classified patients as suffering from:

- anxiety state
- compulsion neurosis
- conversion hysteria
- neurasthenoid condition
- organic conditions associated with psycho-neurotic disturbance.

He considered that most of these conditions had no 'material base', and that the true aetiology was to be found in mental conflict and disharmony in the unconscious mind. Dane derived this idea from Charcot, Freud, Janet and Putnam, but of these, Freud had the greatest influence. In Dane's view, even an intimate knowledge of the brain and the 'layers of ganglia and associated fibres' could not bring this understanding. Dane believed that sooner or later it would be revealed that there was a sexual origin to inner conflict. His analysis of cases revealed 'narcissistic and homosexual trends' as with any inner conflict basis of psychic trauma, and supported the common belief that 'there is no difference in the psychic mechanisms involved in the neuroses of peace and war'. Evaluation of 145 of these war neurosis cases led him to believe that hypnosis and suggestion were the most effective methods of treatment.

Spurred on by his experience with World War One soldiers, Dane immersed himself more deeply in the analytic field. In 1928 he travelled to Europe for analysis under Joan Riviere, and returned to Melbourne to continue his practice and help form the Melbourne Institute of Psychoanalysis.

By the 1940s, when World War Two soldiers began to appear as neurotic casualties, Dane became closely involved in their treatment, and in the training of repatriation psychiatrists. He rued the fact that still, at the beginning of World War Two, the medical profession had neither understood nor accepted the ideas of Freud, and 'medical personnel of the army, and psychiatrists in general, were unprepared for the proper evaluation of the possible psychiatric casualties of the war'. In World War Two he was shocked to find that electro-shock treatment was being used to treat the psychiatric casualty: 'These patients had of course in many cases lapsed, and their second state was worse than their first'; the advances in psychotherapy of the previous 28 years were being ignored, and psychotherapy was little practised. Dane again advocated that 'the only rational treatment for such disorders is to restore to consciousness the lost memory, and allow an appropriate motor reaction for the affect [abreaction]'. He considered that the best results were achieved if this was done as soon after the traumatic impact as possible.[54]

Attention to traumatic war memories was central to Dane's theory, but unconscious conflict rather than the traumatic event was still the most cogent explanation. Towards the end of his life he shifted slightly in diagnostic orientation when he made a distinction between traumatic neuroses and ordinary psychoneurosis. He described men who had experienced a single 'severe traumatic experience, presenting as irritable, sensitive to light, having headaches, insomnia and battle dreams, who were easily fatigued, and had bouts of amnesia'. In these cases he considered a diagnosis of shell shock appropriate, but still maintained that a long term disabling condition could only be explained by a repressed unconscious and distorted sex drive. 'Those who are to experience intense psychic trauma without developing neurotic symptoms are those who have been able to surmount successfully all infantile traumatic experiences, thereby allowing a smooth and harmonious development of their Ego'. All phenomena could be explained in Freudian terms. Battle dreams, for example, were a result of a partial return of the repressed event at a time when the ego's defences were weak. For Dane the only effective treatment was to address the amnesia by recalling the event through hypnosis and abreaction. Even unsuccessful treatment could be accommodated on the grounds that the patient had a Freudian death wish.[55]

Paul Dane was never fully acknowledged by the establishment and he made no direct contribution to policy formation. This may be fortunate, since any entrenchment of Freudian ideas in policy and later psychological practice may have served to focus attention on constitutional pre-disposition, rather than on the nature of the stressor. On the other hand, had he been accorded more credibility, more consideration might have been given to the importance of traumatic memory as a factor in treatment.

CHAPTER 3

Nothing New in World War Two

Now that we are in the throes of another war, in which fear-inspiring influences will be no whit less than in the previous struggle, the neuroses as seen in war will attract additional attention. It is as well to realise that the term war neurosis does not connote some new nervous disorder which does not have its counterpart in civil life.

C.C. Minty, Senior Medical Officer, Repatriation Department, Brisbane, 1940 [1]

With the outbreak of World War Two medical authorities had to establish a medical service to underpin the huge AIF contingent sent overseas, but there were no adequate models and few ideas for the psychiatric services. At the beginning of World War Two there was within the Australian Army Medical Corps (AAMC) no articulated body of knowledge and no official policy to deal with the mental casualty.

A.G. Butler's medical history of World War One, which had a substantial section on the 'moral and mental disorders' of the Great War, was not published until 1943. His experience from the First War was therefore unavailable to medical practitioners in the Second, and though Butler did publish a few articles in the *Medical Journal of Australia* prior to 1943, he appears to have exerted minimal influence on World War Two thinking.[2] As many thought that 'the war to end all wars' would not be repeated, and there would therefore be little need to prepare for future psychological casualties, little development in theory or practice had taken place. The 1922 British Inquiry had virtually buried any critique of psychological wounds of war in its rejection of the term 'Shell Shock'.[3]

Despite the World War One experience it was later acknowledged in the official medical history of World War Two that medical authorities were not prepared for psychiatric casualties. Brigadier G.W.B. James, the consulting psychiatrist to the British troops in the Middle East, admitted that:

> The doctors of the empire, no matter where they were trained, were, with few exceptions, bewildered by the psychiatric casualty; they looked on him with distaste, and were quite unable to deal with him effectively.[4]

This unreadiness was also reinforced in a later report by Hurt and Nettle, who concluded that 'medicine was quite unprepared for the magnitude of the psychiatric problem'. Selection of service personnel was inadequate and the number of trained psychiatrists was far too small to cope with the number of psychiatric cases that swamped the wards.[5] While the best ways to perform medicine, and in particular, psychiatry, were not always clear, the purpose of psychiatry and medicine in war was clear. Medical personnel were there to support an efficient fighting unit and at the same time minimise losses through efficient treatment of casualties. A.J. Sinclair, a senior psychiatrist in the Australian Army Medical Corps said this of the role of the psychiatrist:

> his duty is to keep them fighting, as well as to care for those who are mentally incapacitated. Every patient represents a potential unit of fighting power.

Despite the initial unreadiness, a psychiatric medical system was eventually established. The way in which medical ideas were eventually applied in the field is illustrated in the experience of Arthur, a flying officer who at the age of 22 was posted to Papua only a month after the fall of Singapore.[6] On his squadron's flight to New Guinea, two pilots in Arthur's group died when their planes crashed in low cloud north of Sydney. In Papua he slept in a tent without adequate protection against malarial mosquitos, rose at 3 am nine days out of ten and 'stood by' all day at the airstrip ready to scramble. As food and sanitation were poor, Arthur was seriously ill many times with malaria, dysentery and sub-clinical beri-beri. He described this time as 'living on death row'. After only eight weeks of flying, six out of 20 of the more experienced pilots in his squadron had been killed in action and only two from his own school of ten recruits were still alive. He had helped retrieve bodies after crashes and came to dread fire in the cockpit. His senior officer publicly berated any pilot showing signs of weakness, such as reporting sick with dysentery. One fellow pilot suicided after being accused of a 'lack of moral fibre'.

Arthur's encounter with ideas about psychiatric illness came a few months later during his second tour of duty in Dutch New Guinea in December 1943, when he reported to the squadron doctor with 'an intractable itch' but no sign of rash. He 'couldn't bear to wash himself'. Arthur, who became a medical practitioner after the war, reflected on his treatment:

> I went to see our doctor in Merauke. And I remember he really dressed me down on this business of neurasthenia.
>
> [O]ur doctors didn't know anything. But what was more, at the end of 1943 the doctor was saying that I was 'troppo' ... I've shown you [interviewer] the medical book that said that nebulous symptoms were to be treated as neurasthenia. They were intent on always putting it back on neurasthenia, without thinking or listening; and therefore no one had learned anything and people went on being made sick and it not being recognised.[7]

The 'medical book' Arthur referred to was Allan Walker's official history, *Medical Services of the RAN and RAAF*. After the first air raids on Port Moresby in 1942, Walker reported that a number of airmen complained of 'nebulous symptoms which they hoped would cause them to be boarded out of the danger area', but he believed that:

> It was unwise to be too sympathetic, as this would have encouraged imitators. On the other hand discretion had to be used, as their condition was infectious. Eventually the worst cases were evacuated south with the diagnosis of neurasthenia, and thereafter evacuations from this cause were few.[8]

Obviously Arthur was under stress at the time, but the interesting question is not whether he had a 'real' complaint, but that he was diagnosed with one of the 'nervous affections' of the nineteenth century, which was defined by American neurologist George Beard in 1868 as 'exhaustion of the brain and spinal cord'.[9] In civil life neurasthenia had been a diagnosis for excitable women, like Alice James, who were drained of energy by reading too many novels, and for men who were given to excessive onanism.[10]

Neurasthenia was in fact one of the range of diagnoses that had been drafted into military service in World War One to frame the experience of men who were unable to adapt to the mayhem and destruction in places like Flanders and Gallipoli. It was included as a minor classification of illness in the classic British text *The Neuroses in War* by Emanuel Miller in 1940, where it was described as exhaustion, mental apathy, with vague aches and pains and dizziness, mostly following periods of intense strain. So the legitimate skin complaint of the pilot was interpreted as an unconscious or conscious attempt to escape his duty, just as Ernest White had suggested over 20 years previously.[11]

The experience of Arthur encapsulates the role of psychiatry in the services. Malingerers had to be weeded out. Little sympathy could be afforded to nebulous complaints. Medical labels reflected the view that individual weakness was the primary aetiological factor. These features are clear in the texts of the time. In 1943 John Bostock and Evan Jones published the only textbook produced specifically for army doctors and officers to assist them in fulfilling the dual roles of preserving military morale and discipline, and healing the mentally ill.

> There will be quiet days when it will profit the Medical Officer to dally with his patients, extracting the story of their lives so that they appear not as men in uniform, but as human souls striving from infancy through the trials of youth and the perils of adolescence to a near stability endangered by the cataclysm of war. It is your privilege to be able to disentangle the threads and to restore stability.

But on the other hand:

> Army efficiency is a matter of life and death for the community. Whenever in doubt it is wiser to consider that a man is a malingerer rather than that he may be a neurotic.[12]

The medical officer in Arthur's case had been assigned a clearly defined role in manpower management and the maintenance of military morale. In another document, the manual for the Australian Army, *Handbook for the Prevention, Detection and Treatment of Nervous Invalidity,* Bostock and Jones listed the neurasthenic as one of the personality types likely to develop a neurotic reaction to stress in battle. Neurasthenia was also included as a diagnostic category in the *Hints to Medical Officers* for handling psychiatric casualties issued by General Headquarters in the Middle East in 1942.[13]

Treatment of soldiers on the front line was informed by psychiatric diagnoses and treatments of the time. Most disorders were basically seen as a form of neurosis, a condition where there was no physical basis for a person's inability to function. Their problems were 'all in the mind'. According to the official medical historian Allan Walker, the standard labels of psychoneurosis, anxiety state and conversion hysteria were the most commonly used. The official medical guidelines for General Headquarters, Middle East Forces (1942), emphasised the place of individual inadequacy in a breakdown and listed the causes of breakdown as the three Ps:

- *Parental* – 'the whole family history, the patient's nurture and upbringing and what is vaguely described as his constitution, in fact his whole life story'
- *Psychological* – the interpretation of events, attitudes, distress
- *Physical* – physical weakness, illness, fatigue, high blood pressure etc.[14]

No great concern was expressed about the mental casualty in the civilian medical literature. It was predicted that the majority of men would not break down because they were so well balanced, and 'great stress will be needed to create a morbid state'. According to Bostock and Jones, inherent personality weaknesses could be observed in anxious folk, neurasthenics, hysteroids, paranoids, mental defectives, schizoids, psychopaths, over-conscientious types, and morbid and moody types, so these needed to be weeded out, preferably during training. When looking for the likely weak types, the medical officer needed to watch for fatigue, moodiness, hypersensitivity, unsociability, sullenness, and a long list of other unpleasant behaviours.

This practice would enable men to be sorted into three broad categories or 'pigeon holes' by the medical officer at the front line:

- Normal nervousness – the jitters, shakiness, and other normal reactions
- Psychoneuroses – organically based disorder, anxiety state, hysteria, malingering, and delusional state
- Acute psychosis – grave anxiety, acute mania, acute melancholia, schizophrenia, paraphrenia, confusional state, alcoholic state, head injuries, epilepsy, and commotional shock.

Shell shock, a term from the early days of World War One, was never to be used as a diagnosis in World War Two except in cases where some form of explosive shock had been sustained. The Enquiry into Shell Shock in 1922 by British army and medical experts had reviewed all the evidence on the validity of the diagnosis 'shell shock'. Their exhaustive deliberations resulted in a rejection of the term 'shell shock' and a recommendation that it be only used in the case of commotional shock. Only a small proportion of mental injuries could be attributed to the physical shock of battle. This report had also recommended that:

> No cases of psycho-neurosis or of mental breakdown, even when attributed to a shell explosion or the effects thereof, should be classified as a battle casualty any more than sickness or disease is so regarded.[15]

In terms of treatment, Bostock and Jones argued that more sophisticated treatments could only be applied away from the front line. They listed a full range of possible interventions: persuasion, suggestion, hypnotic suggestion, simple analysis and hypno-analysis, narco-analysis, and shock therapy (with cardiazol or phrenazol), narco-therapy, faradism, physiotherapy including relaxation methods, isolation, and re-education and occupation. Traumatic memories could also be recovered through narco-analysis. Above all, the medical officer was to adopt a firm supportive role, paying great attention to taking a careful life history to achieve an understanding of the nature of the man's condition. A key therapeutic activity was to draw out the suppressed 'terrifying emotional experiences'.[16]

In effect, Bostock and Jones offered many possibilities for medical officers in World War Two, but it is doubtful that any front-line medical officers other than psychiatrists put these ideas into practice. Their book was not readily available, and few medical officers would have been trained in the whole range of treatments proposed, and it is unlikely more than a few specialist psychiatrists would have had access to the book. Training for army psychiatrists did not start until the beginning of 1941, and even then it was no more than a crash course of twelve weeks. There was no systematic training for regimental medical officers on how to deal with the psychiatric casualty.

Love, a Major in the Australian Army Medical Corps, placed more emphasis on the psychobiological basis of neurosis. He drew on a number of prominent theorists (Pavlov, Walter Cannon and Paul Wood) to explain the dynamics of fear and anxiety states, which comprised the majority of casualties at the front. The symptoms of men admitted to casualty stations with insomnia, exhaustion, tremulousness, dizziness, anorexia, headaches, abdominal discomfort, nausea, blurred vision, weeping, enuresis, or inability to concentrate, had a neuro-physiological explanation. Under the stress of battle soldiers had two competing emotions – fear (producing fatigability, muscular exhaustion, and depression) and anger (promoting muscular power).

This mechanistic explanation, based entirely on an intra-individual psychobiological dynamic, had implications for prevention and treatment. First the potentially weak individuals needed to be detected and sorted at recruitment. Further 'weeding out' could be achieved during initial training, where troops were put under pressure to expose any vulnerability. Those who remained needed to be well-equipped and instilled with *esprit de corps* and a fighting spirit. Nervous conditions in the field (nervousness, restlessness or moodiness) needed to be recognised and treated early. Treatment for 'fully developed neuroses' initially consisted of rest and sleep, which could be induced by doses of hot drinks and the sedative Luminal.

The medical officer would learn to 'strengthen such as do stand; and to comfort and help the weak-hearted; and raise up them that fall'. Evacuation was only to be a last resort and every medical officer should aim at a 'nil return'.[17]

Retrospectively, Walker (1952) provided the most comprehensive account of psychiatric services and ideas in World War Two. In *Clinical Problems* he detailed the psychiatric provisions in the army against a background of the history of medicine in Australia. On the one hand medicine had become much more specialised, but the public also had more access to medical information and products, which was a threat to the authority of the doctor. In terms of mental health, this trend was decried by Walker who argued that 'positive harm could be done by publicising certain aspects of some subjects, such as neurotic types of illness.' This had led to such evils as the 'universal aspirin in the handbag' and 'numerous proofs of self-drugging in the sanctuary of the bathroom cupboard'.[18] Walker detailed how, prior to the war, medical services in civilian life were provided largely on an individual, private level, and this style was to some extent transferred to the war services.

The Army Medical Corps became much more organised in the provision of psychiatric services. Management of the psychiatric casualty occurred at five levels:

Regimental Medical Officer
Field Ambulance Station
Central Clearing Station
Psychiatric Clinic
Australian General Hospital.

In the ideal field situation, the Army Medical Corps would have established psychiatric centres. The term 'psychiatric centre' rather than 'war neurosis centre' was deliberately chosen to deflect attention from an 'inaccurate name for conditions not necessarily associated with the war'.[19] These centres provided more specialised treatment after casualties had been sorted at the field ambulance station and Central Clearing Station level. Medical officers were instructed (e.g. No 17 Middle East Series) on how to provide initial treatment in the field and make decisions about further referral. The primary purpose of such efforts was to involve the medical profession in more systematic measures 'to control mental illness' and to create a more efficient fighting force.[20]

A few studies were undertaken in Australian Army General Hospitals, one of the more notable being that of Cooper and Sinclair at 104 AGH at Tobruk in 1941. Alec Sinclair was a significant figure in the Australian Army mental health system, and his study provided a particularly interesting site for exploring the application of psychiatric ideas.[21] A number of Australian battalions, including the 2/10th and 2/43rd, were part of a garrison assigned to hold the coastal town of Tobruk on the Mediterranean Sea, from early April 1941 until October the same year. The German siege was maintained from the land, but supplies could be brought in under enemy aerial bombardment by sea. Casualties were housed in the General Hospital established in the town. Cooper and Sinclair surveyed 210 psychiatric patients in this AGH, where they could observe men under extreme stress of bombardment, strafing, machine gun attacks, monotony and helplessness, as well the annoyances of fleas, poor food, flies, and limited water.

Psychiatric casualties presented with over-alertness, loss of concentration, fearful half-waking imaginings bordering on hallucinations, frequent need to micturate, and profuse sweating and tremor. They were diagnosed with hysteria, fugue states and mimicry, depression, psychomotor retardation, sense of unworthiness, hypochondriasis, exhaustion states, psychopathy, mental instability, congenital mental defect, malingering, and psychoses. The most common explanation for these conditions was constitutional inferiority.

The conditions and length of the siege allowed little more than careful history taking and talk therapy. The primary purpose of interviewing was to articulate the immediate circumstances of the breakdown and carefully examine prior experiences to establish the 'root causes' of the soldier's weakness under pressure. Fear states, for example, were said to occur in men with 'less well integrated personalities', and with 'long-standing fear reactions dating from childhood'.[22] The primary focus in diagnosis and treatment was on the individual patient, not the traumatic events.

The classification of casualties was similar to those in the Middle East, with a slight increase in psychopathic states – anxiety states (35 per cent), psychopathic states (20 per cent), fear states (15 per cent), hysteria (15 per cent), psychotic disorders (10 per cent), and depressives, hypochondriacs, mental defects (5 per cent). A careful examination of prior experience of patients led Sinclair to conclude that weakness in character was the root cause of these breakdowns. Less than half of these casualties could be linked with battle experience, but those with no battle experience were more likely to have had features of psychological breakdown in their past history.[23]

The treatment of soldiers in New Guinea was no different from that offered in the Middle East, but medical facilities in the field were very primitive. Medical officers were overtaxed with more pressing demands to treat wounds and epidemics of sickness such as dysentery and malaria, so treatment in the field was far more pragmatic. According to Sinclair, the most common condition, anxiety, could be alleviated with physical exercise, mild sedation, psychotherapy and occupation. A major component of the treatment was education about the nature of the anxiety. Modified hypoglycaemic treatment was given to acute cases of anxiety and 'functional' dyspepsia cases. Evacuation by air of psychotic patients presented a particular problem for medical authorities. They required more physically invasive treatments, such as cardiazol-induced shock therapy and restraint, for the men to be safely transported. These could only be administered in the large base hospitals in Port Moresby and Lae and were more readily available in the latter stages of the war.

In a major essay in 1944 Sinclair synthesised his experience in four major theatres of war, which included the Middle East and New Guinea.[24] He based his views on observations of more than 1,000 men, and summarised ideas and practice in the field and in rehabilitation. This paper was a statement about what psychiatry had achieved in five years of war. He had no illusions about the role of the psychiatrist in the armed forces, which was to 'keep men fighting, as well as care for those who are mentally incapacitated'. Every patient 'represents a potential unit of fighting power', and in wartime the psychiatrist 'returns his patient into a rude world peopled by men whose business is warfare'. Sinclair was adamant that pensions should not be granted for neuroses. On the basis of his experience he was clear that the 'folly' begun during World War One of pensioning a soldier with psychiatric problems should not be repeated. He did not deny that men developed post-war neuroses, but 'there seems no doubt that to shackle the neurotic to his symptoms and disabilities by a monetary dole is a poor solution to his problems'. He maintained that the interests of the veteran would be better served by an 'army of psychiatric social workers' giving the veteran 'constructive, creative and sympathetic service than by paying him a fortnightly pension in an endeavour to forget him'.[25]

A key statement on the neuroses of war appeared in a paper delivered by Sinclair at the Beattie-Smith lectures at the University of Melbourne on 22 and 29 November 1944.[26] In his view, becoming a soldier was a process of socialisation, in which the recruit entered a world where he would lose his individuality and become a member of a fighting machine. The majority of men successfully integrated themselves into 'this new social pattern of war', but those who failed to adjust were 'psychologically damaged individuals'. Consequently, 'the psychoneuroses are, in the ultimate analysis, social disorders of the individual'. Sinclair's explanation of how this failure came about was relatively simple. To adapt, a man had to accept authority, and become part of the fighting unit. He dismissed nerve concussion, physical exhaustion and illness as significant causes of neurosis. Rather, the neurotic state was a result of 'conflict between the instinctual urges towards survival and the pursuit of the community goal'. Those who had the 'right background and breeding' (neurological make-up and psychological constitution) could withstand the fear of annihilation in battle. He ended his address with speculation that the fundamental explanation of breakdown might be found in Grinker and Spiegel's theory of defective regulation of stimuli in the hypothalamic area.[27] Grinker and Spiegel, in their analysis of the experience of US pilots and troops in World War Two, provide a classic example of the integration of psychiatric ideas into the business of war. They described war as an 'unnatural experiment' which enabled them to study the ego in various stages of dissolution and repair. War neuroses had offered them the 'best opportunity for the study of ego functions and their interrelation with biological and psychological drives'.[28]

In Sinclair's view there was little place for an examination of traumatic memory. Sinclair's accounts suggest that there was nothing new in diagnoses and ideas in World War Two. The only major difference was the increased range of treatment options, but this development merely took the effects of war further from being accorded a significant place in the aetiology of psychiatric conditions.

Walker considered that during 1939–1945 there was a shift in the role and status of psychiatry.[29] This was a shift from a 'detect the malingerer and bash back the neurotic' role, to a more organic role in the maintenance of an efficient fighting unit. During wartime the psychiatrist had come down from his scientific perch and circulated among the ordinary men in the ranks, and psychiatric influence filtered into every level of medical service, from front-line treatment to the general hospital and rehabilitation services.

Walker reiterated the dominant idea that the fundamental 'cause' of the breakdown was individual weakness. 'Speaking in the most general terms, influences stretching back into childhood are probably of more significance than recent or present domestic or social maladjustments: the former may supply the key to the latter'. These 'maladjustments' determine how a person will react to the strain of events such as war. Like many of his contemporaries and predecessors (e.g. Butler, Springthorpe), Walker believed that the experience gained in recognition, prevention, and treatment of mental illness in the army could be effectively applied in the civil field. Walker thus provides a setting for the further exploration of the discourse surrounding mental health of combatants and veterans.

Walker and others did not support the policy of granting a pension to the psycho-neurotic casualty, believing that this only exacerbated his problems. It was a policy based on an erroneous, non-medical view that 'damage through the violence of war is alone responsible for the mental disorders of service men and women'.[30]

One obvious outcome of World War Two was the view that only civilian labels should be used for battle casualties. Although there was some modification and refinement of labelling, psychiatric terminology shifted little between the two major wars. The common view was that the primary diagnosis was a form of neurosis or functional disorder.

Few new diagnoses emerged and breakdown was explained primarily in terms of the inherent weakness of the individual, and problems of adjustment in war-time were construed as individual medical problems. No medical labels recognised the effect of exposure to battle conditions. The only significant development in psychiatric treatment during World War Two was more efficient organisation in the medical military structure, and the application of the physical psychiatric treatments developed in civilian practice. The application of these practices to rehabilitation is described in Chapter 9.

* * * * *

This brief review of the psychiatric ideas and practices provides a setting for a closer look at the experience of Australian soldiers under stress. The dominant explanation for breakdown or inability to cope with the strain of battle was individual weakness. As Sinclair, the most experienced senior Australian psychiatrist of World War Two, argued towards the end of the war, the psychoneuroses were primarily 'social disorders of the individual'.[31]

CHAPTER 4

New Guinea 1942: War, Tours of Duty and Sites of Memory

> They enlisted as boys, and as Kokoda unfolded in front of us and the magnitude of the mountain became clear, the strain of the Kokoda Trail has to be experienced to be believed.[1]

In 1942 New Guinea became a central battleground in the Pacific War. Before describing the combat experience in New Guinea and its immediate impact, it is important to have a sense of how men prepared for their tours of duty.

A war or major battle is not a random event as many acts of violence are. While some military actions have been spontaneous or chaotic, waging war is normally organised and strategic, requiring a great deal of planning and human ingenuity. War is, necessarily, an arena for killing and destruction. When young men volunteer, or are conscripted from civilian life, to join an army, they have to be transformed into men who are prepared to kill and effect destruction. They must be prepared to face the gravest danger; the enemy also kill. Bourke points out in her extensive analysis of killing in wartime that soldiers learn to do things that are condemned in civilian life.[2] In civilian life, taking life is a crime severely punished. In wartime, killing is necessary, sanctioned and rewarded. The young men in the AIF and militia units in World War Two, who were trained to be part of the fighting force, came directly from civil lives where they were not violent.

The men who told the stories of their time in New Guinea for this book were decent men with no record of homicidal or criminal behaviour, and good pre-war work records. A few had received some training in pre-war militia units, but most had moved directly from civilian occupations into uniform. The transformation of these ordinary men into dutiful aggressors had physical, organisational and psychological dimensions. Training and the formation of a cohesive company provided a foundation for the men from which they were able to develop psychological survival strategies, helping to contain anxiety and mental stress in battle. This training was reinforced by a sense of loyalty to country and kin. According to Fred Burr, a commissioned officer in the 2/27th Battalion, a high school teacher and father of two children before joining up, going to war was

> something more than fulfilment of duty. We are training to fit every officer and every man to overwhelm, destroy and slay the aggressor who aggressed from us our liberty, our land, our homes and womenfolk and there is no true Australian man who is not prepared to die to prevent this. The whole object of our training is to build up such a spirit that will force our way to victory or death.[3]

A battalion is a highly structured organisation, normally made up of five companies, a headquarters company and four infantry companies. Infantry companies, at full strength consisting of about 100 men, are divided into platoons of about 30 men with a commanding officer. Platoons in turn consist of sections made up of an officer and 10 men. Other sections provide logistics support such as intelligence, signals and mortar platoons. Battalions make up brigades, which in turn have their own hierarchical structure. Infantry training is centred on the company, and the duty of the company commander is to drill his men into an efficient fighting force.[4]

The army has to produce physically and mentally fit men capable of enduring hardship and performing highly skilled tasks. Training was a matter of both mind and body, and the corporate spirit – '*esprit de corps*'. This spirit was developed in exercises such as marching in formation, during which the companies were encouraged to sing. For example the 2/27th companies would sing *Old King Cole* and *Mademoiselle from Armentières* during route marches. *Esprit de corps* and teamwork were also enhanced by rivalry between units, particularly on outside exercises, where they could come to blows. Aside from physical training, the other component of the training was skill development. Such skills included the use of weapons, map reading, operating and repairing vehicles, the use of codes, wireless operating for senior officers, and tactics and battle planning. Within a company each platoon commander took an intense interest in the 30 men under him, not only in their training and development but also in their general welfare.

Training, and the development of strong cohesion within sections, platoons and companies, was also intended to provide a sense of personal strength and invulnerability. The effectiveness of training had to be tested under battle conditions. Units in the 7th Division, such as the 2/27th Battalion, achieved this successfully in the Middle East. The more hastily raised units such as 39th Battalion had much more limited training opportunities and no testing ground before being thrown into battle in New Guinea in 1942. In his history of the unit Vic Austin noted that the 39th was raised in October 1941 and 'training had scarcely begun under a nucleus of 1914–18 veteran officers and NCOs when, during the night of 7–8 December 1941, the Japanese struck Pearl Harbor'.[5] By 3 January 1942 the 39th had disembarked at Port Moresby, where they were assigned to labouring tasks such as trench digging, airstrip construction and unloading ships, with little opportunity for training. Poor medical facilities, combined with inadequate clothing and poor hygiene, led to a high incidence of tropical diseases and dysentery.

There was no fixed term of service in the AIF, so tours of duty were extensive, and could last up to six years, with an option of applying for discharge after five years of service. When it became clear that Australia was under serious threat from the Japanese after the fall of Singapore, legislation forced the militia units, mostly comprising conscripts, overseas. A tour would normally consist of periods of intense combat interspersed with long periods of training, waiting, recreation, leave and travelling. Unless wounded or ill, a World War Two veteran could have spent up to six years in service and have fought in at least two theatres of war. After the New Guinea campaigns many units took part in the invasion of Japanese-occupied territories in South-East Asian sites such as Balikpapan and Tarakan. Some men joined the occupation forces to maintain order and repatriate thousands of Japanese soldiers, and oversee the transition of occupied territories such as the Dutch East Indies.

Overseas tours exposed troops to new experiences and cultures, as well as to battle. For example the 2/27th Battalion, formed in May 1940, sailed for the Middle East in October 1940 to fight against the Vichy French and Germans,

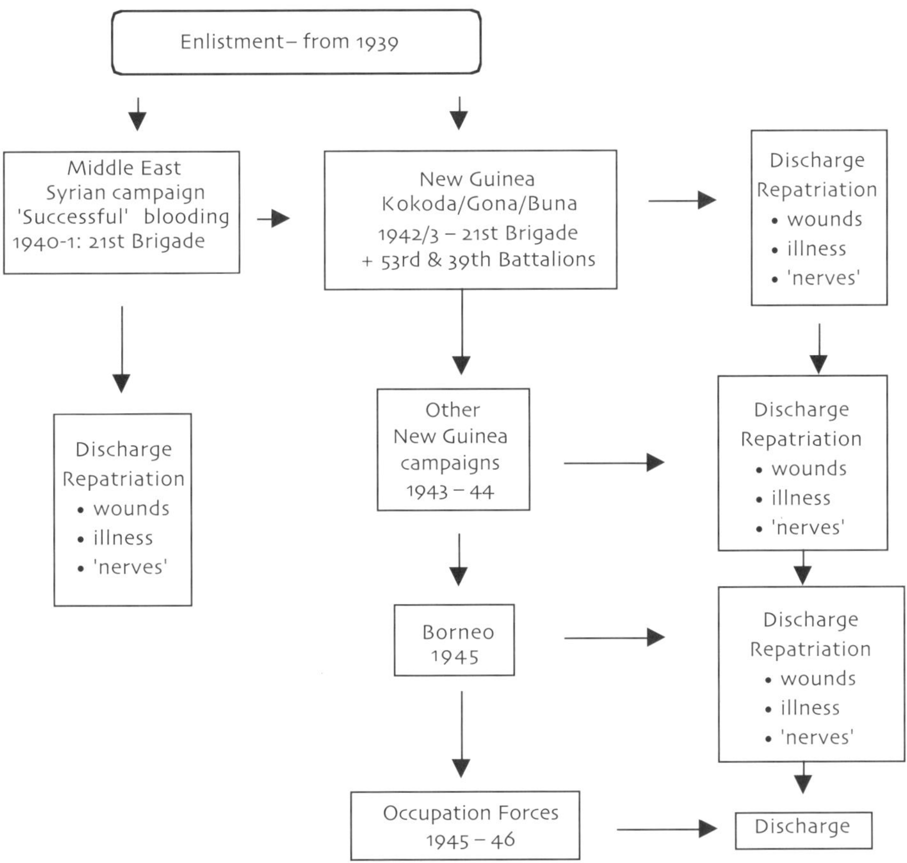

Tours of duty in relation to New Guinea campaigns.

returned to Adelaide on 26 March 1942 after the Japanese entered the war, and were sent to New Guinea in July 1942. Just like their predecessors of the First War they visited ancient exotic places like Colombo, Egypt, North Africa and parts of the Holy Land. Those who survived this intense period came back for 14 days recuperation leave in Australia in February 1943 and returned to New Guinea in the following August. Their last campaign was in Borneo in June/July 1945.

Active military service has been described as 90 per cent boredom and 10 per cent fear. Even though not as traumatic as battle, the times of boredom or inactivity could sometimes cause as much strain as battle. For example, David Sheppard of the 2/27th Battalion found that waiting around was very boring and stressful, especially when there were no books to occupy the mind. At night in New Guinea when there were no lights for writing and reading, the lack of mental challenge left him only with his thoughts and he would get very depressed. Waiting, according to the 2/27th medical officer, often brought an increase in psychosomatic complaints.[6]

New Guinea 1942–43

The New Guinea campaigns presented great potential for battle strain. Because there was no defined front line in the early campaigns, all men were in danger of being killed, or were required to engage in dangerous patrols and close fighting. All carried weapons and could be called upon to fire, and would be fired upon. Even medical personnel and some chaplains carried a side-arm. All senior officers, many of whom were killed or seriously wounded in New Guinea, were directly exposed.[7] For example, Lt Colonel W. Owen, the Commanding Officer of the 39th Battalion, was shot through the eye while throwing a grenade early in the Kokoda campaign. Another 39th senior officer, Captain S. Templeton, died at about the same time. In almost every aspect, the New Guinea campaigns were potentially traumatic for all participating. The general features of New Guinea campaigns were:

- serious combat (observable, stereotypical warfare experiences, such as receiving enemy fire, seeing injured or dead colleagues, going on special missions, and firing weapons)
- exposure to atrocities or episodes of extraordinary abusive violence (observable events that might be considered extremely deviant or beyond normal war experiences, including wounding of non-combatants or mutilation of bodies)
- high risk of contracting debilitating diseases such as malaria and scrub typhus
- the harsh or malevolent environment (the extent to which the veterans rated daily war zone living conditions as bothersome, annoying or uncomfortable, including lack of privacy, inadequate food, bad climate, insect infestation, disease, and filth).[8]

The men on whom this book focuses entered the New Guinea campaign at different points, but all were exposed to similar conditions, especially on the Kokoda Trail. For individuals this meant all or some of the following:

- losing comrades and sometimes witnessing their deaths
- being strafed
- being ordered to finish off a wounded enemy soldier
- collecting and burying putrid bodies
- leaving a dying mate
- being caught in cross-fire with no escape
- observing, hearing about or experiencing atrocity
- fear of being caught alive by the Japanese and being tortured and mutilated
- sustaining serious wounds.

The most intense engagements in New Guinea for the 2/27th, 39th and 53rd Battalions were between July and December 1942. A full account of the battles can be found in military histories such as Brune (1991) and McCauley (1991, 1992). Here I focus on significant features. It was estimated that by August 1942 Japanese forces outnumbered Australians by about 30:1, and that the Australian troops would not be able to withstand their attack. For example, on 29 July the 39th was overrun, and their commanding officer Colonel Owen was killed in the Japanese attack on Kokoda. In a counter attack, the 39th ran out of ammunition and food and had to withdraw. As Don Simonson and Len Suckling recalled, the Japanese:

> had their drill – as soon as they struck us they were out and around and we would be cut off from the back. They would strike and then surround you. They would outflank you all the time. So I think that was a lot of the cause for the withdrawing. Early in the piece these Japanese were so good they could find their way in the jungle. If we went off the track we would get lost. Afterwards we learnt all sorts of little ideas about going down ridges and going up rivers. Not that we had maps. They must have had maps. They would infiltrate and come up in all sorts of places where you would least expect them. [9]

The Kokoda Trail was the centrepiece of the drama that unfolded from July 1942 onwards. This rough track through mountains and jungles was described in the medical report of the Seventh Division recorded in January 1943:

> The intense jungle, inducing feelings of claustrophobia, its intolerable quietness rent by eerie sounds, the crashing of enormous rotting trees, the narrow tortuous tracks, the knee-deep mud with its vice-like grip, and the torrential tropical rains. Into this awe-inspiring scene with its oppressive heat by day and bitter cold by night place the infantryman clad in jungle greens, the only clothes he possesses, assail him with dysentery, malaria and mite bites which ceaselessly itch.
>
> Every few miles bring the track through a small patch of Kunai grass or a small native garden and every seven or ten miles build a dilapidated group of grass huts

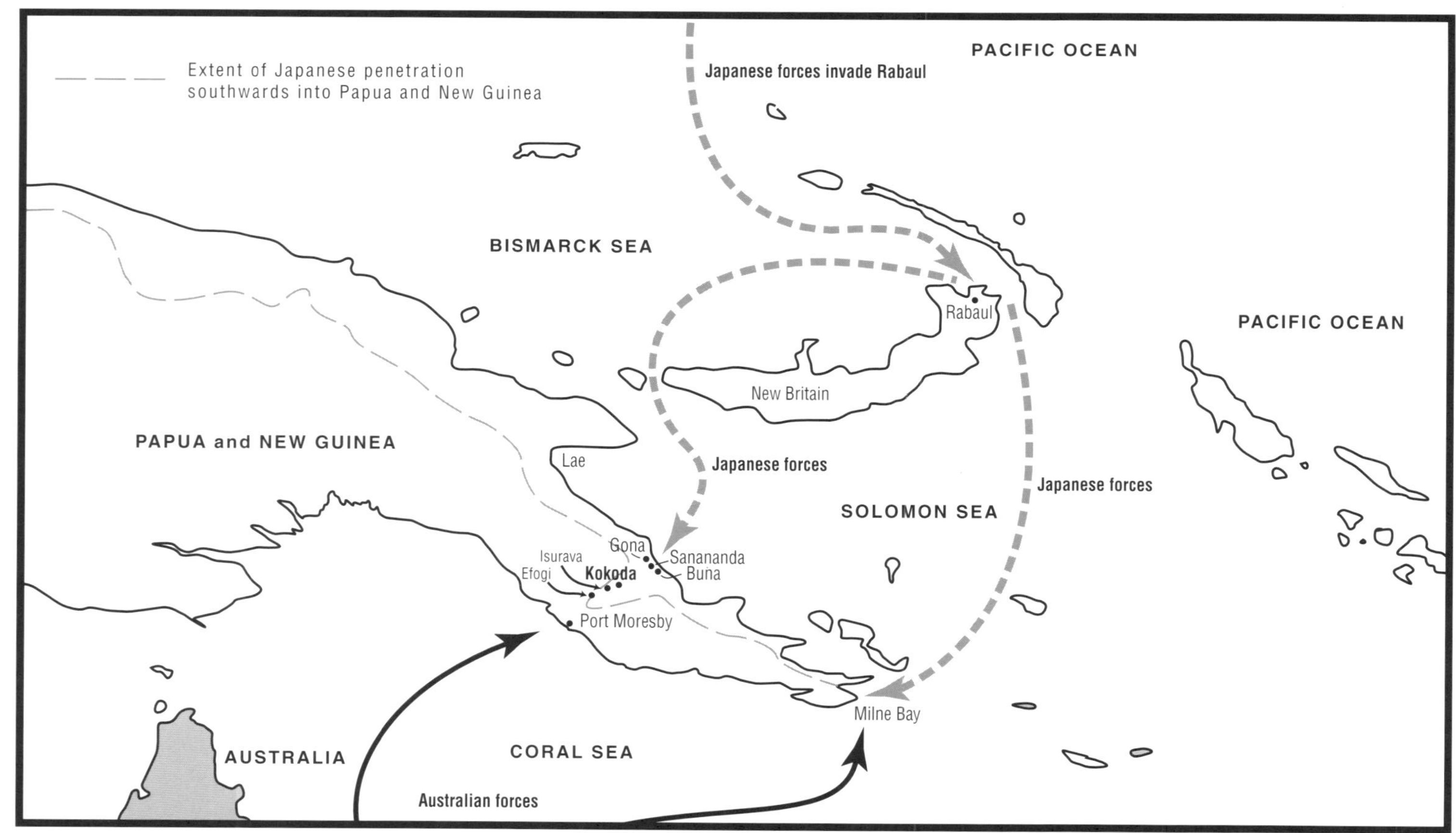

Map of Papua and New Guinea showing course of war 1942–45.

> as staging shelters, generally set in a foul clearing. Leave beside the track discarded putrefying food and occasional dead bodies, and human foulings. On this track day after day followed the walking sick and wounded, stretcher cases being carried by native carriers with improvised stretchers. From each staging post at dawn the walkers, the lame and the halt would be on their way while the native bearers would assemble for their task.[10]

Harry Katekar recalled how different the conditions on the Kokoda Trail, where he first encountered the Japanese, were from those that had prevailed in the Middle East. The 2/27th had only just dug in at Efogi, using their bayonets and steel helmets, when the Japanese attacked with weapons that outranged anything the Australians had:

> The first night was the eerie sight of the Japanese moving down the opposite ridge using flares to enable them to move. We were virtually sent in with Middle East garb – standing out like proverbials – with Middle East weapons that did not work well in the jungle. The battalion was under continuous attack for two days. We suffered 80 battle casualties.

After several weeks of fighting, the headquarters of the Australian 21st Brigade was surrounded, and the battalions were forced to withdraw. Katekar again:

> The overall effect on the troops was that they always wondered why this had to happen. There was a high degree of uncertainty in the troops because there was no-one to inform them. They were left with the opinion that the command had failed to communicate the full situation, particularly why they were not able to rejoin the brigade.

During the withdrawal the battalion broke up and each man had to fend for himself and find a way back. This meant three weeks of deprivation, starvation and exhausting trekking through dense jungle and terrain. They had no aerial support, no supply line, no medical supplies, no mechanical help, and no communications. The majority contracted malaria and dysentery, and in some cases beri-beri and scrub typhus, a normally fatal disease. Managing the sick and wounded was a major problem. The only means of medical evacuation out of the Kokoda area was on a stretcher carried over mountainous terrain, with many river crossings. Often men watched helplessly as their mates died of untreated wounds, disease, starvation or exhaustion. There was a high probability of further injury or wounding, and if caught by the Japanese, torture and execution.

Survival became a matter of individual struggle. Bert Ward, for example, could think only of food, having only one day of emergency rations to last three weeks. He tried leaves and grass to keep him going. He also gave up smoking in that September of 1942 as a way of increasing his stamina and chances of survival. He survived by looking after himself physically as well as he could, keeping his head down and persevering. He did get pretty low but was not prepared to give up. He had to focus his thoughts on each next step.

Lt Colonel Cooper, Commanding Officer of the 2/27th had to make a decision about a group of men who were too sick or weak to travel. Consequently, a group of stretcher cases was left behind in a clearing in the jungle. Signaller John Burns and stretcher-bearer Alf Zanker, who had no medical training, had to care for those men. The only way Jimmy Moir survived was by having maggots eat the rotting flesh in his wounds. David Sheppard developed beri-beri and was near death most of the time. Two men died before they were rescued. Burns was awarded a Military Medal for his efforts:

> Most of his citation [after referring to a mention at Gona when he maintained radio communication despite being wounded] was devoted to an earlier time when he was one of a party cut off and forced to take a difficult track, carrying several wounded men. For ten days Burns worked untiringly, encouraging comrades to keep going and keep carrying the wounded. Once comparatively safe from enemy patrols, the wounded were left in the care of Burns and one other man [Alf Zanker] while the rest of the party – desperately short of food – went on. Through another ten days Burns cheered the wounded, found food for them, kept them comfortable in heat and flies, wet and cold. He gave them talks on the Bible and other topics he could think up. Two men died and Burns [and Zanker] scraped graves for them with bayonet and tin hat … So gentle care, determined cheerfulness and talks on the Bible helped win a Military Medal for the baker's boy grown quickly into a man.[11]

The survivors were found by a patrol. Captain R. Wilkinson described their condition when they were found:

> They were naturally delighted to see us. The stench and the flies were terrific. The party had moved slightly to get away from the flies but they had followed. I was given two hours to work on them. Many of the blankets were fly-blown and I only had acriflavine to use on the wounds. The party had run out of dressings; fortunately we were carrying plenty. Altogether there were nine patients. Two of these were weak and malnourished after dysentery but could walk, the rest were on stretchers, and most of them were suffering from severe gunshot wounds.[12]

The remnants of the withdrawing units reformed in Port Moresby, but soon had insult added to their injury. At the assembly the survivors were publicly humiliated and accused of cowardice by their Commander-in-Chief General Blamey, for withdrawing.[13] Once they had reformed, the units were sent across the Owen Stanley Range to attack Gona, Buna and Sanananda.

Casualties

Fear of death or wounding was dominant in the Owen Stanley Range, at Gona and Sanananda. The 2/27th lost 39 killed and 50 wounded (one-sixth of the battalion strength) in the first two days of fighting on the Kokoda Trail, while 200 enemy deaths were recorded.[14] In the Owen Stanleys–Port Moresby period 625 Australians died and 1,055 were wounded. Of the original Middle East 2/27th Battalion strength of about 1,000, only 330 were fit for the attack on Gona in November 1942. Of those, only 70 men survived the battle unscathed; not even

AWM 013876

Japanese soldiers killed during the Gona action: 'a grim sight'.

the senior officers went unharmed. The 2/27th Battalion commanding officer Lt Colonel Cooper was wounded, and Adjutant Harry Katekar was the only senior officer to survive unscathed. By Christmas Day 1942 the battalion strength had been reduced to three officers and 83 men. In all, seven officers and 59 men were either killed in action or died of wounds in less than a month. John Burns described the aftermath of Gona, where at least 500 Japanese were killed:

> The whole enemy position was a grim sight. Dead were piled high; in many cases they were in an advanced stage of decay, for the enemy had made little effort to bury his dead, and in some cases they were part of a fire step in his defences.[15]

John Manol recalled a Japanese taken prisoner after the 39th Battalion had recaptured Haddy's Village [Gona]:

> He spoke perfect English and showed remorse for what the Japs had done so far in the war. The last thing I remember about Haddy's Village was the bodies of Japanese soldiers left in the open clearing between the huts and the sea. There were at least 100 or 150 of them.[16]

AWM 013845

Exhausted Australian troops resting after the capture of Gona. 16 December 1942.

The 21st Brigade itself sustained serious casualties and by the end of 1942 was reduced to 41 per cent of its original strength.[17] The 49th Militia Battalion, which served in the same period, was reduced, through death, wounds and illness from a strength of 646 in August 1942 to 316 in December of the same year. The total Australian casualties at Gona, Buna and Sananda for the period 14 November 1942 to 22 January 1943 were 1,261 officers and other ranks killed and 2,209 wounded. In comparison, for the whole period of Australian involvement in Vietnam, where 46,000 Australian personnel served, 396 died in battle or from wounds sustained in battle, and 1,952 sustained battle injuries.[18]

Encounters with the enemy and terrain were not the only life-threatening events during this period. Some men were killed by the 'biscuit bombers' – the DC3s that dropped supplies. Heavy bundles containing tins of bully beef and biscuits that had to be dropped without parachutes became lethal missiles. There were also more serious accidents which men found difficult to forget. For example, at Jackson's airfield:

> there was this four-engine Yank plane taking off fully loaded with bombs and fuel and it just touched some trees and ploughed into a truckload of troops – it was devastating.[19]

The circumstances of Gona and Sananada warrant special mention. It was an unnecessary strategy to send men across an open area of burnt kunai grass to attack the well-entrenched Japanese when the objective could have been achieved in less costly ways. As well as snipers, there was enfilading fire from machine guns. The order to 'attack and capture' Gona, it is now argued, was a political decision that overrode sound military planning, and survivors believe it came from much higher than the divisional headquarters in New Guinea. This added to the bitterness felt by the men as they later tried to make sense of their experience. Lt Tom Kimber described the first wave attack on Gona:

> The manner of the attack at Gona was so unnecessary. After the Gona Mission the 39th was detailed to go to Gona West and cut off a force of about 160 Japanese and we had to knock them off – at our own pace. We buried over 150 Japanese with about 20 Casualties – it was murder at Gona Mission. We had to do an attack through Kunai grass and were mown down.
>
> I was in the middle of my line of 30 men. I lost 11 killed and nine wounded, and two of those died of wounds. I stood out like a country shithouse in the middle and all these blokes falling around me. One man had his face shot away and he was only three feet away.[20]

After the battle, Australian soldiers had to collect, identify, and bury their own dead as well as the Japanese. In the official history of the 2/16th Battalion, Malcolm Uren described the conditions when cleaning up the 640 Japanese who were buried in the area after Gona. One task confronting Australian soldiers was clearing a bunker that had been stacked with bags of rice and bodies of dead enemy soldiers, with ammunition on top. The rice was green with mould and the bodies were in advanced stages of decomposition.[21]

A platoon leader in 39th Battalion who participated in a bayonet charge on the day before the final 'bloody stupid' assault on Gona recalled that only 26 of 90 men survived. Military Cross recipient Ron Plater related his worst experience at Gona:

> Having to move forward foot by foot against heavy machine gun fire and well concealed Japanese defences, eliminating one stronghold at a time, in effect hand to hand fighting; then being carried out wounded on a stretcher for two or three days.

The same officer had captured a machine gun post single-handed, led his platoon to take out another post, and was shot while dressing the wound of a fellow officer.

Being wounded, however, was not always perceived as traumatic. A survivor described his experience at Gona Beach:

> I was in a very shallow hole with one of the officer's batman and this bloody sniper

AWM 013861

Wounded troops from 21st Brigade after the battle for Gona

was after us, and after a couple of shots I said 'This is no bloody good, we'd better get over to this tree over here'. I only got about two or three crawls and I got it. It was a feeling I will never forget [at 87 years of age]. It was just a feeling as if I was hit with a stone wall, and gradually and slowly going backwards on my back. The two of us struggled up to the tree and I was going every few yards and falling over. My left hand and arm were broken and I kept pulling it over but next time I fell, over it went again.

Strangely enough I did not have any feeling at all. Did not even feel it hit me. I think I slept the night in a field hospital. Bill Badser, a bloke from Mt Gambier, died alongside me that night. Next day they put me in a jeep and it was just like going over steps. By Hell it was rough. When I got back to Popondetta they sent me back to Port Moresby.[22]

Another survivor, Bert Ward, recalled his experience with no distress. As a Bren gunner during the Owen Stanleys campaign he had to make a stand while the rest of the unit retreated, and he had the distinction at that point of being the northernmost Australian in the Owen Stanleys. Ward was hit with shrapnel early in the Efogi battle but at the time he did not worry about it. This sniper's bullet ended his service.

> It felt like a sledgehammer. There was this blackness – I thought I was dead – I had no feeling anywhere – complete blackness – what comes next – there is none of this life passing before your eyes – after a while there was a kaleidoscope of colour flashing across my eyes and then it settled down into nice soft greens and blues and I thought 'This heaven's a lovely place'. I was flat on my back looking up to the blue sky and palm trees.[23]

Ward was able to turn over and crawl back through the kunai to the Regimental Aid Post (RAP). He had some movement in one leg. He actually walked by himself back to Soputa and arrived there about 12 hours after he was wounded.

Being exposed in helpless positions was extremely stressful, especially during strafing attacks. Robert Johns remembers being caught in the sea with nothing on and being strafed. In these circumstances there was nowhere to hide and you were 'completely exposed, and could not fire back'.[24]

Take no prisoners

Knowing what the Japanese were capable of meant that men had few qualms about killing the enemy in New Guinea. Knowledge of atrocities committed by the Japanese fuelled the Australians' distrust and hatred of them, making it easier to kill. The Japanese themselves showed no mercy and were brutal with both soldiers and civilians. The extent of the atrocity and brutality is well established from eyewitness accounts and verified in war crime trials. Paul Hope recalled:

> I think we absolutely hated the Japanese. Because on our walk up to the bivouac area ... we saw the result of their treatment of some of the militia boys they'd caught and some natives. There were some of the Seventh Brigade members who had been tied to a tree with signal wire – I saw this with my own eyes – and they had obviously been bayoneted, all marked all over their body – dead of course. There was a native woman with her breast cut off. There was a native boy with his hair burned off with a flamethrower. I thought he had just been shaved.[25]

'Take no prisoners' was an unwritten policy in the early New Guinea campaigns, mainly because of the lack of prison and medical facilities and the refusal of the Japanese to surrender. Reports in the Murdoch Sound Archive and my own interviews established that in some circumstances no prisoners were taken and wounded enemy were disposed of. John Morgan, an Anglican army chaplain in New Guinea who later became a bishop, recalled seeing the body of a Japanese soldier who had been brought in earlier as a prisoner. He did not see him killed, but he heard the shot.

> How could they have got him out? ... there were times in which you can say no prisoners of war are taken. Because you can't look after them ... And that has to happen. This was something that was never discussed.[26]

William Refshauge of the Australian Army Medical Corps objected strongly to orders 'not to bring back any prisoners', and threatened to court-martial anyone he found disposing of prisoners. He understood the order was a form of retaliation for the practice of captured Japanese blowing up themselves and captors with grenades. Refshauge believed the Geneva Convention should have been honoured.[27]

In rare, extreme situations when the only choice was to leave a wounded fellow soldier to the hands of the Japanese, the decision was made to hasten his death. This is not recorded in any unit histories, but there are sufficient testimonies to confirm that it did happen. The practice of killing wounded Japanese soldiers is more readily admitted, but again it is not recorded in histories.

Before going into battle for the first time some men knew of the Tol Plantation massacre of 23 January 1942. Their company commander Colonel Owen, who had escaped from Rabaul, was there at the time of the massacre. Owen took command of the 39th just before the Owen Stanleys engagement, and he warned his men that they could 'expect no quarter': 'if they catch you that would be the end of you'.[28] In their first attack on Gona Mission, the Japanese carried out similar atrocities to those of the Tol Plantation: nuns and children were among civilians massacred at the mission.

John Burns remembers his mates Teddy Churchett and Victor Knot getting 'nabbed' on the Kokoda Trail. They were later found tied to a tree and bayoneted. Owen Curtis related to his Murdoch Archive interviewer that he had heard of two officers who had been bound with their own dressings, tied hand and foot with signal wire, bayoneted, doused with petrol and left to burn. He had also heard about a native boy who had been bayoneted in the anus, a woman with a breast removed, and a native tied to a tree and killed. He had also heard of men having to shoot their own men rather than leave them for the Japanese.[29]

Japanese planes bombed the main dressing station of the 2/4th Field Ambulance, and the 126th United States Combat Clearing Station at Soputa on 27 November 1942. Twenty-two men were killed, including two Australian majors.

Despite the hatred expressed above, killing a captured Japanese, wounded or not, could have lasting effects. Lawrie Howson, whose story is told in more detail in a later chapter, was ordered to shoot a wounded Japanese soldier, and it affected him deeply for years afterwards. Jim Ashton (2/27th), who had a wife and two children at home, found a photograph of a wife and two children on the body of a dead Japanese soldier. After this, he could no longer sustain his commitment to the war and after a bout of dermatitis was transferred home where he spent the rest of the war on guard duty in an internment camp.[30]

Standing the strain

Medical officers and chaplains provide another perspective on this strain of battle and how men coped with it. Chaplains were exposed to helpless situations, particularly in their role in burial services. Unlike the doctors, they could not mend the bodies of men, only bury them. Harold Norris was chaplain to the 10th Central Clearing Station and the 2/10th Battalion between March 1942 and March 1943. He recalled that one of his first duties at Milne Bay was to bury men who had been incinerated when a Bren gun carrier had blown up on a mine. He became known as the 'chief grave-digger' in New Guinea.[31]

Witnessing death and illness was always painful, but for those, such as medical officers or stretcher-bearers, whose job it was to help but who were often powerless to do so, the impact was even stronger. John Burns, who was left to care for a group of stretcher cases for ten days with little food and no medical supplies, recalled, 'the worst thing was watching your mates die knowing there was nothing you could do'.[32]

Jim Fairley, who was initially assigned as medical officer to Base Hospital at Port Moresby, vividly remembers the aeroplane ploughing into three truckloads of men at take-off. Most of the men died. He regarded treating the men burned in that incident as one of the worst experiences of his career. He recalled how he felt helpless and just had to watch them die. Don Duffy, RMO of the 2/14th Battalion experienced the same reaction in similar situations:

> It is extremely distressing to have your close friends, both officers and other ranks, brought to a RAP dead on a stretcher and know there is nothing one can do to help.

In such conditions the official record indicates that there were few breakdowns in the field. There is some evidence of what might now be called Combat Stress Reaction (CSR) occurring in the field. This is a complete breakdown under battle conditions and has been recently defined by Solomon, a researcher with the Israeli army, as:

> A psychiatric breakdown on the battlefield ... during which the soldier ceases to function altogether or/and functions in such a manner so extreme that he becomes a danger to himself and his comrades.[33]

Such a breakdown could be a response to a single event or a combination of fatigue, intense fear or extreme danger, and is a different experience from someone functioning adequately under pressure of battle but experiencing a stress reaction much later. CSR does not cover the other possibility of someone who functions on the surface but is on the edge of breakdown. An example of a breakdown in the field occurred early in 1943:

> [It was] very rough. They sent about six of us under escort from the infantry chaps, because it was in the Jap territory, and we got through to there and three of us up on the plateau where they were going to drop the supplies, which we planned out. The Japs let us all in and then surrounded us, and it was a hell of a mess. My two

Padre A. Begbie attending to the burial of soldiers killed at Gona.

mates up there were hit, and I covered them while they got out and then I jumped over the edge.

I dodged around the Japs and jumped over the edge, and went bush. I didn't know where I was. That was when I got lost and things weren't too good after that. I was lost for a couple of days, but it seems 12 months when you're out there in the Jap territory. I could see Japs all the time, and I'd hide and then go through. I knew the only way to find my bearings was to get to the top of the hill and look around. When I got back there, well I just broke up.

Things were not too good – I just broke up. I was in a terrible state. I couldn't stop crying. That was a good thing the doctor told me. He said you don't want to feel ashamed at that, that's nature's way of getting rid of it. I just got to the point where I could not take any more – I don't know whether it was fatigue or nerves – a bit of both I suppose. I got back to the unit and I cried and cried and cried. I realised then I was in a bad way. That's when I met Dr Fry and he said – 'You are finished son.'[34]

Among both officers and the ranks, there were cases of men not being able to cope, though a different language was used to describe strain and its effects. In interviews, participants preferred to talk 'off the record' about any such cases. Stress reactions were often fused with references to fear and an inability to face up to particular situations, or to displaying cowardice in the face of the enemy. It is difficult to distinguish a breakdown from an outright fear reaction, when a soldier is simply unable to face battle. One example was a young man who was overcome with fear and hid behind a tree until rescued by his older companion. The young man was not given any treatment, senior officers refused to allow him to be re-located, and he subsequently 'suicided' by running into machine gun fire at Gona. Terms such as 'messed his pants' were used to describe temporary experiences of fear reaction.[35] A man 'who did not acquit himself well', had either broken down or had temporarily given up. In one case a young man was described as not having 'handled himself well' and was later killed by the Japanese. My informant had the difficult job of visiting his mother after the war and telling her that her son was a good soldier.

Young soldiers even saw some of their leaders break down under the strain. Captain Jack Reddin recalled having to take command when a senior officer broke down just before his unit went into the Owen Stanleys:

> At that point I was in charge of Don Company. What caused the original collapse of that officer [was that] he realised that his company was not as well trained as some of the others by reason of the young men who had enlisted. His men had Lewis guns from World War One. They may have been all right then but not in World War Two. The officer concerned completely cracked and had to be shipped back to Australia and discharged ... It was the initial shock hit everybody – we are now going into action. It became evident that many of the men who had come on the *Aquitania* should never have left Australia before another six or eight months' training.

Mick Scanlon recalled:

> There was a fellow up in New Guinea who went troppo. I thought he was alright. We were trying to set up our Vickers one night and he came along with this bit of plant and was convinced that it would make my sights luminous. He seemed to be serious.

Trevor King of the 53rd/55th Battalion recalls that one officer completely cracked and was repatriated: 'His nerves went; he just could not control himself, or his men, or anything appertaining to it. Just a complete mental breakdown.'[36]

Other breakdowns may have been temporary and would not have even been recorded at a forward Aid Post. Paul Wright, for example, recalls the combination of poor preparation and conditions at Kokoda leading to a temporary collapse. He was 18 years old ('18 going on 12, couldn't even drive a car') in May 1942, when, with minimal training and no battle experience, he and members of the 53rd Battalion were sent in to take on the Japanese. He recalled the stress of

> having to kill a man three feet in front of me and seeing the look on his face when your bullets enter his body; seeing your mates lying dead on the ground; having to bury a mate that has been killed; going into the jungle to bring back the bodies of mates killed in ambush; smelling the stench of dead bodies from both sides; having to fight the jungle conditions, sickness and weather.[37]

The strain of these experiences, along with bouts of malaria, did tell and during a night patrol he 'saw things no one else saw and shook uncontrollably'. He recovered after a few days away from the fighting.

For the individual, succumbing to strain was a last resort. A serious breakdown would mean being separated from the battalion, a personal loss and a source of shame. To give in meant you had failed the test and were letting your unit down. For the individual psychological casualty who was evacuated, there was no victory parade – just a quiet return to an overcrowded hospital where treatment was limited and often invasive. Some of the facilities were only tents outside the main general hospital wards. While they could, soldiers kept control of their minds, even under terrible stress.

Medical perspectives

Walker, the medical historian of World War Two, acknowledged the conditions of severe strain and constant threat under which men operated, but concluded that 'nervous disorders were on the whole uncommon' during the Owen Stanleys campaign.

> During the Owen Stanleys campaign few neurotic casualties were seen; Robinson records that he saw only three who needed evacuation. In an action which called for fortitude and unselfish endurance of a high order, this again reflects the spirit of the men and their leaders.[38]

In general, Walker tended to discount the contribution of actual battle stress to these casualties. He noted that in one hospital, of the 343 psychiatric casualties for May–October 1945, battle stress was non-existent in half the number. In other words, only half had a 'just cause' for their condition. He also pointed out that psychiatric 'casualties' increased in non-combat areas as well during the war, some of them correlating with the increase in troop numbers.

The psychiatrist in charge of the Australian General Hospital at Port Moresby, Alec Sinclair, surveyed 310 psychiatric cases admitted between September 1942 and January 1943. These men had been involved in the Owen Stanleys and at Gona and Sananda. He noted that these battles were of 'psychiatric significance', where men 'were tested to the limit of their endurance', and 'their primitive aggressive tendencies were exposed'. These campaigns were quite distinctive in terms of the terrain of steamy jungle and rugged mountain ranges and the type of warfare – patrol-oriented jungle warfare with no armoured support. Consequently, troops had to be constantly alert. In Sinclair's opinion this type of fighting heightened personal aggressiveness and courage.

Even under such trying circumstances, psychiatric casualties comprised only 2.1

per cent of admissions to the general hospital. Admissions were classified as suffering from anxiety and fear states, hysteria and personality inferiority. Inferiority encompassed the inadequate soldier, schizoid or paranoid and psychotic types. The majority of cases were classified as exhibiting anxiety states, distinct from fear states. Of all psychiatric admissions, 54 per cent had not been in combat situations, thus confirming Sinclair's view that 'combat is only one of the factors causing or initiating breakdown'.[39]

The principal causal factor in breakdown identified by Sinclair was the make-up of the soldier, and he estimated that only 14 per cent of the anxiety states could be wholly attributable to war service. The least desirable patients were those with the 'medical liability' of personality defect, and 'the neurotic officer' who was a 'bad medical investment'.

Captain David Ross of the Australian Army Medical Corps noted that the number of psychiatric casualties requiring hospital treatment increased towards the end of the campaigns. By then psychiatric casualties accounted for 7 per cent of all admissions. A new ward was established in August 1944 in the General Hospital (possibly in Lae, although this was not clearly stated) to cater for seriously disturbed patients, and provide treatment that would previously have been available only in Australia. The new working conditions for the medical officer, three sisters and 12 medical orderlies were 'now pleasant and easy and the patients were comfortable'. This new facility did not, however, reduce the numbers requiring evacuation, and with the limited means of sedation, such as sodium amytal and mild coma induction, restraint during flights to the mainland was still problematic. This led to the decision to establish convulsive therapy facilities in the unit.[40]

A more descriptive account of the effects of the stress of battle is found in the recollections of medical officers who served in New Guinea, and in unit medical diaries. These accounts confirm Walker's view that breakdown in the field was the exception rather than the rule, despite the extremes endured by combatants.[41]

In field medical practice, there were good reasons for not placing too much emphasis on, and even discouraging, stress reactions. With losses from illness, wounds and death already high, units could not afford to lose any casualties from mental breakdown. Such losses were a threat to fighting strength as well as to the morale of the unit. For the most part military doctors were understanding, but they could not afford to be too sympathetic nor encourage unwounded casualties. As Sinclair stated:

> It is the important duty of the army psychiatrist to attempt to return such men to service, even though he returns his patient into a rude world peopled by men whose business is warfare.[42]

Sinclair's survey demonstrated how a stressful situation can act as a filter for sorting out capable soldiers and how the medical service becomes the sorting agent. Most men returned to their units, and to active duty.

In February 1945 Brigadier Kingsley Norris of the Australian Army Medical Corps described the New Guinea campaigns at a meeting of the Victorian Branch

The Sun
DAILY AT DAWN
NEWS — PICTORIAL

Largest Net Daily Sale in Australia 264,823

No. 6058 Melbourne : Friday, February 20, 1942 20 Pages. 2d.

JAPANESE RAID DARWIN TWICE

93 Bombers Used With Fighters: Four Shot Down

SYDNEY, Thursday. — In the first enemy attack on Australian territory powerful forces of Japanese aircraft today launched two heavy raids on Darwin.

The Prime Minister (Mr. Curtin) announced tonight that the raids caused considerable damage to property, but reports so far to hand do not give precise details of this damage, nor is there accurate information as to loss of life.

Earlier reports, however, indicated that there had been casualties in the first raid.

The first raid was launched at 10.5 a.m. Darwin time (10.35 a.m. Eastern Australian time). It lasted about 40 minutes.

The attackers comprised a force of 72 twin-engined bombers, which came in in waves. They were protected ...

The ... by 21 twi... received ... the attac...

The ... vigorous ... four ene...

The ... indicates ... probably ... Indies no...

[When ...

GUNS LIKE THESE were in action against the Japs yesterday. Australian-made anti-aircraft gun at Darwin.

RED ARMY Birthday

Japanese Push Into Burma: South To Java

Special Sun Service and Australian Associated Press

LONDON, Thursday. — The Japanese are pushing their forces west into Burma, threatening Rangoon, and south from Palembang, threatening Java.

Latest reports from Rangoon say that the Battle for Burma has begun in earnest. The invaders, in spite of severe losses, have obtained a foothold on the west bank of the Bilin River. Fighting continues with undiminished ferocity.

It is stated authoritatively in London that there is no reason to think that our forces in Burma are not holding their positions. British and Indian troops are fighting side by side.

The Chinese forces, who are stated to have invaded Thailand from the South Shan States, are reported to be still progressing in the direction of Chiengmai.

In Sumatra the Japanese are driving from Palembang to Oosthaven, the port of Telok Betong (on the southernmost coast of Sumatra) which will bring them to within ...

MY WAR
PART 32

The Sun
DAILY AT DAWN
NEWS — PICTORIAL

Largest Net Daily Sale in Australia 271,705

No. 6232 Melbourne: Friday, September 11, 1942 (20 Pages) 2d.

JAPS ADVANCING ON MORESBY

Cross Gap: Win Vital Ground

SOMEWHERE IN AUSTRALIA, Thursday. — The Japanese have won vital new ground in their drive across the Owen Stanley Range towards Port Moresby.

For the first time since the invasion of New Guinea, the Japanese are now on the Allies' side of the gap on the highest point of the mountain range, which had been officially described as "almost impassable."

[Osmar White, The Sun's correspondent with the forces in New Guinea, says, "While we must admit that the Japanese have won the first part of the battle for the Owen Stanleys, it is still true that Port Moresby cannot be blitzed by such methods as have given them success so far.

"There is not even the remotest question of the fall of Port Moresby being either likely or imminent," Osmar White adds.]

From Myola, about 5500 ft. above sea level, the Japanese have pushed up through the gap (8000 ft.) and down the trail past Efogi (4600 ft.)—a distance of 12½ miles.

Efogi is only 53 miles by trail from Port Moresby.

Australian brigades under Lieut.-Gen. Rowell are reported to be fighting back tenaciously and gallantly under conditions of extra-...

... vicinity of Efogi, and the fighting now to the south along the narrow trail which leads across the mountainous divide.

Allied air attack units are giving strong support to our troops by bombing and strafing the enemy ...

THE TALL TREES and jungle surrounding these Australian administration outposts in New Guinea give some idea of the type of country where fighting is in progress. —(Dept. of Information photos.)

GERMANS STRIKE AGAIN

THRUST CLOSER TO STALINGRAD

The war approaches Australia, but Australian troops eventually push back the Japanese tide.

SYDNEY

No. 162. SYDNEY, TUESDAY, NOVEMBER 3, 1942. PRICE, 2d.

KOKODA CAPTURED AS ALLIES DRIVE ON

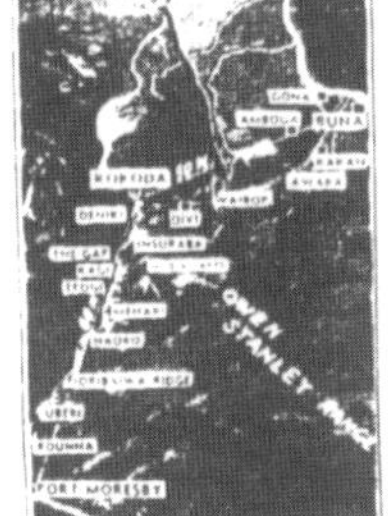

Landing Attempt At Buna Smashed

(Daily Mirror World Cables and Special Correspondents.)

CAPTURE of Kokoda, Japanese stronghold on the northern side of the Owen Stanley Range in New Guinea, 60 miles from Buna, is the highlight of today's news from the north-eastern area, where the Allies are harrying the retreating Japanese with a series of telling blows on land, on sea and in the air.

- A Japanese attempt to land large reinforcements at Buna, on the northern coast of New Guinea, was frustrated by Allied bombers, which battered the convoy and forced it to retire to the north.
- Washington announces the destruction by U.S. submarines of another seven Japanese ships and damage to three others in the western and southern Pacific. A converted aircraft carrier was left in flames and a destroyer damaged.

Kitty Bluett's Letter On Alleged Blue Jokes

Replies To Radio Chief

Miss Kitty Bluett, popular comedienne, who is faced

MY WAR PART 34

Largest Net Daily Sale In Australia 273,585

No. 6343 Melbourne: Wednesday, January 20, 1943 (16 Pages) 2d.

AUSTRALIANS TAKE SANANANDA

Situation Now Hopeless For Japs Left

CAPTURE, after a two-days' battle, by an Australian force, of Sananada village and Sananada Point, on the northern Papuan coast, was officially announced at General MacArthur's Headquarters last night.

Sweeping past Sananada Point, our forward elements have reached Girawa, about 1500 yards further south-east, liquidating the last Japanese beachhead on Australian territory.

On the coast the enemy is now restricted to a small pocket 500 yards north-west of the Soputa-Sananada Road terminal, which

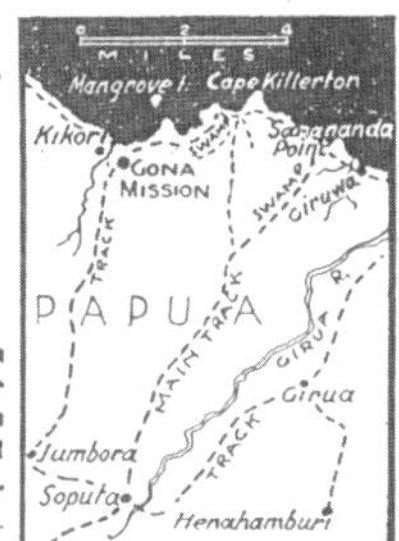

Best Russian News Of War

Siege Raised At Leningrad

Special Sun Service and Australian Associated Press

LONDON, Tuesday. — The relief of Leningrad and the capture of Kamenskaya on the Donetz, which has been crossed by the Russian Army, were announced in two special Moscow communiques.

The lifting of the siege is described as the best news of the war so far from Russia. Russian progress is reported to be far more than the communique discloses.

South of the Don the Russians forced a crossing of the Mainich River and captured the town and railway station of Divnoie.

The offensive on the Voro-

RAPID PROGRESS TOWARD TRIPOLI

MONTGOMERY SWEEPS WEST

of the British Medical Association.[43] Most of his rather florid account focused on the history and topography of the islands, though he did mention some battle history. His graphic descriptions reinforce the stressful nature of the battles, particularly the encounters in Gona, Buna and Sananda. He does not describe any aspect of psychological strain or casualty, and medical perspectives were confined to the disposal of the walking wounded on the Kokoda Trail, where the 'courage and cheerfulness were wonderful – beyond praise – almost incredible'.

Other personnel who served in the Owen Stanleys during 1942 and 1943 present the same view that high morale, discipline and training prevented serious mental casualties. Each unit and brigade kept a medical diary that set out the history of the health of the unit during combat and training. These diaries describe the stressful conditions and make much of how inadequate the material support for the brigade was. Consequently, heavy casualties were sustained, but reports of psychological strain or 'fear' reactions such as self-inflicted wounds were 'rare'.

Dr K. Norris's medical report in January 1943 of the 7th Australian Division, which included the 2/27th Battalion, gives a clear account of the trek over the Owen Stanleys and the conditions encountered along the way. He listed eight major diseases: malaria, scrub typhus, diarrhoea, skin conditions, urti, haemorrhoids, track trauma (physical), and wounds. The only mention of mental conditions was a small number of 'Not Yet Diagnosed' (NYD).[44] The main emphasis is on treatment of the sick and wounded and improving the appalling sanitary conditions: 'The incidence of psychiatric conditions was reported to be very low. On 30 November 1942 there were 13 cases of NYD and 207 other'.[45] The 21st Brigade Diary mentions psychiatric cases, but without explanations. The chief medical complaints (apart from wounds) were diarrhoea with blood mucus, foot disabilities and psychiatric cases. H.D. Steward, the Regimental Medical Officer (RMO) of the 21st Brigade, does not mention psychiatric casualties.[46]

Other indicators of mental strain such as low morale can be found in records of units such as the 53rd Battalion, which withdrew from the mountains with very low spirits. When it was relieved by the 2/27th, the 53rd Battalion was 'very low in morale, their boots were rubbing, they had blisters, and their socks were adhering to their feet'. On 1 September 1942 'some companies appeared to lose control' and there was 'far too much straggling and independent movement of troops'. By the time they reached Port Moresby, 10 per cent of the men paraded sick each day. After they had time to recuperate they were flown back to the north coast at Sanananda where they knew they 'were to kill as many Japanese as possible before they were killed'.[47]

> By the third week of December the nervous strain of the two attacks (on a Japanese post) was beginning to tell on the troops and that, together with heavy losses suffered plus the appalling conditions under which troops lived, caused a lowering of morale. The effort of trying to retrieve two mortally wounded men (Coote and Henderson) was particularly stressful.[48]

The 39th Battalion diary documents a number of incidents that, for men in their first battle, were distressing. In their first encounter on 25 July 1942 they lost six men. On 26 July McLean reported that the whole force had been surrounded and lost and they were subsequently ordered to withdraw to Oivi:

> At 1730 hrs on 26 July Capt Templeton was caught in a burst of gunfire and not heard of again. He disappeared without trace. By 30 July they were very tired and 'morale was low' and there were still 20 men missing. Then on 2 August a personal tragedy also struck when Private Hughes was shot [by his own sentry] and killed when he did not answer a challenge.[49]

Medical officers in the Owen Stanleys did not regard psychiatric casualties as a major problem, and each had his own theory about how men survived the extreme stress. Keith Viner-Smith, RMO for the 2/27th Battalion in 1942, recalled only a low incidence of breakdown or loss of nerve:

> There were at least 3 or 4 soldiers who suffered from combat neurosis but I can remember only one – a sergeant whose normal duties did not include active fighting. In the rather torrid conditions I certainly had no time to diagnose and treat. I used him with probably three other men to carry a wounded man back down the track for several hundred yards to a place where a white officer was holding some native carriers away from the more dangerous area. Unfortunately this team was the first to meet with the Japs behind our unit and had to return to us with the wounded man.
>
> I would try to assess the man concerned. If there was any hope of him regaining his nerve I would keep him in a relatively safe position, keep him busy and hope he would regain control. If there was no hope I would try to evacuate him from the area.[50]

In August–September 1942 Jim Fairley, as medical officer at the 2/9th AGH in Port Moresby, treated casualties after the withdrawal from the Kokoda Trail.

> I think the main reaction was the relief. They were out of it. No, Alec Sinclair was there – the 2/9th AGH psychiatrist – and he was never very busy – at least I didn't think so. From my memory there was no dramatic casualty rate. There was a psychiatric ward. You were always very reluctant to write someone off as a psychiatric case. Another thing with the 2/27th, the originals had been through it and they would support the new blokes. In Balikpapan [Borneo, July 1945], there were no mental casualties as far as I know. It was nerve wracking when we were on patrol.[51]

Fairley was himself exposed to direct threat of death later in his career at Balikpapan, where at night the Japanese would creep in and spear men with sharpened bamboos while they were asleep in their hammocks. 'There were a hell of a lot of blokes who never got to a psychiatrist, but had potential psychiatric problems – more like acute attacks'. He believed that only 'unstable' men would have a breakdown under strain, but there were 'normal' men who under 'abnormal strain' sometimes became dysfunctional.

According to Fairley, comrades, NCOs, the RMO and other officers kept a lot of men off the psychiatric casualty lists. An officer 'would need to be convinced that his reactions were in the normal bracket – a normal person reacting in a normal way in an abnormal situation. The affected man might weep, become incoherent, have tremors, vomit and be unable to eat'. Good officers understood this well, without any formal training, and doctors were reluctant to write a man off as a psychiatric case. If handled properly in the field, these men could get better without gaining a psychiatric label. Fairley believed that officers generally accepted the man who 'could not take it':

> At that stage there was complete understanding. I did not see any of my nursing staff who did not understand what had happened to these 'kids'. We knew from the units they came from, what they had been through and how good they were. We all thought 'there but the for the grace of God go I'.[52]

The 39th Battalion experienced the worst of the Kokoda conditions, particularly in their first encounter with the Japanese. However, there is little evidence of an elevated level of psychological distress in this unit. Major J. Shera, who was RMO of the 39th Battalion on the Kokoda Trail, Gona, Sanananda, and served with other units at Finschhafen and Tarakan (Borneo), has a similar version to that of other medical officers:

> As far as I can recall, there was not a high incidence of combat stress in the 39th Battalion during the Owen Stanley campaigns. Before we started the climb there was a slightly larger attendance at sick parade but no obvious attempt to avoid the climb. There was one youth who presented with sore eyes. His eyes were full of grass stalks. I considered this was self-inflicted. The lad later performed with exceptional bravery near Deniki.
>
> At Isurava when Battalion headquarters looked like being overrun, one young man became hysterical. Fortunately at the time the 2/14th marched in and took up defensive positions.

Shera had received no training for assessing and treating psychological casualties. His explanation for the low number of casualties was the youthfulness of the battalion and the high quality of leadership. However, he did acknowledge that in another New Guinea unit with which he later served with there was a higher incidence of 'combat fatigue' in men who had also served in the Middle East. At least one man suicided. He believed that the longer a man served, the more likely he was to have psychological problems.

Shera had a strong view on modern perspectives on stress, and adopted a more practical, organisational view on how to reduce psychological casualties:

> The buzz word these days is counselling. It is important to eliminate factors such as inadequate clothing, inadequate diet and to make sure that there has been proper military training. Morale tends to drop a little when a meal would consist of a stew of taro roots and a little bully beef mixed up; not a good preparation for combat under dreadful conditions.[53]

At the age of 28, Douglas Leslie was assigned to the 2/4th and 2/6th Field Ambulance units to establish staging posts along the Kokoda Trail during the return over the Owen Stanley Ranges after the Japanese had retreated. He was also surgeon with the 2/9th Australian General Hospital near Port Moresby. He treated men in the field and also received casualties from Gona and Buna. Even though his focus at the time was on treating physical injury in very primitive facilities, his recollection of the experience is that psychological casualties were low. In 1993 he wrote:

> My impression throughout was that the morale of our soldiers was very high indeed and very few of them showed signs of psychological problems. However at Myola I was so busy surgically that, apart from routine post-operative care, I was not able to make any psychological assessment of the troops. One of the most stressful times must have been during the retreat over the Kokoda Trail. My only experience of this phase was in treating the patients who arrived back at Moresby.[54]

Alan Bentley, who became a physician after the war, served as a medical orderly with the 2/6th Field Ambulance on the Kokoda Trail and could recall few instances of psychological breakdown in that period. He was distressed by the extent of the physical casualties and in later life was reluctant to recall details of the period.[55]

Don Duffy was medical officer with the 2/14th on the Kokoda Trail at the height of the Japanese assault. Like most of his fellow medical officers, he had no training in detecting and treating psychiatric casualties before being assigned to the Middle East and New Guinea. Although this may have influenced his observations, he could recall little evidence of psychological disturbance and certainly no psychotic disturbance either in the field or with the 2nd Australian General Hospital. The only mildly psychotic behaviour was considered to have been a side effect of the malaria suppressant, Atebrin. His preparation for the extreme conditions of New Guinea was rather brief:

> I had no special training in the army directed towards the handling of mental cases and my preparation for NG was limited to my meeting with the Director, Australian Medical Service HQ on the wharf at Brisbane on the night of our departure. He said he supposed I knew where I was going. I said, 'not for certain'. He replied 'well it is New Guinea, and as the place is malarious [*sic*] I have put two large tins of quinine tablets on board which you had better distribute to the troops in cigarette tins before you leave Moresby'. He then faded into the darkness.[56]

Duffy's theory was that unit discipline, training and strong leadership minimised the possibility of breakdown under duress, and that any potential problems would have been eliminated early in their training. This is borne out in his observations of the 39th:

> Perhaps there was some degree of anxiety among troops going into battle for the first time but the certain support of trusted reliable mates carried them through. There was an instance of an inadequately trained battalion – which means badly officered and led troops – who did not complete a fighting patrol, did not contact the enemy and gave misleading information on return, some men having left their weapons behind. This unit was rapidly returned to Moresby. The blame lay not with the troops but the HQ administration who had them loading ships in

Moresby at the expense of this basic training and secondly the poor standard of officer command from the CO down.

Duffy considered that the idea of a traumatic neurosis induced by some form of physical shock had some credence, but did not think the New Guinea conditions were likely to produce it. He regarded the stressors in New Guinea as less severe than those in World War One, where the shock of heavy artillery barrages could temporarily interrupt 'coherent thought and action':

> In a battle scenario the tremendous noise and shock wave of exploding artillery and mortar shells has been a stress factor which stuns or temporarily interrupts the coherent thought and action. In the First World War, the circumstances were bad enough to have completely disoriented soldiers walking aimlessly about in no man's land. Such circumstances did not prevail in New Guinea where automatic small arms fire and exploding hand grenades provided most of the noise.[57]

These reflections of medical personnel support a view that it was not just the individual's internal resources that determined survival. Organisational and contextual factors such as training, support, morale and physical resilience also affected their ability to cope, and the notion of a single traumatic incident dislodging a soldier is not part of their analysis. They believed that cumulative stress, which built up over several tours of duty with the exposure to danger, tropical diseases and wounds, was more likely to take its toll.

Surviving

There appears to be a consensus among veterans that surviving the strain was not an accident. As well as mental and physical preparation through training, individuals took actions that allowed them to rise above their fears. One had to adapt quickly or be overwhelmed by stressful experience. The experience of these New Guinea men suggests that this adaptation is more than just individual resilience.

When speaking of their experiences, veterans did not always distinguish between managing mental and physical strain. This is not surprising as the two were often seen as connected, and one was more likely to withstand mental strain when physically stronger and not ravaged by illness, such as dysentery or malaria. Diseases such as dengue fever, cerebral malaria and scrub typhus often produced emotional disturbance in addition to the physical pain. There is a qualitative difference between a temporary inability to cope because of fatigue, and a more permanent breakdown of defences, succumbing completely to the fear and strain. It was fear – the fear of breaking down in front of one's mates – that gave a powerful incentive to 'hold on'. As one participant put it:

> I suppose the main thing that enables you to rise above your worst fears is simply that there is an even more fearful alternative – the fear that your mates will see you are afraid. You really would rather die than let this happen. The question arises – what is courage? Well, I would never have had the courage to show fear in front of the other men. So yes, you all help each other and the very best way to handle stressful periods is to be busy. If you have time to pray or think of home then you

are very probably not attending to something that needs to be done. Yes, I guess we all send up silent prayers at times, but personally I'm not a prayerful person.[58]

Clive Edwards reinforced the view that training can prepare you for stressful experiences and with application you can survive:

> I would be a disappointing person to gain information from because of my war experiences. Nothing really occurred which was worse than my training and reading had prepared me to expect. For example, my first sight of a corpse with the entrails gaping received no reaction from me for I'd expected to see such things. I spent several days this week with a mate of mine who had been three years with me and we both agreed that we were glad we volunteered and he went through Gona from start to finish.
>
> Contact & thoughts of home were very important – writing & receiving letters. Support of mates & Esprit De Corps. It's hard to believe in religion during war but I attended church parades & always kept a copy of the New Testament with me – it seemed a mark of respect to say a short passage from it over a dead mate's body.[59]

Another strategy was to dissociate from the war situation and fantasise about more pleasant memories and associations. The most common thought or fantasy that kept men going in extreme times was about home or loved ones. Stirling Ashenden expressed his thoughts in a poem:

As I was sitting in my tent wondering what to do
I saw in the doorway standing a vision dear of you
You were wearing one of the most beautiful dresses
All covered in gorgeous lace
Your hair hung in wonderful tresses and surrounded your lovely face

Your voice as you sang our favourite song
Was sweeter than a dove
Your smile was like that of an angel and shone like the stars above
This alluring vision was just a passing myth
But made me realise what I truly miss.[60]

Survival sometimes meant taking some practical action in a dangerous situation that would keep the mind focused or the body alive. Many veterans reported very simple strategies and mental tricks as ways to survive critical times. For example, during the Efogi withdrawal:

> I must admit that I was feeling down. No particular reason, the only thing I'm conscious of is that I had not smoked. I realise this afterwards. I noticed that the heavy smokers were feeling it worst. All I could think of was the lack of food. I had tried to eat grass or leaves – I did not consume much. We dug up a few potatoes – got a bellyache. All my thoughts were centred on food.[61]

Another survivor of the Kokoda Trail and the march back over the mountains with Cha-Force kept himself well by always keeping a change of dry underclothes.

(How this was possible in the jungle and rain is not clear.)[62] Among other things, mateship and humour also played its part, although some of these 'funny bits' do not seem funny at all 50 years later. John Burns related a story that graphically illustrates battle humour. He was standing one morning with Lt Colonel Cooper and Harry Katekar preparing for a bayonet attack at Gona. John was the radio operator and had to put his left hand up to adjust the aerial to get better reception. He was hit by a sniper and sustained a minor wound that produced a lot of blood. The Regimental Sergeant Major (RSM), who was known as 'Loopy', became very agitated and, as was his habit, started to jump around and wave his arms. One of the men called out 'Get down you silly bastard!'. The RSM demanded that the soldier identify himself: 'Who said that?' Sixty voices cried out in unison from the kunai and jungle: 'I did!'[63]

Incidents like this are claimed to have sustained men through the strain of close combat. Jimmy Moir recalled:

> At one stage during the Owen Stanleys campaign my mate on the Bren gun and myself were on guard duty at night and were lying in our groundsheets. After a while my mate said he was going to have a nap. Shortly afterwards a couple of objects landed near us and I realised it would be Japs trying to attract our fire and give our position away. I reached over to put my hand over his mouth to prevent him speaking. Then I put my mouth to his ear to tell him what was going on, to which he replied 'Thank God it's you, I thought it was a Jap crawling over me so I was pretending to be dead'. (Not very funny at the time but we had a few laughs later on over a beer or two.)[64]

The other perspective is that many men actually found the whole business a challenge and enjoyed the experience. Often they were too busy to be frightened, and for many soldiers combat was an exhilarating experience and the idea of being stressed did not occur to them.

> We were that busy we were not frightened. The adrenalin flows and unless you have been in action you would not know what it is like. You can do superhuman things. You get so fired up. The worst thing is waiting. Some blokes messed their pants once it was on. In the Owen Stanleys it was different.[65]

* * * * *

This brief account of the period of battle in New Guinea provides an insight into the conditions that men endured. There is no doubt that this was a period of intense physical and psychological strain, during which heavy physical losses were sustained, but the participants were often able to make light of the psychological pressure. Medical personnel, officers and combatants all acknowledged the stress of this period, but there is very little official record of psychological damage. There was no epidemic of psychological breakdown and the majority of participants, while admitting it was very difficult, were more likely to emphasise their personal survival and unit morale. Subsequent chapters describe what happened after these men returned to civilian life.

CHAPTER 5

Remembering the War

> Only a few veterans raise the subject of war, so the distressing memories are rarely discussed. Items covered [at reunions] are sport, family matters, general ailments, news of other veterans, etc. If war memories are raised they are almost always amusing stories – probably embellished with faulty recall.
>
> *Bert Ward* [1]

> I now feel that the years are closing for many of us who fought in the Pacific war and we could perhaps record and perhaps talk more, something we have been reluctant to do in the past. No front-line troops would want to talk about actual warfare, something they would rather forget, although for many that would be impossible.
>
> *Maurice Little* [2]

The New Guinea story did not end in 1945 and I take up the story from 1990 when I began to talk with survivors. One of the men I met was Bert Ward, who was seriously wounded in the head at Gona, and has regularly attended functions of the 2/27th Ex-Servicemen's Association. In the comment quoted above he was reflecting on what happened at these gatherings. This association is typical of many hundreds of ex-service groups throughout the world. Some have formed out of a particular experience, such as being prisoners of war (Ex-Prisoners of War Association), or being in a particular event, such as the Siege of Tobruk (Rats of Tobruk Association), but most are based on the formation of the original regiment. Unit and Division associations function independently from the general veterans' associations such as the Returned and Services League (RSL).[3] The shared collective memory of the members of these unit associations emerge out of the specific events of the battles they fought together, and the times they experienced serving together.

Associations are held together by strong bonds of friendship, tradition and shared memory. This bonding of veterans might be understood through the words of Jimmy Moir, who was close to death in 1942:

> When I was wounded [shot through the buttocks] no one saw me fall, but fortunately our company commander Capt George Wright, who had been creased on the side of the head, was going in the wrong direction calling on the company to follow him. When I called to him to say get me a stretcher, this seemed to bring him back to reality. Soon after, our stretcher-bearer, who was about three stone lighter than I was, arrived and because he could not lift me, he crawled under me

> and crawled off with me draped over him. When he got to where some of our troops were they put me on a bush stretcher and although the Japs were no more than 50 yards from us they blasted away at them until they could get me away from the main trail and into the jungle from where the 30-day epic began – that brings about affinity.[4]

Unit associations provide a forum for exchanging information, maintaining networks, and offering moral and material support to members and their families. They also provide a space to construct a cohesive narrative about a period that at the time was confusion and chaos. Associations and their gatherings also provide a space where military tradition and the culture of the unit can be upheld. They are therefore very much sites of memory.

The most poignant and binding memory for the 2/27th Association is their service in New Guinea, particularly in the Owen Stanley and Gona campaigns during 1942 and early 1943. This association has a regular monthly meeting, an annual general meeting and dinner, and on commemorative occasions, such as ANZAC Day, its members participate in the march and meet for reunion luncheons. These gatherings maintain rituals, create a collective military narrative, and perform a gate-keeping function to contain memory and ensure that the exchanges within the association are restricted to relatively 'safe' topics and focus little on the stressful side of war.

It was at one of these functions that I began my search for what happened to the men who fought in New Guinea over the 50 years since they returned home. The reality of that story emerged gradually over a number of years, as I scraped away the layers of the veterans' memories. I discovered layers of memory in such things as a set of unpublished poems by Stirling Ashenden, which included this portrayal of his troubled mind as he was recovering in a field hospital in the Markham Valley in 1943:

> *The wounds they cop in war time, are not always blood and bone*
> *Others cannot see them – you are on your own*
> *It starts above your shoulders, and only you know it isn't right*
> *'Cause these weird and wondrous happenings are only for your sight.*

These 'weird and wondrous things' were the New Guinea experiences. The fact that Ashenden's poems had remained hidden characterises the protective reticence that veterans have maintained about their war stories. This was particularly true in relation to the experience of strain and breakdown. In some cases I had to wait for several years to gain an insight into their experience. For example, I originally interviewed one man in 1991, but I did not find out until 1995 that he had had 'nerve' problems, and that his brother had experienced a more serious mental breakdown, from which he had never really recovered. Had his first interview been taken at face value my version of his life story would have been much different. This is something he would never have talked about at reunions, nor discussed within his family.

The reticence was not just about 'nerves'. The bad New Guinea experiences had been buried for many years. Veterans preferred to talk about the 'funny bits'. Even after finding men willing to discuss their experience, getting access to what really happened was sometimes difficult. Some veterans still found it distressing to talk, and good sense and professional judgement dictated that these were secrets that should be left untouched. Others had put their memories so far away that even they had difficulty accessing them. One of the early respondents returned a scantily completed questionnaire with 'NO PACK DRILL' [i.e. 'no names'] scrawled across the top of the page. I learned from his colleagues that he had been a heavy drinker after the war. However, his responses in a questionnaire stated only that he had 'never settled down', and that he had been forcibly retired from teaching on grounds of invalidity eight years after the war. There was no mention of a breakdown in his questionnaire response and only a brief mention of some treatment at the Repatriation Hospital. However, there was some further information in his diary, which was made publicly available through members of his unit association:

> After returning to my civil occupation I suffered a breakdown in health, was discharged from the Education Department on medical grounds in 1953. This was the first of momentous happenings since 1946. My wife left me in 1959 and got a divorce in 1961. As a consequence the two boys left me too. I was made TPI after my breakdown in health but during the last few years have learned to live with my disability.

In fact this man was treated exclusively in the Repatriation Hospital psychiatric ward. In his diary he had hinted at some form of breakdown in his time in Borneo in May 1945 – 'I wonder if I was beginning to show signs of cracking up even then' – and he was visibly changed on his return home in 1945:

> and when I staggered along the platform at Adelaide in jungle greens looking like a shivering rat, E [my wife] and company hardly knew me. I was sent to Daws Rd for a medical but wouldn't listen to their idea of a pension; all I wanted to do was get back to a civilian job of work.

In veterans' narratives there might be other brief references to strain in the form of comments like 'most of the chaps have problems', or there were 'years of nightmares', and 'only another soldier would understand'. Maurice Little, the second soldier quoted at the beginning of this chapter, was writing in response to an article in a rural newspaper saying he had experienced 'stress problems' after he had settled back into rural life, well away from the jungles of New Guinea. His letter indicated that he had been stressed in his early years, and in retirement he thought a lot about his lost mates. He admitted that 'I myself suffered some moments of stress for a period of a few years, but [they] appear to have little effect now', and:

> Perhaps sometimes we should say a bit more. I don't mean about actual warfare itself, but where we were, some of the experiences and that. Another 10 years and most of us people will be gone. I suppose it's difficult for anybody else to understand.

AWM 059004

The platoon commander, No. 7 Platoon, A Company, 2/27th Battalion issuing mail after the Trevor's Ridge action. Second from the right is Lieutenant R.D. Johns (see photo on opposite page).

In a later interview with him and his wife he elaborated on his undercurrent of stressful memories, which had been submerged for most of his life.

By and large, understatement was a key characteristic of the veteran narrative about New Guinea. For example, in his letters from the front line Clive Edwards (2/27th Battalion) maintained that there 'were no heroes – just men doing a job'. His laconic style, even allowing for his regard for the censor, is reflected in a letter he wrote to his father on 24 September 1942:

> The barest and most essential facts are that I have spent the past three weeks in action once again, this time amongst the wildness of New Guinea and that at present I am in a back area resting and recovering. As with the previous state of action, the sound and threat of bullets and bombs didn't perturb me greatly but I did find it a physical effort to keep going because the country is indeed difficult. You would have difficulty recognising me at present because I have lost a great deal of weight and down to around about nine stone.[5]

Edwards was seriously wounded in December 1942, and 'the bullet chewed a chink of flesh out of my leg about nine inches below the knee – about three inches in diameter':

> It was a couple of miles back to the dressing station and believe me I only just made it. The track was crook leading through jungle and mud in places and open in

Robert Johns (at right) pictured in 1993 at a re-union with fellow veteran Gordon McDonald. [Photo: John Raftery]

> others where the sun belted down on a poor bloke and the noodle whizzed a couple of times on that 10-mile journey.[6]

Edwards' understatement contrasts with a flamboyant account in a letter sent by a soldier to his fiancée shortly after the withdrawal from Kokoda in November 1942. His story is supported by my analysis of the battle and conditions, but his account is much more graphic than was the norm. He wrote:

> the terrific battle against odds by men who refused to be beaten. Often surrounded, we would escape into the jungle and reform and fight at another point. It's not that the enemy defeated us, it was the hunger and awful jungle-clad mountains.
>
> It was ambush or be ambushed, crawling snakelike through the undergrowth to get at the enemy, often being surprised in our turn and firing madly into the undergrowth or tearing insanely on with the bayonet, for Japs do not like cold steel. The ferocity and mercilessness, at first, amazed me, but with such hate, where can there be pity. And we were fighting for our homeland and those who are dearest to us, in three months I saw only one Jap left alive and heard of three more. Most of which were never recovered from the jungle and so our bodies took on a new thinness. Gaunt, bearded, mud-covered men, clad in rags, we pushed on.

> How could we let these savage yellow swine live? We who saw some of their treatment of native women and have learned from eye-witnesses of their treatment of captive white women, of the awful fate suffered by the poor creatures.[7]

Strain, stress or mental breakdown are not topics covered in any battalion association literature, nor in the official battalion history of this unit.[8] The reticence that was observed in the original 2/27th official war diary, which contained no mention of atrocities or the effect of extreme conditions, is continued in contemporary discourse.[9] In the collective battalion memory, expressions of grief and loss *are* permitted. On commemorative occasions, especially the monthly luncheons, grief and loss are acknowledged in the ritual remembering of deceased veterans, both in wartime and current life. This grief is formalised in the *Ode of Remembrance*, which is recited after the reading of the names of the recently deceased. *The Ode* reads,

> They shall grow not old,
> as we that are left grow old:
> Age shall not weary them,
> nor the years condemn.
> At the going down of the sun
> and in the morning,
> we will remember them.

Death was acknowledged in the histories of the 2/27th and 39th Battalions, with detailed lists of those killed and wounded. However, there was no information on mental strain or psychiatric casualties.[10] John Burns's history of the 2/27th Battalion, for example, focuses on morale and survival and does not contain references to strain or stress, or events that would have caused distress to former members and families. Burns did not record an event that occurred in Syria when a member of the unit on sentry duty killed his mate, who did not give the correct password when challenged. The soldier was known to his mates to have been in 'a mess' since the war, but none of this was part of the public memory. Other unrecorded events emerged during my research, which clearly indicated a submerged side of the individual and collective narratives.[11]

This reticence to confront publicly the distressing side of war may be partly explained by a comment by Clive Edwards:

> I was at a party recently where a lady of high social standing said 'All soldiers love to glorify war'. I asked her, rather heatedly, if she would like to see one of her friends run over and killed by a car. Naturally she answered 'No!' I then challenged her by saying, 'Why then do you consider that we glorified in watching our mates killed or injured?' 'Nuff said! War is a dreadful thing, so dreadful that only those who have experienced it can really know how bad it really is![12]

Evidence of the careful containment of memory can be found in the newsletters of associations, such as 2/27th Association newsletter, *The Brown and Blue*

Diamond, which is a storehouse of association culture.[13] Publications such as newsletters preserve a collective memory of a unit's history, and place boundaries on what that memory may contain. In such publications there is regular reporting on members, including their latest physical illness or frailty, and in every issue, the 'Last Post' – a commemoration of those who have died in the previous month. The newsletter provides opportunities for networking between members in each state and even overseas. There is the occasional comment on modern society, reflection on the unit history, philosophical statements, sometimes poetry written by members or quoted from somewhere else, and there are occasional instances of humour. Again, there is no evidence of discussion among veterans, either in the newsletter or other settings, about mental health and illness.

A sense of pride and noble service is perpetuated in the association, where only physical weakness is acknowledged. Illness and admissions to hospital for physical treatment can be reported, but not bouts of depression, nor admissions to the Repatriation Hospital psychiatric ward. Mental health crises are not part of the illness discourse – only physical crises such as strokes, heart attacks, and cancer. This avoidance of any reference to mental health in association transactions is replicated in other unit associations. The 39th Battalion Association, for example, based in Victoria, produces *The Good Guts*. A review of issues of *Guts* for a three-year period revealed no reference to mental health problems among veterans, even though such problems were clearly evident in the interviews I conducted with a number of 39th veterans.

By and large, the memory of the battalion is focused on patriotism and commitment. For example, in September 1987 Major Harry Katekar, the former 2/27th adjutant, wrote a feature 'The Adjutant Reminisces' in the newsletter. At this time he was free of the obligation of silence imposed after discharge, especially on senior officers, and could speak his mind. Katekar had established himself as a very successful businessman, having turned his back on a career as a lawyer in 1946 to support his father on their rural Riverland property. He buried his personal memories of the war in hard work on the property, and in community involvement. In his first public statement on the New Guinea campaigns he briefly touched on the potential distress of war:

> I prefer to keep fresh the memories of those with whom I served. I do not like to see them growing old and enfeebled. Nevertheless I always remain interested and ever keen to help. Even though we have served in war, we do not want anyone else to be involved in another war. In hindsight, those of us who had the unexpected, perhaps unwarranted, and certainly hazardous, experience of serving in a unit like the 2/27th Battalion AIF, especially those with responsible positions in the section, platoon or company, in circumstances where our lives were in peril, must rate that experience as unforgettable and enduring.[14]

In the newsletter of March 1995 the editorial reinforced the strong bonds and pride in the battalion:

> The bonds that were forged between members of the 2/27th back in those

wartime years have remained with us ever since. They can best be illustrated from the following extract from H.D. Steward's book, *Recollections of a Regimental Medical Officer*.

> The spirit which grows up in a battalion when it has been welded together into a true fighting unit is a comradeship almost supernatural in its strength and intensity. It springs from the hardships shared equally, risks run by all in common, and its power exceeds most of the emotions that an ordinary man will ever know. The care of the soldiers for one another, their sure and calm dependence on each other are hard to understand by anyone who has not known it.[15]

Burns expressed the same sentiment in his regimental history, *The Brown and Blue Diamond at War*, in which he concluded:

> Yes, almost every man who wore the brown and blue diamond to war has taken back into civilian life the spirit of comradeship and torch of service kindled during his service days, and has spread the ideals, the standards and traditions of the 2/27th Battalion into the community. And now, instead of fighting a physical enemy, they are serving freely, generously and vigorously in a very wide field of public duties so that Australia may be a better country so many gave their all for.[16]

Behind this veil of bonding, honour and sacrifice there was a cost. In private, veterans like Maurice Little would admit to a more distressing side of war memory:

> Many people in this day and age having never experienced a wartime situation and probably find it difficult to understand what mateship meant in time of war, something you would have to experience to understand. I, like many of the front-line troops could never, I believe, eradicate from our minds the loss of our mates. I remember them every day and the terrible circumstances under which many of them died.[17]

Other sources suggest that the memory of New Guinea was more stressful than generally acknowledged. The Murdoch Sound Archive in the Australian War Memorial houses audio recordings and transcripts of 365 interviews with veterans of all ranks and roles and service arms. The intention was to record personal accounts of military involvement, and many interviews cover the post-war settlement period. As an unintended consequence, there are references to strain, stress and neurosis in some transcripts. An analysis of these transcripts revealed evidence of post-war strain and breakdown among 2/27th, 39th and 53rd Battalion members.[18]

The current memory of the war years is more constrained than the discourse that emerged in the publicity given to war strain in the years immediately following the war. Print and other media at that time contained an undercurrent of concern about the disturbed returned man that was never fully acknowledged. An interesting example was the popular radio serial *Blue Hills* (1949–1976), which was a mirror of Australian post-war life. It portrayed post-war families, one of which was the Gordons, headed by Dr Neil Gordon. One of the four children was

Bruce, was a 'medical student back from the war, and suffering still from its effect on his nerves'.[19]

Elements of the post-war print media created a public forum to publicise the plight of the war-damaged veteran. For example, the following article appeared at the end of 1945 in the *Sun* newspaper:

> When Private Bill Smith came back from the jungle and just couldn't fit into the old life again, his mates shook their heads a little, and said, 'Bomb happy' or 'Troppo'.
>
> Perhaps he can't settle down at home, is irritable, impatient, restless. He's a difficult man to get along with, and lacks the confidence and patience to master his old job again.
>
> He might run through a lot of jobs, and it's possible he will become estranged from his wife, family and friends. In the extreme he might end up in the padded cell or under restraint.
>
> There are now a lot of Bill Smiths about, and there will be many more when the harvest of this savage jungle war and the Jap prison camps is gathered in.
>
> Major H.R. Love MB, BS AAMC, in the *Australian Medical Journal* (1942) states that: 'Neurotic illness in soldiers is a potential source both of serious wastage of manpower in the field and of prolonged and refractory post-war disability'.

According to the journalist, this disability was widespread – the 'nervous wrecks might come home, be afraid of large crowds and confined spaces, be irritable, rebellious, irresponsible or even dishonest'.[20]

The influential *Smith's Weekly,* a champion of the shell-shocked World War One veteran, devoted significant attention to mental health problems among veterans from World War Two.[21] The *Weekly* (1919–1951) had a history of being highly critical of the government's treatment of returned soldiers from World War One. Even though much of the reporting was polemical and somewhat sensationalised, the paper did reveal a significant amount of concern for the mental health of veterans. This stance reflected the views of the main financier of the paper, Sir James Joynton Smith. During and after World War Two the editor's strategy was to focus on specific cases of apparent injustice in order to expose and highlight government inadequacy. One example of the type of case *Smith's* would take up was JES, aged 24, who had served in Syria, Palestine, and New Guinea. His discharge papers stated that the nervous condition that had developed during the war was not attributable to war service, even though a psychiatrist argued it was at least aggravated by it. This man was passed A1 on enlistment, and after the war was diagnosed with schizophrenia. Such cases of injustice were 'legion', and the Repatriation Department was described in *Smith's Weekly* as 'slow, unsympathetic and stingy' in dealing with such cases.[22]

A sample of issues from 1944 onwards clearly illustrates that there was a great deal of public concern about mentally damaged men returning from the war. One major topic was the acceptance of neuroses as compensable injuries. On 20 May 1944, Minister for Repatriation C.W. ('Hoar') Frost was reported as saying: 'It

July 22, 1944

SHAMEFUL TREATMENT OF ARMY MENTAL CASES

NOTHING more disgraceful has ever been disclosed in the whole history of the Federal Government's d... with ex-service-men than its callous, horrible treatm... and bomb-happy soldiers, as reveal... Queensland United Council of Ex-ser... Such action by a Federal Departme... with full powers to deal with such m... doubt in the mind of every Austral... the Government knows how to use... it has them.

FACTS and opinions asserted in letters by ... Forde and Minister for Repatriation Frost ...

AND THEY SAID THIS MAN WAS MAD

ALLEGATIONS about misuse of Government labor and materials, made by a former RAN Petty Officer, have led to a remarkable exchange of letters between Mr. Kim E. Beazley, Labor MHR for Fremantle (WA), and the Minister for the Navy.

After these accusations had been made the Petty Officer, W. J. Paramor, alleges his sanity was questioned.

Smith's —— Page 3

HOW ARMY TREATS ITS MENTAL PATIENTS

CONDITIONS under which soldier mental patients are being treated at 102 AGH, ... bane, call for immediate investigation.

HOSPITAL has been set up to cater expressly for soldiers who are suffering from mental disorders, with the object of nursing them back to normality.

Mental condition of some of the patients is such that they require constant care and attention, without which there is little prospect of their regaining mental health.

But some of ...

Mother Saw Her Son Assaulted

IT would be easy for members of Parliament to go over Army's Kenmore Hospital at Goulburn, NSW, to see what soldier nerve and mental cases have to go through. It's only across the way from Canberra.

NO REPATRIATION FOR NEUROSIS

It would be harder for them to go over some of Repatriation Department's psychiatric hospitals where ex-soldiers can have their treatment continued into civilian life under skilled psychiatrists who can build up their health and confidence while they are getting back into civilian jobs.

There aren't any such hospitals.

MP'S WOULD THUS DISCOVER THAT SOLDIERS DISCHARGED WITH NEUROSIS GET NO REPATRIATION BENEFITS AND ARE EXPECTED TO SAVE THEIR SANITY AT THEIR OWN EXPENSE.

April 17, 1948

STOP THESE SUICIDES!

Nerve Clinics Demanded

The tragedy of men whose war-shredded nerv... make life a nightmare for them is being tackled ... problem is acute, for the number ...

SOLDIER, HEAL THYSELF!

MINISTER for Repatriation, Mr. C. W. ("Hoar") Frost, is anxious not to spoil ex-soldiers with his Department's munificent pensions ...

Page 22 —— Smith's

A "SMITH'S" SURVEY

Neurosis Is Our Biggest Post-War Problem

COMPARE these figures of pensions granted from the annual report:—

Wounds (gunshot).

No grim... war's ... ists the disrega... neurosis" cases.

Official figures in the Commission's own annual ... this appalling fact — that ...

Smith's Weekly going in to bat for veterans, from 1944

would not be equitable to automatically accept mental disorders suffered by all ex-members of the services as due to war service when such a principle does not apply in respect of other disabilities'. Later reports covered the 'callous, horrible treatment of mentally-sick and bomb-happy soldiers', and on 29 July it was argued that 'humane US methods where the "maladies of the mind" were entitled to treatment the same as men wounded in action' were in stark contrast with Australian treatment.

Smith's Weekly was a sensationalist paper, and it often used risqué and sexist humour, as well as exaggerated reporting, to make its case. In relation to the treatment of veterans this sometimes allowed otherwise hidden or contentious issues to be given a public airing, and could even exert an influence on government policy. For example, its August 1946 reporting of the Repatriation Commission's claim that it had granted more pensions for psychiatric disorders than for physical wounds was juxtaposed with a claim by the Air Force Association that 67,000 [*sic*] applications for pensions on grounds of war neurosis had been rejected. This prompted an inquiry and action from both of these bodies.

The most dramatic issue, highlighted in a number of newspapers, was suicide. One horrifying incident occurred in Adelaide in 1948:

> This case was so shocking as to provoke comment from the South Australian coroner, Mr Cleland. The victim was H, aged 47, of Adelaide. He was decapitated by a railcar at Mile End on March 5. H had been arrested for drunkenness on February 16. He tried to take his life in his cell by slashing his wrists. After two weeks at Enfield mental home he was released on March 2, and arrested the same day for drunkenness. The Coroner said his condition was due to war captivity. He had been a POW for three-and-a-half years. His body was lacerated with torture marks.[23]

This type of media publicity brought a negative response from veteran organisations, but at the same time provided an opportunity for medical and other authorities to repress any public discourse on war stress. One Adelaide veteran mounted a personal campaign to change community attitudes. He complained to the *Sunday Mail* about the lack of support in the community, saying that the attitude of some people 'made me feel unwanted. I seemed to be running into unsympathetic brick walls', and:

> The public attitude toward war neurosis frightens them away from treatment. The people who can help these men are ordinary people, their workmates, the people in their street. Medical clinics and psychiatrists are all very well; but it is the understanding of our fellow men the war neurosis victim needs most.[24]

The editorial in the same issue of the *Sunday Mail* used the suicide incident to call for more community support for 'war neurosis victims'. The prime need of the victim was 'the stepping in of ordinary men and women to help and cheer him up after the specialists have done their job'.

Calls had also come from other quarters to improve the services for returned soldiers. Early in September 1949 the South Australian Wheat and Wool Growers'

Association approached Repatriation authorities to address the plight of mentally damaged returned soldiers. In particular they complained about ex-soldiers being placed in mental hospitals 'where they had no hope of recovery'. The association argued that the needs of ex-soldiers could best be met by the provision of a special clinic for 'returned soldiers suffering from psychiatric ailments caused by war service'.[25]

This public discussion about war neurosis brought a reaction from the Returned Sailors, Soldiers & Airmen's Imperial League of Australia (RSSAILA). In response to these criticisms and other publicity, the RSSAILA called a meeting on 6 September 1949 to address the 'many irresponsible and unfounded statements regarding the treatment of war neurosis cases'. The meeting, convened by the President of the League (a Victoria Cross winner), included service organisations, Legacy and Red Cross, and representatives from the SA Hospitals Visitation Committee as well as the National Council of Women. At the outset the chairman made it clear that 'irrational statements on War Neurosis did not help anyone, least of all the patients and their relatives'. Two 'medical men' gave their interpretation of the term war neurosis. The meeting then made a number of statements and recommendations. One conclusion was that there were relatively few cases of war neurosis 'directly due to actual battle experience', and most conditions could more accurately be attributed to instability before enlistment, and these cases should have been screened out at the time. Post-war problems of veterans were explained as problems arising from the challenges of readjustment to civilian life rather than from the trauma of war experience. While the meeting recommended some changes to services, the final resolution was:

> That this meeting representing all servicemen organisations, Australian Red Cross and other bodies interested in the Ex-servicemen and women expresses its confidence in the government and its medical officers and Staffs [sic] in the approach they are making to this very vital matter and pledge themselves to cooperate and assist authorities in all matters appertaining to the welfare of Mentally Ill ex-service personnel.[26]

In effect the RSSAILA was saying that there was no case to answer, and any problems with neuroses were to be kept within medical confines. From that time no representative body made an issue of mentally damaged World War Two veterans. It was to be left to the medical experts in the Repatriation Commission to deal with it as a clinical problem on an individual basis. This early containment of potential problems may go some way to explaining why mental health issues were pushed well away from the public arena. The other contributing factor was that veterans just wanted to forget.

* * * * *

In the overall assessment of the post-war period, mental health issues did receive some attention, but this was short-lived and focused on the complaints of individuals. Mental health problems of World War Two veterans have not been the subject of public discourse since the early post-war years, when the media took up the cause and elicited action and public interest. Memorialising has been directly focused on loss and bereavement, not on the mental health consequences of such loss. War-related mental health issues only became more publicly acknowledged when Vietnam veterans adopted a political stance in order to have their needs met. This coincided with the emergence of a more acceptable diagnosis of post-traumatic stress disorder, and the emergence of the American and Australian Vietnam veteran movement.

The discourse about the mental health of the largest population of war veterans in Australia has been carefully contained and suppressed for most of the post-war period, and has not been part of the culture of veterans themselves. Any dysfunction has been managed within the medical framework of the government agencies and kept away from public view.

This historical context provides a background for the discussion that follows, on the post-war lives of Kokoda veterans. Behind the façade of the contemporary memory and in the suppressed post-war discourse there is a clear indication of that the New Guinea experiences were carefully submerged.

CHAPTER 6

Life after War

> I wish you all on returning to civilian life, every success and happiness and the very best of luck. It is my sincere hope that you will find little difficulty in re-establishing yourselves in the community back home and that you and yours will get just reward for your sacrifices that you have made for Australia.
>
> Speech to troops, August 1945[1]
> Brigadier Ivan Dougherty, Commander, 21st Brigade.

Dougherty's statement, made shortly after the end of the war in the Pacific, suggests that some difficulties may have been anticipated for veterans re-entering civilian life after years of strain in the jungles of New Guinea. This chapter outlines what happened to 65 of those men.[2] Dougherty was partly right; most of the men did re-establish themselves successfully, but many were troubled by ghosts.

There are common threads through the lives of these men, but there is also much difference. The commonalities and differences are illustrated in the narratives of two men discharged around the same time in 1945. The first is that of a senior officer, a veteran of five campaigns who had sustained several wounds, been ill with malaria, and been exposed to multiple battle experiences. He acknowledged the strain but did not think it was an issue that needed special attention. He also did not acknowledge the possibility that a veteran could not adapt:

> After living on your nerves for some years, it does take a while – I reckon about a year – to stop over-reacting to a tap on the shoulder or a sudden noise. However, I get disgusted with some of the rubbish they produce on TV and films about disturbed returned men. I do not know anyone like that. No-one at all. No doubt there is the exceptional case. Again, any normal person doesn't need special help. The human species is extraordinarily adaptable. Anyone returning to a good family gets whatever help is needed. And really it's no big deal.[3]

The second view is from an infantry private who was only 20 years old when he was thrown into battle against the Japanese in New Guinea in 1942, with very little preparation. He too had been wounded and been ill with malaria and was in front-line combat for most of 1942. He recalls his most stressful time in New Guinea and its lifelong effect:

> One Japanese bloke had his arse and legs shot away with machine gun fire. The officer at the time did not have enough guts to kill him and he said to me, 'Right-oh Smoky, finish him off'. I have lived with those eyes looking at me from that day to this. I shot him between the eyes. Bloody terrible. I dreamed about it for 20 years or so – very bad with me nerves at the end of the war, I'd have nightmares about that chap. I nearly choked my wife. God knows what it does to you and it's the first four or five years that's the worst.[4]

In these narratives there is a common thread of the strain of combat, and the difficult period of adjustment that immediately followed discharge, but the accounts of life after that military period are quite different. The officer believes that while a stressful experience does have a short-term effect, it dissipates without the need for expert intervention or particular adjustment. The militia soldier confesses to a lifetime of struggle. His traumatic memory continued to disturb him long after discharge, affecting his relationships and work.

Both informants grew up in poor households during the 1930s Depression. The officer lived in difficult and deprived areas to which his father, a minister of religion, had been assigned. The family survived on what the parish could provide. As one of 19 children subsisting on a market garden, the private was also poor. Pre-war poverty was a common experience, but they had little in common after discharge.

As the officer had completed high school in his youth, after discharge he was able to go on to become a successful farmer and businessman. He built a large comfortable house where he lived all his married life with his wife, and enjoyed the material and social benefits of a successful career and a felicitous choice of partner. His life was one of rich variety, with much satisfaction from work and family and in later years from serious hobbies. He has produced several books, and maintained a strong interest in agriculture and viticulture. His main contact with medical ideas came when he had a heart attack at the age of 70.

The officer's narrative was not dominated by his war experiences. When telling his story, he chose not to emphasise his traumatic experience, and while he admitted to some distress when reminded of lost mates, he highlighted his ability to overcome his fear. In a later interview he recalled incidents that were painful, such as when he lost a close friend at Soputa hospital when it was overrun and patients were bayoneted. Other events included seeing two of his mates after they had been found strung up by their hands and used for bayonet practice. He had also watched helplessly as a mate took three hours to die at Gona. None of these events assumed a central place in his post-war narrative, even though his wife said that he was 'nervy' just after the war and the family had to be very careful in those early years.

The soldier, on the other hand, whose life will be described in more detail in a later chapter, never settled down, and found life after war a continual struggle. He was an angry and aggressive man, his marriage failed, he continued to be tormented by nightmares and war dreams, and he struggled with mental and physical health problems for most of his life. Although he did well as a builder for some time, in later life he had few possessions, not even a house of his own. Ultimately he was a survivor, but his war experience and his efforts to remain mentally and physically healthy dominated his narrative. What he has gained in later life is always overshadowed by his struggles for stability.

Veterans' post-war experiences fall between these contrasting perspectives. Not all men struggled, but many did conceal their difficulties. The collective life story reveals the complexity and variety in these experiences.

Collective life story

Individual accounts such as those sketched above provide a sense of the individual, but life stories can also be incorporated into a collective life story, in which there are two major elements. The first is the *outer life*, comprising the outer tasks of resettling, finding work, establishing relationships, finding/building a house, starting and supporting a family, and engaging in recreation and community activities. The second strand is the *inner life*, which is the psychological and emotional experience of the veteran. This inner experience includes the remnants of war, which surface in thoughts, feelings and behaviour, and in the subconscious in war-related dreams, particularly nightmares. Remnants like nightmares were reported by the veterans and by family members who lived with the veteran and knew of the night-time ghosts. Evidence of this inner life can also be found in behaviour like avoiding reminders of war, or becoming teary when recalling war memories. War remnants surfaced in different ways at different stages of the life span – immediately after discharge, at midlife, and in later years. Of particular interest was the experience in later life when memories suppressed at an earlier time re-emerged unsolicited.

The collective story is taken up from the time soldiers entered the army. When these men went into the New Guinea action at the beginning of 1942, most were under 25: ages ranged from 18 to 40 years, with the average age just under 24 years. The soldiers from militia units were relatively young and few had any previous battle experience. On enlistment all of these men had passed a basic medical examination and been declared physically and mentally fit. Although their statements cannot be clinically evaluated, they had testified that they had not had a nervous breakdown and had never been diagnosed with shell shock or neurasthenia.[5] Most had been to school in the 1930s, when opportunities for higher education were limited. About a third had completed primary school, 22 per cent had completed some secondary schooling and 32 per cent had completed Intermediate or three years of high school, three per cent had trade qualifications, and a small number had trained for professions with university-level education. These men had survived the Great Depression of the 1930s as children or teenagers, and 21 per cent remembered this as a distressing time. Before the war they were labourers, farmers, bakers, butchers, school teachers, company managers, bank clerks, journalists, sales men, and there was even a lawyer among them. Although a number had been in the militia only one was a career army officer.

By the end of the war 23 per cent were commissioned officers (Lieutenant Colonel, Captain, Lieutenant), 43 per cent were non-commissioned officers (Warrant Officer, Sergeant, Corporal), and 34 per cent were in the ranks. Between them they boasted one Military Cross and Bar, four Military Crosses, three Military Medals and five Mentioned-in-Despatches. In the Owen Stanley Ranges and on the northern coast of New Guinea, all ranks were directly exposed to the enemy and to front-line fighting The sample included a commanding officer, adjutant, company commanders, platoon commanders, section leaders, those with support roles such as stretcher-bearers, cooks, quartermasters, signals, and intelligence officers. Specific combat roles included machine gunners, mortar operators, runners, snipers, and riflemen/infantrymen.

Discharge

The men in this sample were discharged at various stages after 1942. Bert Ward was discharged in 1943 after months of recuperation from a serious frontal head wound received at Gona. On the other hand, men like Glen Williss and Ray Baldwin served their full five years and spent extra service with the occupation forces after 1945. When they were formally discharged, they were all examined medically and details of disabilities were noted on the Final Medical Board AA Form D2.[6] Any medical condition arising during service was noted on the Service and Casualty Form AF B103, which was a record of every investigation and treatment undertaken during service. On discharge there was no questioning or examination about mental conditions, such as nervous break-downs, shell shock or neurasthenia during service, as there had been at the time of enlisting.

This medical examination addressed only the soldier's physical condition – eyes, ears, nose, throat, cardiovascular system, lungs, abdomen and nervous system. If any abnormality was detected the soldier could be presented to a Medical Board for examination and determination of eligibility for compensation. A key question was whether the 'member has any occupational restriction, or requires treatment'. In this case, appropriate referral was made with a Medical Rehabilitation Advice Form. There were thus two decisions to be made. The first was regarding the need for rehabilitation and the second was whether the soldier could apply for some form of compensation.

Service in New Guinea took a very big physical toll. Only 10 per cent of the 65 men escaped being seriously wounded or contracting a serious illness. Seventy-six per cent were treated, at least at an aid post, for serious illnesses such as malaria, scrub typhus, dengue fever, dysentery, and beri-beri. Of the total sample, only two emerged unscathed with no wounds or illness at all. All of those involved in the withdrawal from Efogi had lost significant body weight.

Being wounded or contracting disease often meant the end of service, followed by lengthy recovery and rehabilitation. John Burns, who had gone from 16 stone

Medical History Sheet of (Army No.) [redacted]

Surname (in capitals) [redacted] Christian Names [redacted]
Age 22 years 4 months Date of Birth [redacted] Birthplace [redacted]
Occupation MOTOR DRIVER I.C. Religious Denomination R.C.

Complexion Fair Colour of hair Light Brown Colour of eyes Blue

Distinctive marks, and marks indicating congenital peculiarities or previous disease: Scar on left shin Bone / Scar on right eyebrow

TABLE I.

1. Are you now suffering from any disease or disability? No
2. Have you ever suffered from any of the following illnesses?
   - (a) Rheumatic Fever No
   - (b) Weak Heart or Heart Disease No
   - (c) Tuberculosis or Consumption No
   - (d) Spitting of Blood No
   - (e) Pleurisy No
   - (f) Asthma or Shortness of Breath No
   - (g) Venereal Disease or Stricture No
   - (h) Neurasthenia or Nervous Breakdown No
   - (i) Kidney Disease No
   - (j) Skin Disease No
   - (k) Malaria No
   - (l) Dysentery No
   - (m) Ulcer of the Stomach or Indigestion No
   - (n) Piles No
   - (o) Have you ever had any other serious illness? Corns on the feet/Corn on right small toe
3. Have you had fits of any kind? No
4. Have you had discharge from either ear? No
5. Have you had a broken bone or been seriously injured? Yes
   If so, state nature and date Broken right leg. 1937 Broken Left wrist 1934
6. Have you been operated upon? Adenoids and Tonsils Removed
   If so, state nature and date 1935
7. Has any member of your family suffered from Pleurisy, Tuberculosis, Diabetes, Stroke, Nervous Breakdown, or Mental Trouble? No
   If so, give particulars (relation and when)
8. Have you been rejected or deferred for Life Insurance? No
9. Have you been rejected or discharged as unfit for service in any branch of His Majesty's Forces? No
   If so, give date and reason
*10. Have you been wounded, suffered from Shell Shock, or Gas Poisoning? –
   If so, give particulars

† I declare that I have read the answers to the above questions, and that to the best of my knowledge they are true.

Station M.P.T. & R Depot Padd.
Date 9-10-1939 Signature of Recruit [redacted]

Examined on 9 day of Oct. 19 39
at M.P.T. & R Depot
Height 5 feet 9 inches
Weight 155½ lb.
Chest Measurement: Girth when fully expanded 37¾ inches; Range of expansion 2¾ inches
Urine
Slight defects, but not sufficient to cause rejection (Details in Table VI)

VISION
Without Glasses: Right 6/6, Left 6/9
With Glasses: Right, Left
Vaccination Marks: Right Number; Left Number
When Vaccinated not vaccinated
Blood Pressure, Systolic Diastolic

Examined by me and classified as follows:—
Classification‡ I Signature David Adcock Date 9-10-39

Subsequent Medical Examinations:—
Classification‡ Class I Signature D. M. Salter Maj 14 Dec 39
D Signature Percy Williams Capt. Date 14-12-39
Anxiety State (Mild) Signature W Cockburn Lt Col Date 6-11-44
J. W. Fotheringham Capt.

* Only to be answered if the recruit has had active service.
† The recruit will be warned that should he give false answers to any of these questions he will be subject to heavy penalties under the Defence Act.
‡ In accordance with S.O. A.A.M.S., reasons for unfitness to be stated.

On enlistment soldiers had to attest that they had not suffered psychological problems; see questions 2(h), 3, 7 and 10.

4 pounds to 10 stone 6 pounds after the Efogi withdrawal, was shot in the elbow at Gona and then contracted scrub typhus. John's mate Thommo had died from typhus. John survived but was unable to return to duty. Peter Sherwin lost part of his leg at Gona and lived the rest of his life with an artificial leg. At the time of discharge, most were still recovering from some form of illness and would experience periodic bouts of fever from malaria. Others had to adjust to more serious losses, such as an amputated leg or having part of the scrotum shot away.[7]

The men felt an urgency to return to normal life and therefore often hid medical and/or psychological conditions that may have entitled them to compensation. There were occasions when, if ignored, such a condition went away, but for many, they developed into something more serious

Pension entitlement was an indication of the effect of war service, and was awarded on those grounds only. A returned soldier had to show that the illness he suffered was a result of stress or wounds suffered during war service. Determining the connection between illness and war service is governed by strict protocols that can, in some circumstances, be questionable. For example, if a veteran had smoked in response to the stress of service, a consequent heart condition could be acceptable grounds for pension entitlement. The protocols state, however, that the veteran had to have smoked for a certain period following the war, even if he had taken up smoking during service. If he did not meet the criteria of duration and timing he would not be granted entitlement. Many conditions, such as tension headaches, were not so strictly governed by protocol, and were more difficult to assess for their relation to war service. After examining a number of files, it appears that no pension was awarded to any of the veterans solely on the grounds of mental illness.

Among the men in this sample, 80 per cent were awarded pensions on grounds of physical illness. Of the total sample, over half of the men (52 per cent) had received either 100 per cent pension or TPI/Extended Disability Allowance (EDA).[8] A further eighteen men (27 per cent) received part entitlement, which ranged from 10 to 80 per cent. Five men (8 per cent) received a service pension without a disability component and eight had no pension at all. A service pension is granted purely on the basis of service, and is basically equivalent to an aged pension but has additional medical entitlements. In the sample there was only one case in which a pension, awarded for total and permanently incapacity (TPI) following a review after 1980, included a part entitlement for post-traumatic stress disorder.

I was unable to discover the success rate in entitlement applications, but on the basis of evidence gleaned from a few case studies it is reasonable to suggest that a significant number had their applications either rejected or allocated at a reduced rate. Some men with serious illness did not seek pension entitlement, but in general the seriousness of health problems emerging over the years correlated with pension grants. A reasonable conclusion is that these men were officially recognised as damaged men, but this recognition did not acknowledge the full extent of the distress that they experienced over time.

Transition to civilian life

> Make sure you tell them what it was like after the war – we had been married in June 1944 and our first child arrived in May 1945. I married one fellow and another came home. He went away a nice boy and came back a big rough man. At the end of 1945 we had no money, an eight-month-old baby, no car, no telephone, living with parents, and he was having bouts of malaria. He returned to his old job at Elders on the same wage as in 1940. There were no 'frilly aprons'.[9]

Rosslyn Russell's personal experience highlighted the fact that husbands, sons, brothers and lovers had gone away as healthy boys or young men but had been changed physically and mentally by war. Physical and psychological remnants took a long time to work themselves out. Most men tried to just put these things aside and get on with life. Indeed, 'getting on with life' was a first priority and a main strategy for forgetting the war.

Four out of five men in my sample found life difficult or very difficult for at least six months after discharge, some taking up to two years to feel as though they were back to 'normal'. Only four individuals claimed that they found adjustment relatively easy. Veterans had to start over again in several important areas of their lives. The two most pressing tasks were to get back to work and establish the family unit, with all that that entailed. Housing was limited, and most had to live with relatives or in shared housing. Parents had aged, often prematurely, during the war and many needed care. For some the difficulty of starting again was the challenge they needed to bury the memories of war, a view expressed by former Adjutant Major Harry Katekar.

> [Stressful memory] fades with time. What causes it to immediately fade is that when you come back after 5 or 6 years away from family and relatives, and having just got married, there is an urgent need to earn a living, and to get involved not only in your occupation, but also if you are that way inclined, to get involved in community service, to be on just about every committee that is around the place. And to do that I think you drive yourself in a frame of mind. Because the busier you are, the more tired you get and less likely to dwell on war experiences and the friends that you lost and the bitter thoughts that you had about things.[10]

For those who had been more seriously unseated by their experience the memories did not so easily fade:

> When I first came back – oh I'd be in bed and out of bed, and my wife used to nearly die of fright and I'd be standing on my feet then I'd open my eyes. Probably a noise, just a bang or something – a crack, you know, or something, slam a door ... When in action there was a rifle shot that used to warn you of an impending air raid ... And I came back very badly affected by war neurosis. Of course, being on an Observation Post with the mortars, I think the shelling probably did some of that, I don't know ... I couldn't work. I was sick. My nerves were gone and I was a wreck. I've still got trouble with my stomach. I've still got an ulcer which they said was from war service but still I get very bad pains and it's anxiety state; that's what they call it, anxiety state.[11]

Making the transition back to civilian life. Bob Johns with his wife Faye (above), and Jim Fairley (right). They are pictured with war-time photographs of themselves. Jim Fairley was the RMO, 2/27th Battalion. [Photos: John Raftery]

The distress and disturbance during the transition to civilian life was attributable not just to coping with the remnants of prior traumatic experience or the difficulties of starting again. There was another dimension to the transition – leaving the unit to which men had become so strongly bonded. It was argued that this could have been as distressing as reliving war memories. Former platoon commander Bob Johns MM, a very experienced campaigner, put the view:

> I've got another theory … I wonder whether the trauma was as much going from the army environment, where you were owned by a unit. 'I'm a part of it' – you were part of a body of men you were proud of. Whether transferring from that to the traumas of civilian life, not the war itself, and the change from one style of life, a disciplined proud life, to fight for yourself in the civilian life where there was a lack of feeling of purpose and pride – that was as much a trauma as the war itself.[12]

In spite of the post-war transition problems, the majority of the men were able to find satisfactory work or resume old jobs and advance their careers. The majority also found stability in relationships, and could enjoy their grandchildren in later life and retire in relative material comfort. Marriages were largely stable, and during the 1960s, while the next generation was experimenting with relationships, they remained settled in their marriages and jobs. Perhaps for many, it was, as Hugh Dalby put it, that they had 'had enough excitement for one life'.[13]

Work

Returning to work was a major part of re-adjustment and finding satisfying work was a significant factor in re-establishing a civilian identity. This was the men's most significant outer task and was closely linked with the male imperative to provide for the family. They had worked in a variety of occupations prior to enlistment. For some, the army had provided secure paid employment for longer than they had experienced during the 1930s. Some men had established positions or careers to return to but the majority had to start again. One-third of them had been in unskilled occupations before enlistment but all moved into skilled, sales or managerial work after discharge. There was a wide diversity of vocational settlement patterns. On the surface the majority of the sample were successful and took up responsible positions in private companies or in the public service, and many established their own businesses.

The initial settlement into work was not always a simple transition, particularly for men who had been away for five years where they had achieved status and recognition. For example, Robert Johns found a different world in his bank.

> Robert had returned to the Bank. He did not intend to stay there, but his sense of responsibility kept him there for long, weary hours, and Saturday mornings, of course. At the Bank, young men had been given unusual promotion opportunities because of the staffing drain to the Armed Services. Rob, as a decorated and distinguished officer of the Australian Army, was given menial tasks and a lack of concession to the traumas that had undermined his health.[14]

No one lost status in the transition, and the majority made significant gains, such as Bill Russell who started his working life as a wool classer in a stock and station firm and eventually managed a large finance company. He worked his way into several managerial positions in different companies, and in the last phase of his working life took over a struggling teachers' credit union, transforming its annual turnover from $300,000 to $20 million.[15] Others took a radical turn in their lives by taking up soldier settlement blocks and establishing themselves as successful farmers and graziers. Life events also caused a shift in life course. Harry Katekar turned his back on a successful law career and returned to the country to manage his father's property. He became a very successful and wealthy primary producer and retired in comfort to the city. The training and responsibility in the army was a significant factor in the careers of some men. This was the case with John McKinna, who had distinguished himself as an officer in the 2/27th and then as a brigade commander. In later life he was head-hunted to be the commanding officer of a state police force, even though he had had no police training.

Relationships

Forming new or taking up old relationships was another major factor in the transition to civilian life. All the men were married at some stage, either before, during or after the war. The decision to get married was often taken during a short period of leave, or even amid the violence of battle. Robert and Faye Johns made the decision at the height of the 1942 campaign, which Robert recalled in vivid detail:

> And running back to our platoon Joe was hit alongside me, poomp! Through the heart – massive hit through the heart, he hit the ground and he was dead when I rolled him over … I joined the battalion from having arrived back in Australia late. I arrived just before they went off to New Guinea and was given to Joe as his Sergeant and we became very good friends. And on the boat [to New Guinea] – he'd got married on his return from the Middle East – he was extolling the virtues of marriage and I told him I'd met Faye. He said, 'Get married! You know, the war, grab your chances while you can, get married'. I wrote to Faye when we then got to Koi-Taki, prior to going into the Owen Stanleys. We talked about it further and then I wrote this long letter asking would she become my wife.

Marrying during war-time was very difficult, with limited opportunities for time together. George and Ronda Raftery, for example, decided to get married in 1943, but did not get to live with each other for several years after that. She had started writing to him when he was in the Middle East, and George proposed in February 1943, six weeks after the Gona battle, in which he had been shot through the upper thigh. After a week's honeymoon George returned to duties. Ronda was posted to Victoria with the Air Force but had her career interrupted by rheumatic fever. They could not resume a normal married life until the end of 1945.

Despite the challenges of life after war, only five marriages of the men in my sample ended in divorce. Satisfaction with marriage was difficult to determine accurately, but few expressed dissatisfaction. One couple in their seventies for example, who expressed some surprise at the low divorce rate among other veterans, were in fact going through a period of tension in their marriage at the time, but would not discuss it openly. There also appeared to be much more tolerance of men by their wives because they had 'been through so much'.[16] A widow who had been abused and deprived by her alcoholic husband admitted that she still loved him despite his failings. One veteran did not want it known that he had actually been very unhappy for many years but had remained loyal to his wife. Fourteen per cent remained in the same marriage while admitting to some tension. Divorce occurred only in extreme cases, such as serious violence against a member of the family, or in one case where the wife was an alcoholic.

Often children formed a bond that kept couples together:

> And so, therefore we have a mixed bag of a family and because we love them all – their difficulties are our difficulties. Now that we're not free of difficulties even though we have a lovely house by the sea and stuff. We've had lots of hard times through our family. I think the family held us together when things got tough. Because we couldn't … I mean, you've got five kids and they're dependent on you, you have to stand by them.[17]

Below the surface

Had the medical examiners at the point of discharge probed below the surface and had the men wanted to reveal themselves they might have found psychological wounds. On discharge men repressed their memories, including those of traumatic experiences unimaginable before the war:

> I find this question most difficult as I have several traumatic experiences. One of the worst was being overrun by the Japs at Isurava [Kokoda Trail]. A small amount of mail had got through [including] a letter for an 18-year-old mortally wounded soldier from his mother. He pleaded for me to read it out, which I did, but he died in my arms. I will never forget the terror in his face, his thoughts of home and his mother.[18]

All men had their own version of similarly distressing experiences. Seventy per cent recounted at least one such disturbing event. The most serious were experiences like being ordered to shoot a wounded enemy soldier, and, in an extreme case, being ordered to kill a fellow soldier. In addition to the physical and social adjustments after discharge evidence of inner torment surfaced in many ways. Individuals experienced more than one type of disturbance, but the primary types were nightmares (44 per cent), war dreams (8 per cent), severe sleep disturbance (5 per cent), behavioural problems (16 per cent), and alcohol abuse (13 per cent – probably underestimated). In some cases early troubles translated into long-term dysfunction or interpersonal conflict, and only six men were assessed as having no major difficulties with adjustment.

The other significant observation is that for the most disturbed veterans distress fluctuated over time. A veteran admitted to hospital periodically for treatment would have bouts of productive work and satisfying family life. The 'disease' did not pervade all aspects of his life at all times. This observation questions a disease model of post-traumatic stress, in which distress or dysfunction becomes appropriated into a permanent pathology.

Veterans reported a range of experiences that in hindsight show clear evidence of strain. Despite such a high level of exposure and strain, the official data records that very few men were affected in the field. Of the 65 respondents, only six were identified as having had a breakdown experience of some kind during their service.[19] Five of these continued to experience difficulties and require some form of intervention at some stage during their lives. There may be reasons for this low incidence of diagnosis. In these campaigns, medical staff worked with very limited facilities, and were pre-occupied with treating wounds and serious illness, which may have resulted in failure to diagnose. Serious wounds and illness, such as malaria and scrub typhus could also have contributed to the low incidence of diagnosis, in that they masked any signs of psychological strain.

This apparently low incidence of stress breakdown during war-time does not truly reflect the effects of war in later life. As well as those who broke down during service, a further 21 men (33 per cent) were judged, on the basis of their narrative, to have had some form of stress problem during the New Guinea campaigns not acknowledged with a medical diagnosis at the time. These men had had temporary breakdowns or were on the edge of breakdown. Others experienced some crisis, either mental or physical, that necessitated a transfer to other duties. Evidence of these types of experience was derived from self reports of experiences in combat areas, and their own and others' assessment of their state on discharge. The following statement describes one man's minor breakdown experience:

> During an advance at night time, two hours on, two hours restless sleep, my nerves became strained; I saw things that no-one else saw; I was shaking uncontrollably; taken back for a couple of days then returned to front line again. No more trouble after that.[20]

One veteran, when he had a serious breakdown after discharge, reported a breakdown experience during service that was not picked up at the time. Seven veterans, not identified as having a breakdown in service, had some form of breakdown in their later lives that required psychiatric intervention. A further 10 experienced serious difficulties but received no psychiatric treatment. In all, 24 men (37 per cent) had serious mental health problems at some stage in their post-war lives. This does not include another 15 who experienced some symptoms such as mild depression, which did not affect their lives to any marked degree. It is clear that during service many veterans suppressed difficulties that emerged in later, civilian, life.

The difficulties that men experienced in later life were not always recognised as mental health problems and could be masked by alcohol abuse. For the returned soldier, this could well have been a form of self-medication to take away the pain no-one else could see. Other presenting problems were chronic non-life-threatening illness (e.g. ulcers, dyspepsia) not related to normal ageing, and relationship disturbances including family abuse.

Of all the men in the study, 70 per cent suffered some form of serious intrusion in their later years. It was not uncommon for veterans to say that hardly a day went by without some memory or dream interfering. The memory of those few years in service had the ability to disturb across time, and thoughts and memories of stressful events intruded involuntarily, without active recall. Nightmares and battle dreams are the more obvious intrusions, although battle dreams are not necessarily distressing. Memories did not fade and in most cases, grew stronger with time.

Collectively, these intrusions in later life are evidence of a residue of traumatic memory. While not labelled a disorder, these memories are evidence of an internal narrative of distress that was never fully aired. When evidence of inner distress did emerge it generally remained within a closed family environment. One widow clearly remembered her deceased husband's nightmares, which were not mentioned outside the family, and especially not to doctors, 'in case you finished up in the funny farm'.[21] Further evidence of a concealed narrative was found in a survey of a sub-sample of 29 of the men using a Memory Intrusion Scale that confirmed the view that 'normal' veterans are still disturbed by intrusive memories. These could emerge in unsolicited fashion (intrusive thoughts, 90 per cent;

reminders from TV/newspaper, 86 per cent) and could be upsetting. Most respondents preferred to talk about amusing memories when with other veterans (90 per cent), and they were more likely to reflect on their battle experiences after retirement (73 per cent).[22]

Most veterans presented a brave public persona, so that an outsider would not see what was really happening within. It is necessary to dig deeper to assess just how their lives worked out, behind their marks of war.

No one was totally unmarked by grief and war memories. The apparently unscathed veterans, however, masked an undercurrent of disturbance arising from searing events that remained a repressed, but important, record of their war experience. In this sense they did not quite 'put it behind them', even though they were not overtly impeded in their lives, nor did they become mentally ill and require treatment. The aura surrounding these men, combined with the stigma of any association with mental illness, dictated that their distress remain hidden.

Finding a balance

The account of life after war illustrates just how far lives can diverge over time after experiencing a similar series of traumatic events. In New Guinea each man developed his own way of coping, and each carried his own perception and inner narrative of his war experience.

After an unsettled initial period, the majority of men adjusted well, received their 'just rewards', and went on to live fairly conventional lives, at least on the surface. What was happening underneath was more complex and varied. One veteran spoke of having learned values and skills from his hardship in war years which helped him in later life:

> You have a lot of experiences. Despite a lot of them being unpleasant, they still add something to your being, to your person. We had a daughter who was born with one leg shorter than the other. She had a lot of time in hospital. That is a tragedy but it adds something if you like to look on the good side; added something to her character. The army was like that – it is not all credit and not all debit. Of all the settlers at W, the soldiers generally were more go-ahead than those who had never been.[23]

Another beneficial outcome of service was the financial and material advantages. For example, on discharge veterans were eligible to apply for low interest housing loans. Other repatriation benefits included farming land allocated under the soldier settlement schemes under the Rural Reconstruction Commission, and retraining allowances under the Commonwealth Rehabilitation Training Scheme (CRTS) for veterans to complete approved education and training. This ranged from a trade course to a medical degree. The soldier settlers scheme opened up virgin country and granted blocks to returned men. The 'blocks' provided were cleared and fenced with some shelter, such as a second-hand hut. Pensions and the accompanying eligibility for free medical treatment added an element of security.[24]

Two strands have run through most of these men's lives, even the most seriously disturbed. The first is that the majority of veterans maintained a positive view of their war service and their involvement in their unit. Positive experiences include comradeship, a broadened outlook, the development of problem-solving skills, a sense of having participated in an important part of military history that 'saved' Australia, and the development of some technical skills. Such positive experiences would even lead a soldier who had experienced a serious wartime breakdown to say that he 'would not have missed it for quids'. The second strand is the outward success, which occurred in all but a few cases, and allowed veterans to maintain a façade over their inner lives. This was rarely removed for any outsider.

Most men continued seeking their identity through contact with other veterans. The close bonds formed during stressful times usually continued in the unit associations and reunions, but not always. Bill Russell, for example, left the army and never joined any veteran associations (something 'best left behind'); he built a very satisfactory life in terms of wealth, career, family and community involvement. He had never 'enjoyed' killing, although he conceded it was something 'you had to do on the spur of the moment'. Nor had he 'enjoyed' seeing mutilation, such as the man in his unit who had been shot through the head, or another man at Efogi who, though still alive, was sitting up trying to hold his brains in his head. He recalled the piles of bodies from both sides at Gona that had to be disposed of. In the heat of battle there was not much time to think about the reality of the fighting, and he did not recall being badly disturbed by memories after he was discharged. He had never sought any help from the Repatriation Commission, and his only complaint was a 'bit of arthritis'. His main problem after discharge was coping with bouts of malaria for a short time. His wife supported his testimony of being stable and free from reminders.[25]

A number of critical stages can be identified in the lives of these men. The first was in the immediate post-war period when they suffered the residual effects of illness, particularly malaria and scrub typhus, while grappling with the immediate effects of combat experience and the transition to civilian life.[26] Many felt lost and confused at this time and were caught between wanting to get on with life and still experiencing anxiety, nightmares, lack of concentration and other disturbances, as well as coping with the severance of their connection with their units. If they survived this period and did not continue to be sick, drink heavily or need psychiatric treatment, the majority adjusted to rebuild their lives successfully during their middle years. Trauma-related memory intrusions were distinguishable from phenomena such as grieving for lost comrades and the process of reminiscing to make sense of their war years.

The lives of almost all these men revealed a submerged discourse of an inner life that has never been adequately addressed within the psychiatric paradigm, either administratively or clinically. The chronically disturbed men had their symptoms appropriated and expressed in foreign medical terms, and those who were treated encountered alienating technologies aimed at expunging memory rather than integrating distress and traumatic memory. Men who were not identified as chronically disturbed but were troubled by intrusions from traumatic memory were indirectly marginalised. They were not dysfunctional enough to be diagnosed as ill, but were not offered a forum in which to explore their difficult memories.

The collective veteran story is complex and cannot be confined to simple clichés. Theirs was largely a story about the search for identity in a world that was turned on its head. This is well illustrated in the story of Ray Baldwin. One of the youngest volunteers in the 2/27th Battalion, he survived every battle from Syria to Balikpapan, and still carries fragments from two hand grenades that hit him during the attack on Gona. He also served in Borneo as a regular soldier in the 1950s, so he saw war from all angles. One of his first post-war jobs in 1947 was to return POWs and internees to Germany, where he witnessed the execution of German soldiers. At Belsen he fell on his knees and wept, and still remembers the inscription 'The earth can seal not the blood shed on thee'. It is not surprising that he carried emotional scars that would fester during the night – 'I still wake up yelling something like "Bring that gun over here" – they are mostly war dreams'.

Ray's sense of identity had been seriously challenged when he enlisted at the age of 19, and discovered that he had been living with foster parents since infancy. Army life was hard but was also a learning experience, and the unit gave him a sense of family, and a renewed sense of identity. He learned a lot about life and it changed him in a way that he would never have thought possible. He learned about loyalty, friendship and supporting your mates. He can remember times in his life when he would draw on the example of his role models, like Ron Johnson, his platoon leader in New Guinea. Ray's toughening up in times of deprivation and danger served him well on many occasions, but this sometimes caused concern to those who did not fully appreciate that early experience.

Ray enjoyed a fulfilling adult life, through work and family life, which continued into retirement. The 2/27th Association remains a central feature of his life. Marriage and family were important to Ray. Like many veterans, Ray found marriage a stabilising influence. Val has been central to his life and still is: 'She is the best thing that has ever happened to me'.[27]

* * * * *

Not all veterans managed the search for identity in a changed world as well as Ray Baldwin did. The following chapters trace in detail three different patterns of experience evident in my sample of veterans: those who lived with significant remnants of war, which did not adversely affect them (Chapter 7); those who had serious problems that were not detected (Chapter 8); and those who had serious mental health problems that were treated within the rehabilitation system (Chapter 10).

CHAPTER 7

Just Below the Surface

The majority of the men in this study managed their post-war lives very successfully, but even for this group there were varying levels of disturbance from their New Guinea experience. This disturbance did not attract a psychiatric label, nor did they seek to talk about it. They sought help only for the physical marks of war like old war wounds or the illnesses of ageing. These men had steady work records and relatively stable family lives and in this sense their lives lacked drama. In their public façade there was no portrayal of struggle and no narrative of illness or distress. However, their outer façade hid varying degrees of disturbance from the past. Most had some disturbance from battle dreams, intrusive thoughts, or nightmares, and behavioural disturbance in the months after discharge, which persisted in varying degrees in later life. Not all individual stories can be related here but a sample will give a sense of the nature of the submerged story, which appeared in many forms. Some of these stories have been mentioned in earlier chapters; here they are told in more detail.

Remnants of the New Guinea campaigns emerged in varying degrees over time, and took a number of forms. For example, the man who bore most responsibility for men's lives, Lieutenant Colonel Jeffrey Cooper, Officer in Charge of the 2/27th Battalion, who had to make the decision to withdraw from Efogi after the Brigade Headquarters was overrun by the Japanese, could never really forget. He had trained himself to put aside these remnants and immerse himself in his demanding work of managing a large family company. He regarded the time in the Owen Stanley Range as something best forgotten, but there had been 'many a time at that dread hour of 3 am when I have turned over and over events of the past.' The memories surface in the dark hours of morning, but 'You kill the dreams'.

At one end of the spectrum is someone like Peter Langsford, who lived a life relatively free of any disturbance. Even though there are individual differences, Peter's life is reflected in a variety of forms in the stories of other men. There is little apparent drama in Peter's story, and superficially it could be reduced to a few phrases such as, he grew up in Adelaide, he went off to the war, he came back, married and settled down in his old job. Eventually he retired to enjoy the benefits of a prudent and successful life. He never troubled the Veterans' Affairs psychiatrist, and discussed only physical maladies with his general practitioner. Peter presented a story of a smooth and unruffled life, with only a slight suggestion of dissatisfaction in that his return to a civilian job was not as demanding as being a senior officer in his battalion. There was no evidence that a particularly traumatic period in his New Guinea service had affected him negatively.

Peter was born in country South Australia on 29 June 1920. His father died when Peter was 9 years old, but he was able to complete a high school education. When he left school in 1935 during the Great Depression he took a job as an office boy in the state transport authority. Five years later he joined the AIF, having served in a militia unit since 1938. He had a feeling that 'something was going to happen', so when he turned twenty in 1940 he enlisted, with his mother's permission.

Peter was originally drafted into the 2/43rd Battalion in 1940 and sent to Officers' Training School at Duntroon. In May 1941 Peter was sent to the Middle East where he undertook further training in the Training Battalion in Palestine. His capacity for leadership was recognised and he was promoted to Platoon Sergeant. He was assigned to the 2/27th Battalion in January 1942, by which time the Middle East action was over and the Battalion was soon on its way to Australia, via Bombay.

The jungle training in July 1942 at Caloundra in Queensland was the only preparation for the appalling conditions encountered in the Owen Stanley Ranges where he had to adapt his thinking to another new environment. He was a Platoon Sergeant in C Company and while in the field was promoted to Lieutenant. Peter's time in New Guinea was not without life-threatening trauma. He survived the Kokoda campaign, but during the withdrawal from Efogi developed dysentery, probably from eating a tin of bacon from rations, subsequently developed beri-beri and was left behind with the stretcher party. This stretcher party was left in a native garden while the rest of the Battalion made its way towards Moresby. In his condition he did not know what was going on. Prior to that he had been able to walk and get along with the help of another soldier. The two men assigned to guard and look after the stretcher cases, Burns and Zanker, had to attend to Peter's most basic needs. There was no medication and limited food, but ample clean water. They were also in danger of being found by the enemy, as well as dying from illness or wounds. Two men died in the garden. By the time they were found, Peter had been ill for thirty days, during which time he lost five of his eleven stone.

How did he survive?

> It was just a matter of when everybody else moved you tried to keep up. There was one occasion when I knew I had to get to the top of a hill and I knew the only way I could do it was by crawling. So I did. It was probably an exercise in willpower.

Beri-beri affected the nervous system in his legs and he remained ill for some months and was hospitalised in Port Moresby, Brisbane, Sydney and finally Adelaide. This meant he missed out on the battle at Gona where losses were heavy and many of his friends were killed.

> I suppose that is the business we were in. You felt it fairly strongly but there was not a lot you could do. It does not pay to reflect too much on these things. That

> is what we were there for and if you were hit, well that was it – you were unlucky. I don't believe that I considered it to be a traumatic experience. I felt sad but not upset. Nobody likes to see anybody knocked. I lost Reg Bastyan up there, an old friend and my best mate at school.

After his recovery Peter wanted to rejoin the Battalion as soon as possible – 'The battalion was your home. You would do anything to get back to the unit' – and went into action again in the Ramu Valley (1943-44), in very difficult terrain with a lot of heavy fighting. In the Ramu Valley and Shaggy Ridge in 1943 he was mainly engaged in patrol work. As many troops went down with serious tropical diseases as were killed or wounded. Here Peter contracted another dose of malaria, as well as hepatitis.

His final engagement with the 2/27th was the invasion of Balikpapan in Borneo in July 1945. Even though this action was planned and executed extremely well with adequate support for the landing force, it was not an easy time. By this time many men were feeling the effects of five or six years of continuous service. Peter had now been promoted to Battalion Adjutant. He saw himself as someone who knew what he was doing, but regarded the appointment with characteristic modesty, saying 'I was fortunate enough to get the appointment'.

After the official end of hostilities in August 1945, Peter joined the occupation force in the Celebes, where he assumed command of C Company for the duration of the occupation. He regarded this as an interesting cultural experience, and quite a change from direct combat. Peter accepted the surrender of the enemy forces at Kendari on behalf of the allied forces.

Despite the danger, action, life threatening illness, and the loss of a lot of mates, Peter did not regard his army career as too exciting. Campaigns that others would be prepared to boast about were something that he could talk about somewhat dispassionately, and even though he achieved a high rank he does not recall the experience with any show of pride.

Most men found it very difficult to adjust to civilian life after 1945 and although not as affected as some, Peter also took a little while to settle, but:

> At that point most of us felt that the job was done and we had to get on with normal life. The war was over. That is not to say that I did not miss battalion life, but that only lasted a certain amount of time. Once the war was over everyone was relieved.
>
> Marriage certainly helped me to settle down. It would have taken a lot longer if I had not been married.

At the age of 25 Peter's initial consideration was to get back to his job and build a support base for his new family. Peter had made the decision not to get married until after the war, even though he had already met his future wife. They became engaged by correspondence, married in 1946 and eventually had two sons. Leaving the war machine was not the difficult part; it was more difficult making the transition from a senior officer to a relatively junior clerk. He had gone away as a clerk and came back to the same job, having been a company commander and seen a great deal of action: 'There was a difference in responsibility. I was adjutant and senior officer – I came back as a relative junior.' The people now senior to him had not seen the sights that he had seen, nor had they had his responsibilities. this situation, while irksome, did not lead him to become resentful or discontented.

> As company commander you were responsible for 150 men – making decisions about whether they live or die. To come back and be subordinate to people who had not had that responsibility – making a big thing of minor issues. It took a little while to get used to this.

The 2/27th Battalion then had to take second place to family and career. There was no report from Peter or his partner that there were any disturbing elements at this time, such as nightmares, flashbacks, intrusive thoughts or anxiety. The only tangible remnants were some ongoing health problems. It took about three years to rid his system of the malaria, and he occasionally had a twinge in his legs from beri-beri, but neither of these problems restricted his work or other activity. He resumed playing cricket, his favourite sport, and continued his army career part-time. He rejoined the Citizen Military Forces with the 10th Battalion, University Regiment, and later commanded the 43/48th Battalion, as a Lieutenant Colonel. He reported all of this very modestly. The discipline of the army seemed to come naturally to him and was consistent with his internal discipline. Although he continued his army association in the CMF he did not remain attached to his old unit as a member of the 2/27th Association. He did join the RSL.

After this initial adjustment he gradually gained promotion in the public service and life seemed pretty quiet to Peter during his mid-life period. He no longer craved excitement and did not strive to climb the corporate ladder too quickly, but he did retire as head of department. 'I'm one who accepts things as they occur and makes the best of them.' He saw a lot of changes in the government department, as it became corporatised, and his experience as an officer, particularly as adjutant, enabled him to contribute to the planning and executing of those changes.

He retired early at age 60 in 1970 'with no regrets'. He got involved in a number of community organisations such as the Save the Children Fund and Meals on Wheels, and believed that 'Service to the community should be seen as a form of service to the country rather than be just a drag'. He and his partner travelled a lot, spending 12 months in the UK after he retired, but he had no interest in travelling back to the old battlefields; England and Scotland were more attractive.

Peter was a taciturn man who did not enjoy talking about his war experiences, even with friends who had had similar experiences. He had been able to leave it in the past. The past was 'history. I am fortunate I have been spared a lot of the problems others have had.' Peter believed that the army developed his character traits and honed his capacity to think constructively and achieve objectives.

> To achieve anything you must have self-discipline It is mainly a matter of thinking seriously about anything you do – working out the result an action will have – if you consider the aspects of any action you have to come up with a reasonable answer. Do not rush into anything without due consideration. There are always

> standards for behaviour – most of them being fairly reasonable. Always consider the consequences of your actions.
>
> Hardship of that nature [the New Guinea experience] tends to build character – I think that trying times bring out the best in people. You had a choice – you could have just lain down and died – it is as simple as that.
>
> I must say that I did not suffer any trauma as a result of wartime experience.

Peter died during the course of this research, and I interviewed his widow two years after his death to talk about his last days. It is a common experience of veterans to experience distress and fierce nightmares during their death, but in the pain of cancer Peter did not experience any distressing nightmares or dreams or intrusive memories prior to his death.[1] His wife confirmed then that his life had been largely free of distress. He did not have nightmares or other intrusions and never sought compensation for mental stress. There was no evidence that the anxiety, fear, grief, and death of New Guinea had disturbing or socially disruptive effects that endured.

Paul is another veteran in the group of men who coped well with their marks of war, but for him, and others like him, the memories were never far below the surface and did intrude in later life.

> The memories of these years and the experiences will remain with me till the day I die, irrespective of what you try to do to erase them from your memory bank.[2]

Paul said this in 1994, over 50 years after he had arrived in Port Moresby at the age of 18. In his time in New Guinea he survived a number of patrols in the Owen Stanley Range and saw his most intense action at Gona, where he was wounded. He could list the memories he had tried to erase:

> Having to kill a man three feet in front of me and seeing the look on his face when your bullets enter his body; seeing your mates lying dead on the ground and having to bury a mate who was killed; going into the jungle to bring back the bodies of mates killed in ambush; the smell of dead bodies on both sides.

Paul settled back into civilian life, and he never became a psychological casualty in the sense of being diagnosed and provided with treatment. He worked until he retired and at the time of my contact with him was enjoying a life of retirement with his family. His inner experience did not prevent him playing bowls, fishing, travelling and taking part in community activities. His health crises were more physical, such as open heart surgery. However, there was always an undercurrent of disturbance, which he and others acknowledged. His wife described him as someone who was 'sometimes troubled', and who in his early years had experienced nightmares and was anxious, but was a very good husband and citizen. His daughter 'never doubted his love', but acknowledged that he was reticent about his war experiences, and in later life would be distressed if he did open up to his children.

Paul is one in a group of men who were outwardly successful in their lives, struggled inside with the remnants of war, but for the most part managed their disturbance well. Usually they could submerge their memories under a heavy load of work, commitment to their families or to community service. Their strong 'getting on with life' ethic, developed just after discharge, remained with them as a coping strategy. The common feature is that they had no space in which they were encouraged to talk about and make sense of the remnants of war. Theirs is not a discourse of discontent, but a neglected discourse.

For these men, intrusions and disturbance could be quite vivid. One 80-year-old said he could still smell the stench of the hundreds of dead Japanese, from when he had been assigned to body retrieval after the battle at Gona in December 1942. Only 26 of his battalion had been left standing after that suicidal charge, and he still grieves daily for the 200 young men who lost their lives in that year. He still experiences nightmares and unwelcome thoughts, after a full work and family life.

Robert Johns's story is similar and his psychological remnants are partly the wages of his heroism which earned him a Military Medal.[3] Robert is rightly proud of his military service and retains many symbols of this in his comfortable home, the result of a successful career and careful living. He has made a success of his life and explained his life-long determination to succeed by referring to his early experience of 'failing' as a 14-year-old cadet midshipman in the navy, which he left after being bullied and subjected to harsh initiation rituals. This 'traumatic and … early defeat' gave him the determination not to accept defeat in the future.

As a young man, volunteering for the AIF was a natural progression from service in the militia, but this did not quite prepare Robert for the 'the terrible reality of war' in their first campaign in Syria, where he was awarded the Military Medal for bravery. The layers of memories, which later emerged in nightmares, were embedded there, in such things as discovering a mate who had been shot with a large calibre bullet, lying in a pool of blood. His wife, Faye, made this judgement later in life:

> My husband went to War in 1940 equipped with a sense of high adventure, a natural physical alertness, a background of motor bikes, militia – a particularly well-trained soldier. I had not met him at this point, but I know that he was both brave and daring and that he was very highly thought of in his battalion and that his family was extremely proud of him. If there were any negatives at all, they were things he did his utmost to overcome.[4]

As platoon leader in New Guinea it was a case of 'kill rather than be killed', and some of his exploits took him to the edge of self-control. Two personal incidents stand out in his post-war recollections. The first was during the retreat from Efogi when the battalion was fragmented into small groups and forced to survive off the land for up to 18 days. One night he was on the point of exhaustion, many men had collapsed about him, and he was faced with the same choice. In a dream he saw his future wife and a child playing on a grassy slope in his home city. As he approached she handed the child to him. He awoke from the dream determined to go on, and from that time he had no further temptation to give in to strain. Getting home to marry his fiancée became his focus for survival.

Faye recalls how the time in New Guinea had taken its toll:

> I [first] met him on his return from the Middle East in July 1942 – It was a contrived meeting, but I was attracted to his litheness and his sparkling grey-green eyes and he liked my brown ones ... We were engaged by September (when he came out of the Owen Stanleys they fed and watered his emaciated frame and handed him my telegram, 'Yes, certainly ...').

Robert was wounded in the ill-fated attack on Gona Beach but he survived and was repatriated for further recuperation in Australia. He and Faye were married but Robert had little time to regain his health before he rejoined the battalion for the Markham/Ramu Valley Campaign.

> When I stood on the platform at the Adelaide Railway Station [mid-1943] and watched his white, strained face gradually disappearing with the train it was the nadir of my life experience to that point; from what he has told me since, his aspirations changed from War to houses with attics, etc, etc. The yearning for a dear little house with an attic and all of the peace and happiness, which he had so clearly earned, became intense.

Robert again distinguished himself in the Ramu Valley but it too took its toll:

> When I saw him next, after the Ramu Valley Campaign where he had contracted scrub typhus, he had lost most of his hair, was highly irritable and erratic, thin and spun out. His depleted fitness was recognised and he was sent to the Jungle Training Camp at Canungra as an instructor. Desperate at the thought that, as an experienced soldier, he would be used and re-used in the battle zones, I decided to join him.

The army did not support wives living near their husbands and 'it was necessary to have a low profile'. They 'talked of everything but War, and he grew strong and I was happy ... and pregnant', but again Robert had to rejoin to the unit. Faye was able to go home where she would be safe, and he was to return to his Battalion and the war.

Robert continued with the 2/27th Battalion until the invasion of Balikpapan in Borneo. Robert could have avoided this because he had completed five years of service, and people recognised that he was under strain at that point. His wife Faye highlighted the poignancy of his decision to participate in the final invasion.

> I was a Sunday school teacher, and I dipped into a little box of texts and came up with 'Thou shall not need to fight in this next battle' ... One of the Senior Officers, noticing his strain, knowing about the baby, soon to be born, offered him avoidance of the action at Balikpapan in Borneo [July 1945]. He refused. I went into labour and he went into his last action of the War on the same day.

He survived the invasion and eventually returned to civilian life, but the transition was difficult. In the bank he was no longer a cocky young platoon leader with challenging assignments. He was then only a junior clerk. He had wanted to pursue a career in the army but damaged elbows, and the legacy of wounds sustained at Gona on 29 December 1942, meant that he was discharged with a D3 health classification, meaning he was unfit for further service.[5]

> He finally came home on a cold, grey, wet day, alone, to an empty Railway Station, met by his father and me and our son, a very young bundle, wrapped in a white shawl. We went home to his father's house! My husband's father died of cancer in 1949. His mother developed Parkinson's disease almost straight away after the loss of her husband.
>
> Dreams were dissipating. There was no accommodation available. It seemed a shameful way to treat soldiers whose dreams had focussed on a house and happiness through all those years. Eventually we made a wretched sort of compromise and accepted a 'flat' ... that consisted of two rooms (not adjoining) and the use of a kitchen.

From then on, the demands of a rapidly expanding family 'pinned him down' to the teller's counter for many years. He had to divert the energy of the warrior into more domestic pursuits with his young family in the relative serenity of suburban Adelaide. Some of the skills learned in training and the characteristics developed as a platoon commander went with him into the bank. He wanted to provide strong leadership and did so by running a bank branch at a profit and developing a team spirit among his staff. He still believed that a unit never really pulled together until they were shot at, and demanded loyalty and commitment from all his 'troops'.

The struggle for recognition and a career in the bank eventually turned into some contentment during a country appointment, where he spent many hours on the water indulging his love for sailing and enjoying his children.

> To escape the situation, in which we found ourselves, we travelled north of Adelaide, where the Bank Manager had said there was a house available. When we inspected the house it had a dirt floor, so we made other inquiries and accepted the use of part of a house in return for caring for a local man with a bad heart – providing meals, etc.
>
> It was a lovely house and we could have been happy there, in spite of some difficulties, except that I was pregnant again. So we bought a dilapidated, deserted house and refurbished it. So we had our house and our second child and then we were transferred back to Adelaide. There were still no houses to buy and we had a third baby when he returned. There were all sorts of regulations in place to cover the shortage of housing.
>
> I must stress that there is a happy ending. After four years of living in this small house and with five small children, we moved, in 1954, into a large house, with garden and a park next door.

Robert remained in the bank and retired as a manager at age 57. This was not the end of his working life, as he took up another career in finance until he was 65. He always took with him the philosophy that 'you always have the choice between submitting to life's challenges or facing up to them and surviving'.

Despite the strain of the early stages, their marriage was central to their life stories, and baling out when things became difficult was never an option:

> Looking back, when most of your life that you've led, it'd be all very well to get sympathy through your war service and all of those things but, people like Faye and I have really been very lucky, when you look back over it all. We've had some very good breaks. We've led a secure life. We had a secure job all the way through. We were able to bring the kids up well enough and give them the basic conveniences of life and holiday houses and taught them how to sail and we always had a boat somewhere, when they were growing up anyway. And we've had three trips to Europe on the *Canberra* and we've got a nice house by the sea. We've got our health, I mean, we can't really look back and say we need sympathy.

Although the war did take an initial emotional and physical toll on Robert, any marks of war were kept private. In fact he has continued healthy and fit throughout most of his life, remaining committed to his wife and family, to his faith and to living life to the full. He can still be disturbed by the dreams of the past but has found an outlet for this in his writing, which describes many of the critical events of his war years. Faye gives a final assessment:

> I do not know at what point our 'settling in' became 'real life'. I also do not know whether a soldier who has suffered the traumas of war is more 'injured' than if he is killed, wounded or emotionally scarred.

Ron Plater was another awarded a Military Cross for outstanding bravery. In his post-war life the strain of war was well hidden under a successful career, and, as in Robert's case, his war experience did not prevent him from achieving in civilian life. Ron was also seriously wounded and bore the restriction of a leg in calipers for the rest of his life. He served in the Owen Stanleys, Gona and Sananada and, after he was seriously wounded, acted as an instructor in a training unit until 1945. By the time I met him in 1994, he had become well known as a successful businessman and leader in his community, particularly as a municipal alderman. His record of achievement ranged from winning the Australian Nieman Fellowship to study at Harvard in the 1950s to the recent successful completion of a Master of Arts from the University of Sydney. All the trappings of success and a degree of affluence surrounded him.

I met Ron at a time of crisis, when he was recovering from the sudden and unexpected death of his wife whom he had married in 1951. She had been a great source of strength to him and he was lost without her. I could not press him on his life story too much as he was still very vulnerable. One of the legacies of his exposure to trauma in 1942 was that he had always thought that he would die first: 'Never thought I would last beyond 60'.

As a young man he been through difficult times. His father, a former naval captain, had only part-time work after being retired from the navy during the Depression, and suffered a stroke and died in 1943. The resilience of his mother, one of the few businesswomen in Australia in the 1930s, pulled the family through. After entering Duntroon in 1940 as an 18-year-old cadet, Ron graduated in June 1942 in time to be posted to New Guinea.

Modesty prevented him from saying that in the final days of the battle for the beachhead at Gona his exploits earned him a Military Cross, the second highest military award for bravery:

> He stalked the post single-handled, killed the enemy manning it, and captured their machine gun. He then led his platoon in a series of attacks. Towards nightfall as he was placing his section in position his section corporal was wounded beside him. Ron began dressing the corporal's wound and was himself wounded in the shoulder. But, wounded as he was, he led the section forward and wiped out the enemy post.[5]

After further service, he left the army on a medical discharge in 1945 with a badly damaged leg. At the age of 24 he was unable to return to his pre-war pursuits of rugby, surfing and boxing, but he was left with two other legacies. The first was a strong determination to overcome any problems. Being trained as a leader and observing others had helped him mature.

The other legacy was some inner vulnerability. Etched in his mind was the shambles of the Kokoda retreat, the memory of being wounded at Gona and fearing he would bleed to death, and learning that his knee was so damaged he would be incapacitated for life. He went through 'a very nervous stage' in the late 1940s after New Guinea. He was still young and 'you put those things in the back of your mind, and we went through that stage of – "have as much fun as you can because you are not going to last much longer." I had the fear of death – the inevitability of death'.

Life after war was a struggle because he had to re-establish himself. His right leg required him to wear a caliper for some years and was eventually stiffened in an operation (arthrodesis). Besides this, his 'nerves' were bad, he lacked energy, and slept badly. He had an inner anxiety that he could never really explain or overcome.

None of these things stopped him going back to study to complete a Bachelor of Arts at the University of Sydney and commencing a new career as a journalist. One of his early assignments as a young journalist was to cover the Japanese war crimes trials at Manus Island in New Guinea. Covering the war trials re-exposed him to war trauma, and he thought that this had a greater effect than his combat experience. As a result of sitting through hearings he:

> had a hate of the Japanese more than I had when I was fighting them. The atrocities were documented even if the Japanese denied them.
>
> I became quite anxious about war and although I was a trained regular officer I developed a strong anti-war philosophy. Human beings are so stupid to have wars – I became very cynical about society.
>
> My whole life has been affected more by what came out of those war crimes trials than the actual campaigns.

Death in the post-war years hit him very hard. 'During war we had a philosophy – "Here today gone tomorrow – doesn't matter mate" – but as you get back into life it does.' Many of his friends from army days had died in the war or in the early years afterwards. One, married soon after the war, died on his honeymoon. Another, a close friend from Duntroon who had been hospitalised in the bed next to him, died just after the war as a result of war wounds, still in his early twenties.

This grief and disturbing memories did not stop him from making the most of opportunities, and his physical handicap increased his determination to get through his year at Harvard University, 1955–56.

> I had to wear a caliper and it was awful – it hurt, it was awkward and made you feel stupid. The Fellowship was awarded for journalistic achievement and potential for leadership in the profession. I was determined to overcome my physical disability and do well at the university and my wife helped me in this. I have done a lot despite the leg.

After completing his studies at Harvard and re-establishing a successful career in journalism, his greatest achievement professionally was to start his own consulting business from nothing and build it into a viable enterprise. The same determination and independence influenced his struggle to overcome later problems. The expected life of easy retirement did not eventuate:

> The whole of my life was organised for my family – I was absolutely certain I would die before my wife – and yet Erica died just a few months ago. I have outgrown that fear [of death] and look forward to it.
>
> I know I have always overcome difficulties and I will battle this one too. I have had this handicap with the leg and the heart – three heart attacks in recent years – and I've always been determined to keep going even though sometimes I feel like giving in. You wonder why you are still here. So many occasions I could have been killed or died.

Ron has never sought any outside help to explore his feelings of anxiety. He has focused on his life tasks and achieved well, despite some loss of confidence. For Ron, war remains a two-edged sword. It contains the seeds of death as well as the potential for personal development. 'I hate war, but it can give a sense of achievement and direction. People who are called get quite a lot out of it.'

Mick's experience was not as dramatic but the remnants of war stayed in his nostrils. He was born on 5 October 1921 in Western Australia, and his story resembles that of Albert Facey, a fellow West Australian: 'I was a bit of a loner as a boy. I was part of two families because my parents married again. You can only expect what you can do for yourself. You can't rely on your family.'

He left school at 14 and worked very hard, mostly in farm work. He worked for an old German fellow:

> I was on a binder. It has a fan that knocks the cut wheat – I was sitting on the combine one day and it picked up a bit of wire. The tractor was making a noise and I was shouting and I couldn't make him understand. It had a tool box in it so I took out a spanner and threw it at old Bill. It hit him in the back. That was the end of my time there.

He worked for several others and then went to the goldfields, having jumped the train at Kalgoorlie. He grew up tough and learned some hard lessons early in life. In Mick's view the fellows that came from an easier life found war harder than bush boys did.

Mick joined up with the 2/16th Battalion when he was only 18 while working in the goldfields near Kalgoorlie, after forging his parents' signatures. He served in the Middle East and in New Guinea. Initially, life at war was 'a great time'. His first taste of battle came at Litani River – 'we were knocking them off like rabbits', but it was not all enjoyable. He was on a Vickers gun when his mate was shot and Mick was covered in blood. This did not faze him, though:

> We were that busy we were not frightened. The adrenalin flows and unless you have been in action you would not know. You can do superman things. You get so fired up. The worst thing is waiting. Some blokes messed their pants once it was on.

At another time he was cut off and was reported as missing in action. Towards the end of the Middle East tour his battalion took over the garrison at Beirut and that was 'fantastic'. Eventually the order was given to return to Australia and they began the 54-day journey back. That was arduous because by that time the Japanese had taken Singapore and the convoy was ordered away from Java and up to Bombay, finally heading for Fremantle.[6] On his return to Adelaide he met his future wife Kath.

After further training he was sent to New Guinea, and 'in the Owen Stanleys it was different'. The worst part of New Guinea was malaria. When he was walking out of Kokoda

> I didn't care who won the war – wanting to die. I was crook; I retched, had diarrhoea, shivered, froze. I don't know what kept me going. It was after my 21st birthday. When we got back we went to hospital. There were wheat bags on sticks. After I got rid of the malaria and was rehabilitated, I was not fit enough to go to Gona.
>
> I'm not sure what kept me going. Something keeps you going.

After he had recovered he went to Wau. Landing there was not easy since the Japanese held the strip. They dug their Vickers guns in and held onto the strip. He had a close shave when a Japanese time bomb went off in their camp. His next campaign was Ramu and Shaggy Ridge, and malaria caught up with him again several times. None of the details of these events are clear.

While on leave in 1944 he married Kath, whom he had met early in 1942, and shortly afterwards left for Borneo:

> The war changed for me then – when you have responsibilities you have to start thinking about what you will do after the war. When you are single you don't think too much about tomorrow. I sort of worried more. I was very lucky – I was not frightened of anyone because I knew I was good. I didn't care how big anyone was.
>
> Towards the end you hope to get hit so that you could be sent home. I had had a bellyful. I used to worry more after I got married.

Being a soldier had been a good life for Mick for most of the time. Having been brought up during hard times and learning to fend for himself he was able to adapt easily. He could manage the more gruesome side of war more easily than most because he had seen blood before. It seemed to be a settling period for him and one that brought many benefits. The battalion was his home and he continues to stay in touch with other members.

The thing that affected him most was seeing 'blokes who were just vegetables – like the bloke who was a sniper whose marbles are gone. A lot of soldiers had a lot of stress, but some survived, because you either have it or you haven't'. Mick did see many who did not manage war so well. He saw some become 'vegetables' and finish up in a home. Some became alcoholics and some 'went troppo'. Many men did not adjust after the war. One man in his platoon drank himself to death.

For Mick the war was a turning point. When it was over he was married and his career eventually took a different turn, but it did not happen all at once. He was very unsettled, and in the first 12 months he had about 12 jobs. He found it hard to get on with people, and was very restless. He did not drink much as his tolerance of alcohol was low. After all this: 'The wife was starting to despair. Then I went and did an aptitude test. I said I wanted to do a trade – a plumber or carpenter.'

He did a carpentry course at trades school in Adelaide and when he was 40 per cent proficient he was sent out with a firm, eventually qualifying as a carpenter with Van, Webb and Parslow. After about two years, he applied for a government position, passed the medical and got a job in the joiners' shop with the South Australian Railways at Mile End.

This was a growth period for the railways and Mick worked his way up the ranks to become a foreman. He did very well, staying with the South Australian Railways for 34 years and getting a lot of satisfaction from the railway stations he built. When he retired in 1982 he was a works manager for the state transport authority. Retirement was a good experience. He was able to work his 2 hectares of rural land, which gave him a lot of satisfaction, as well as spend more time with his wife and family. He was a devoted grandfather. He also spent time in his workshop where he 'was always making something'. He regarded himself as being well off.

On the surface Mick was healthy. He did not lose time at work and worked through until retirement. The only apparent restriction was his leg, which had been injured. After the war he continued to be affected by malaria and was granted a 20 per cent pension.

However, underneath the successful worker and devoted family man was another Mick. He had 'aggro' moods that occurred periodically throughout his life. His wife thought it was somehow associated with petrol, particularly from planes, and he would be particularly affected by fumes at airports. He continued to have severe headaches, which persisted until his death, and although he did not go to the Repatriation Hospital, he was under treatment from his family doctor. New Guinea continued to haunt him – 'that bloody jungle was depressing and demoralising' – and the memories of those times emerged many times in dreams and nightmares.

Mick died suddenly, 24 hours after having been admitted to hospital. There was no warning of the seriousness of his condition other than a night of high temperatures and vague sense of illness. Even though the cause of death was septicaemia, the circumstances of his death returned him to his scenes of battle. He became ill at the time of the Gulf War, when images of desert warfare on television brought back sensations of sand on his skin, similar to what he had experienced when lost in the Syrian desert in 1941. His symptoms of fever reminded him of malaria fever, which he contracted while in New Guinea. He became ill on a night of a summer storm, reminiscent of the nightly deluges during his time in the Owen Stanleys.

* * * * *

These stories provide a sense of the post-war lives of one group of Kokoda veterans, whose marks of war were kept hidden, albeit just below the surface. Their distressing experiences were never made into an illness, and this important dimension of their lives was rarely aired, and only a few found any constructive way of integrating their memories. A few of the men wrote short biographies, for the benefit of their grandchildren, but these concentrated only on external events and the more humorous side of war. Only two men engaged in serious writing in which the experience of strain was explored. Robert Johns, for example, wrote two unpublished novels, and numerous short stories, which were all based on his war experiences. Even then he wrote under a pseudonym, which distanced him from the original events. Unless veterans created this very private forum for themselves there was nowhere they could explore their memories. They certainly could not do so in the public forums of their ceremonies and reunions.

CHAPTER 8

The Hidden Casualties

This chapter is about a second group of Kokoda veterans, who suffered prolonged war-related distress which was never recognised. These men did not find adequate help in the medical system; their difficulties were generally kept private and within the family, or even hidden from any gaze. Physical illnesses, sometimes labelled as psychosomatic, often masked serious psychological disturbances that were never adequately addressed. On the other hand, serious illness was sometimes labelled as a neurotic condition. These troubles notwithstanding, most of these men still achieved well in their outer lives, but their difficulties were severe enough to affect others. Wives and families living with these damaged men were sometimes 'tiptoeing on eggshells' in sharing their distress and supporting them through frequent illnesses and medical investigations. Multiple medical examinations and applications for compensation added to their distress, and partners often paid for their efforts with their own poor health. For example, one widow had spent all her married life accommodating a very anxious and sometimes physically ill husband. He never sought treatment, and even though he built up a sound family business, he avoided confronting his anxiety and anger. She knew he was a very disturbed man after discharge but was never able to fathom what worried him. This woman experienced several breakdowns about which she consulted only her family doctor, and late in life was still managing her distress with medication.

None of the men in this group had a breakdown during war-time. Their service records were sound and they were a mix of commissioned and non-commissioned officers and privates. They all managed to work in paid employment or build up a private business and were able to support their families. Their moderate to very successful outer lives masked chronic illness, nightmares, migraines, periodic depression, chronic anxiety, 'vomiting every day before work', anger and withdrawal. None of these conditions was recognised as war-related. Owen, for example, was only 19 when he was sent to New Guinea. I was the first person he had told about how he was strafed by allied planes, saw his mates killed, and in later life could still smell the stench of the bodies of those killed at Gona. He heard stories of the atrocities of the enemy and remembered sleeping among dead bodies at Wewak later in the war. He took several years to settle down, and never sought any help to manage his nightmares which persisted right into later life. His distress emerged as dermatitis and other physical health problems. On the surface he lived a sober life and worked until he was able to retire reasonably comfortably.

Accounts of these men's stories are presented here to illustrate the nature of their difficulties and the diversity of their lives.[1] Some are told in considerable detail, and are richly textured. Because of the sensitive nature of these stories, some family members did not want the veteran identified, and only fragments of the range of stories can be presented here.

One fragment is found in the case of a veteran whose memories were carefully suppressed, and who struggled for years to contain his traumatic memory, until illness released his demons.[2] This veteran was a senior officer held in the highest regard among his colleagues. Many of them knew that he had physical health problems later in life but did not know of the strain and underbelly of distress that he had experienced or suppressed for much of his life since 1942. From a detailed analysis of a number of sources it was clear that he was badly affected by his experiences in New Guinea. This had not prevented him from maintaining a very successful career and acquitting himself as a dedicated father and grandfather. From very humble pre-war beginnings he rose to a senior rank in his unit, survived the worst fighting in New Guinea and and after discharge re-established himself very successfully in his chosen career.

His army career was littered with searing experiences like leading his company as it 'completed the destruction, blotting out the remaining pockets of resistance'. In the worst of the New Guinea battles he 'led his platoon so dashingly' and 'was first in the rush on the first post where he killed the machine gunner and 7 other Japs'. Finally his platoon wiped out the post, in which there were about 30 Japanese. The Australian troops 'fighting in this stench couldn't bring themselves to eat – it was so sickening'.[3]

His feats of heroism were acknowledged with one of the highest military awards, but he remained angry about what they were ordered to do:

> The manner of the attack at Gona was so unnecessary. After Gona Mission the 39th was detailed to go to Gona West and cut off a force of about 160 Japanese and we had to knock them off – at our own pace. We buried over 150 Japanese with about 20 casualties – it was murder at Gona Mission. We had to do an attack through Kunai grass and were mown down.

And:

> Looking back it is easy to see that there were some very poor decisions made. At the time we took everything for granted. In fact it was only recently when ******* started to uncover what really happened that I felt very angry and upset that so many men suffered and died – there were no plans and no intelligence.[4]

For him, there was nothing glamorous about killing. He reflected in later life that the most horrific thing to experience was killing men at close range, even if you had learned to hate.

> I had the approach that what had to be done I would do. I hated the Japs with their callous, brutal outlook – there was only one good Jap; wounded or alive, there was only one thing to do as soon as possible. Their eyes just about turn up. They're just as frightened of dying as you are. You can call on a wounded man to surrender but then he puts a grenade up to his mouth and pulls the pin out and you shoot him.[5]

The effects of battle were noticed by those close to him:

> At the end [of the war] he was close to a mental breakdown. He was considered by most to be as hard as hell and any man that he lost gave him hell. I think that carried on in his life. It [discharge] was a let down really. His discharge was a 'kick in the arse' and that was that. He gradually started to show signs of, not cracking, but being affected badly.[6]

Memories of experiences such as those quoted above surfaced immediately after the war in nightmares but were soon buried under the load of work and family duties. Memories had to be carefully suppressed and he had to keep a constant watch on himself. 'When I let my defences down and say, "The war's over, you can relax now. There is no need to stifle your emotions" – if you do that – that's fatal.' Life transitions such as retirement were problematic. His wife was well aware of this and remarked that 'when his mind was full of [work] he was OK, but once he retired the nightmares started...it was terrible'.[7]

> My wife reckons I used to have nightmares. I would wake up strangling her. In this dream I had him [the Japanese soldier] right close. I was going to get him with my bayonet – I had it all planned, had it all worked out.
>
> The worst one I had was lying in bed and I had this bloody Jap, it was dark and I was watching him and when he got close enough I leapt at him – and I hit my head on the bloody chest of drawers – he was a dead man there were no arguments about that – I had it all worked out. I was not going to shoot him – I was going to stick my bayonet up his belly button. And I was quivering like an aspirin.

This man had many encounters with the medical ideas of the Department of Veterans' Affairs for physical ailments, and even though his inner struggles were noted in his medical files they were never acknowledged as significant. The veteran died during the course of the research and his records show that his last days were invaded by his repressed experiences. Significantly, there is no mention in the medical notes of the high esteem in which he is still held by members of his unit and the three battalions in which he served. With them he is still revered as a great soldier who did much to contain the anxiety of his young charges when they faced the Japanese in 1942. He carried his own share of post-war anxiety very privately.

William: 'He never talked very much about the war'[8]

Teasing out the influence of war on a life is more complex and subtle than searching for recorded clinical evidence of illness. This is even more difficult when the veteran is no longer alive. In William's story the effects of his war trauma were well hidden and were not the centrepiece of his widow's story. Glimpses of William's difficulty adjusting after the war emerged subtly in his widow's positive account of his life. She had no regrets, and described his life, work and death with warmth and compassion. However, behind her story was a man whose war experience continued to disturb him and seemed to be linked with illness.

William was a hard-working man who left his wife and four children in 1940 to serve with the AIF. Prevented from going to World War One by his mother, who would not give him permission, he lied about his age when enlisting in World War Two:

> Well it wasn't that you could make money out of it [war service], it was just that, and he always felt, he always said to me that, the boys [volunteers for the AIF] come down from the river all blistered, and he said if those kids can go away and fight, why can't I. You see then they all said, well you couldn't on account of your age. Well he put that back. When he applied he was 39 and the upper age limit was 35 years for overseas service. I don't know what age he gave when he went in ... but he said he put his age back.

As a soldier he performed very well. As an officer he distinguished himself as a leader and in feats of individual bravery:

> Yes, he got a Military Medal. He was recommended in the Syrian campaign too; he got mentioned in dispatches for bravery there as well as in New Guinea ... he was that type of man.

His wife in the meantime had to manage with four children while he was away for five years:

> I had my hands full really. Well I don't know how we would have managed. The money wasn't very much and you had to pay your rent. Although we were lucky, we paid a deposit on the place and we were paying it off, and we dropped our rent down I think ten shillings a week. I think if I remember rightly I got about three pounds five shillings or something a fortnight from army pay.
>
> I had plenty to do. I did my washing, I hung the socks on the line, couldn't hang them on the line there was too many, so we had a barbed wire fence and just stuck them on there. People just asked me if I had the centipedes living there. In those days it was all hand washing with a scrubbing board. There were no washing machines. You'd start at eight o'clock in the morning, you'd still be scrubbing at four o'clock in the afternoon.

William's return home was a shock for his son who had never known his father:

> Yes. It was a bit funny [when he returned home]. 'Cause my son was three and he can tell you now, he said he can always remember that man. That man took him out in the shed and he had a lovely head of white curls, and his father took him out and cut his hair all off. He said he'd make a man out of him, he'd been a sissy long enough.

William's son recalled that military discipline was imposed on the home when his father returned:

When Dad just came home, he tied the curtains up in knots. You weren't allowed to have a curtain hanging down. And 'tuck all your beds up', didn't matter if you had bedspreads on them or not. Just like you know they used to in the army, he'd tuck them all up tight. He was shocking till after he settled down for a while and found out it wasn't army life. It's not easy.

His family got only an inkling of what really happened in New Guinea:

He did mention about one lad that was killed there and how they killed him. That was pretty gruesome. He was very close friends to him too, which made it worse. One lad he sent on a message, he saw him shot in front of him. A sniper shot him. That's the only thing he ever said about it …

William would rarely tell his wife what troubled him, but it appears he was sometimes disturbed. He was able to return to his work and enjoy some family life, but his life was dramatically shortened.

That's the only time he'd ever said anything about it. He'd never talk about it. No, I couldn't remember now. It wasn't very long after he came home. I know I went up to the chemist and asked him if he'd give me some medicine to quieten him down. Yes, he got very upset. Many times we had to get him to go to the doctor. It's just one of those things I guess that just takes time to get out of their system really.

And he went to the doctor to get tablets for his blood pressure. I bet you I'm taking the same now, to keep mine at bay.

He was a different man for a long time after he came back. He just wanted to get away with the men again. I often hear the women say that and I often think, well it's just when they've been with them a long time and they miss that company. He took a few years [to get over it]. But then he didn't go to the doctor very much after that. He had pretty good health up until he had a stroke. He was only about, I think, 58 or something like that, he had a stroke. But he was a man that was always into helping people – anybody that had any problems. Go and get them a load of wood or something like that, and help them out.

William's widow and other wives of that time did not seek, nor were they offered, any counselling to help them understand or manage difficult and disturbed husbands. William's widow was ambivalent about whether there was any tangible benefit from her husband's war service:

Well I think probably we benefited from it as far as I've got more security now than I would have had really. Well it's a lot better pension than the age pension. But I don't know about the medical part of it. That's got me whacked a bit.

William's strange behaviour and illness have been left out of the family history, and the next generation is keen to reconstruct a more glowing account of a hero:

I think the children now are more concerned and take more interest in it, the grandchildren, than my own children did I think, and the great-grandchildren. I had some great-grandchildren here a while ago, and they were greatly taken up with Dad's medals and things. Well see, our kiddies just took that for granted. And my grandson, he wore Dad's medals at the dawn service this year. I said it's the first time they've been worn since Dad wore them. And he was tickled pink, he thought it was great to wear Pop's medals.

Lance: The nightmare that never really ended [9]

Lance was another whose troubles were well hidden from others. However, he was significantly disturbed by his war experiences and, after fifty years, he could still not find relief from the daily experience of nightmares and disturbed sleep. Lance was born in 1920, started school in 1925 and left eight years later, having completed eighth grade. His experience of growing up during Australia's worst economic depression was largely positive, despite being in a poor family. He joined a militia battalion and between November 1941 and May 1946 served with three different battalions in several battle zones in New Guinea – the Owen Stanleys and Gona, Markham Valley and Ramu Valley, and Bougainville. For him 1942 was the most critical time, particularly as he was with the first Australian battalion to engage the Japanese on the Kokoda Trail.

There he gathered plenty of material for later traumatic memory, seeing a lot of his mates killed, being strafed several times, being ordered to retrieve and bury bodies. He felt he had been generally let down by his commanding officers. His most distressing experiences were being wounded, being under fire in a heavy machine gun ambush, being caught in a bombing raid, particularly in Port Moresby, and being under fire from artillery, mortar and rifle as well as grenades. Towards the end of 1942 he received a serious bayonet wound and was out of action for two months. He later sustained a gunshot wound, ruptured kidneys, a 'busted' nose and concussion, and contracted malaria, dysentery, hookworm, and tinea.

Lance never talked about these experiences to anyone after the war, and found adjusting to civilian life extremely difficult. He was initially very restless, with his mind always focusing on the war, but was keen to get on with his life, even though he was anxious and had constant nightmares. As well as struggling with these demons, he was restricted by residual debility from wounds and illness.

He took 10 years to find stable work that he could manage, and after a long struggle with temporary jobs he gained a permanent position, with some family help:

> My brother, being in an executive position .... got me a permanent light job without much exertion, and finally I retired at 62 years of age, as I couldn't work any longer.

At the age of 79 he still had health problems related to his war service, including osteoarthritis, numbness in the arms and legs, trouble with his back, deafness and neck trouble. He was receiving 100 per cent entitlement, but at the time of interview was trying to obtain approval for the more secure Extended Disability Allowance. He had never received treatment for any psychological disturbance.

> Yes, six nights a week of nightmares, seven nights a week of sleeplessness and what-

> ever news nowadays brings about the thoughts of war, these thoughts and images are bloodthirsty and gory dreams. No matter how much I win, they never lay down. Should I hack them [the enemy in dreams] up? Each part grows again. I get up and walk around, then back to bed. I never go to bed until midnight and whatever you think of, it always seems to get on the way back to war.[10]

It is not clear exactly why Lance has never sought, nor been referred for, specialist help. While he has continued to struggle with his anxiety and war dreams, he has nevertheless achieved in his outer world. His wife has been his main support in his life, although he has not talked with her about his inner torment. His war experience and his lifelong disabilities, never really adequately addressed, have affected him to such an extent that he has been unable to fully enjoy his family life, for example, being able to play with his grandchildren, even though he is very attached to home and family. For Lance there has been constant tension between his inner and outer life, and this is likely to continue until his death. He has remained outside the direct influence of mental health ideas, apart from the assessment of his eligibility for a pension. None of his narrative is part of his battalion association discourse.

George: Getting it wrong – organic lesion, not nerves [11]

Medical argument about whether symptoms are merely functional or can be explained by an organic lesion has been ongoing since the latter part of the nineteenth century. George became caught up in such argument. In later life he presented to doctors with a range of illnesses and symptoms which were labelled as neurotic, since there was no logical medical explanation of the physical symptoms. In George's case, it was finally discovered that he did have an organic lesion after his symptoms were filed as neurotic for many years, under the label 'Not Yet Diagnosed' (NYD). George's life illustrates how symptoms of illness can be passed off as psychosomatic. Unfortunately, despite multiple investigations, the actual cause of his symptoms was not detected until it was too late.

George was a lieutenant in the Intelligence Corps. He served in all of the 2/27th campaigns in the Middle East and New Guinea, and was a member of the advance party in Morotai before the landing at Balikpapan in July 1945. As an intelligence officer he played a key role in the 'saving' of the 2/27th Battalion when it was forced to withdraw from Kokoda. His senior officer recalled an occasion in New Guinea when, even though George had dysentery, he agreed to lead a three-man patrol to contact all remaining remnants of the unit before the withdrawal. For this he was mentioned in despatches.

War service, particularly in New Guinea, had a serious effect on George's health. He was badly wounded and contracted malaria as well as dysentery. His wife recalled a time just before they were married in 1943:

> George was brought home to a hospital in Enfield just before Christmas 1942. I was in the air force so courting was rather difficult. However, we decided to get married before he rejoined his unit in New Guinea. We were married at St

> Margaret's Church, Woodville on 10 April 1943 and George left a few weeks later [for the Shaggy Ridge and Ramu campaigns].
>
> When he came back here for that Christmas, we went down to the station to meet him. He wanted to come home – he came home in an ordinary carriage – and struggled off. He just had hospital blues on and he had been sitting up.

He was discharged in 1945 with a medical rating of A1 despite a record of malaria, dysentery, a fractured skull, a burst eardrum, broken teeth, gunshot wounds, nerves of the stomach, and epilepsy. He was entitled to a small pension and free medical treatment. When George settled back into civilian life, he is reported to have done it extremely well. His wife recalls, 'We had a short holiday, then he got straight down to studying and living a normal life'. Most of his energy was put into getting started again. He rarely talked about the war:

> George didn't talk a great deal about the war experience except with other returned friends, but he did say that the New Guinea tour of duty was far worse than the Middle East. When he returned from the war, all she knew was that he'd had a very bad experience, but learned few details.[12]

George worked hard to re-establish himself. His post-war career path was a significant change from his pre-war years when he had been unable to get regular work and had gone to the Riverland picking oranges and delivering ice and water. Within a few years George had completed an honours degree in accounting at the University of Adelaide and then spent several years working in New Guinea as an auditor. He returned to Adelaide and began a successful career that culminated as a secretary of a large company in Perth. But his health gradually deteriorated. His epilepsy worsened in his mid years. Investigations of his complaint at the Repatriation Hospital failed to find a cause. The medical specialists attributed his seizures and failing health to stress and psychosocial factors. War injuries were never considered as a cause. As his sister said, 'for many years he had been treated as a hypochondriac'.

George's first encounter with psychiatry occurred in 1966 when he was examined by a Repatriation Department psychiatrist, to whom he had been referred because of recurring headaches and ear trouble and complaints of a feeling of emptiness in his stomach. It was here that he revealed an inner world that could have been interpreted as war stress. He was considered a 'poor, rather vague, informant – everything had to be dragged out of him'. He had been edgy for three or four years, had experienced temper tantrums, and was disturbed by noise and pain in his ear, by which he believed he could predict his epileptic attacks. His most disturbing experience was a 'nightmare during the day', when he 'saw a vision, it was horrible – can't remember what was – lasted five seconds'. These occurred several times a month, sometimes when he was going to sleep, and 'he had an aura and empty feeling in his stomach, then the vision flashes up'. The nightmares he experienced after the war were 'different from these 'visual hallucinations'. Nothing was made of his original post-war nightmares, and temporal lobe epilepsy was accepted as the explanation for his symptoms. While his childhood and earlier life were subjected to scrutiny, his war experiences were left untouched, although it was noted that his brother John had been killed in action in 1942.

There was some argument between the specialists in ENT, neurology and ophthalmology, which centred on whether he had sustained a head injury in a motorcycle accident in 1941. One specialist concluded that he could not 'support the suggestion that the current upset is the result of an alleged fracture of the skull sustained in 1941 when on war service'. The administrative decision was then made not to accept his symptoms and distress as war-related, the Deputy Commissioner concluding that 'the member is not suffering from hot sweats, nightmares and nervousness'. George appealed against this decision, pointing out that the only way he could validate his experience of hot sweats or nightmares was to have a medical practitioner present at the time of their occurrence. He was 'unable to produce physical evidence such as a hole in the eardrum, missing teeth, a gunshot tear or even a heart murmur, which could be detected by a stethoscope'. It was decided that an earlier diagnosis of ruptured tympanic membrane was in error.

At this stage George was only 52. Even though he was well educated and had a good work record, he was described only as an 'easily excitable man, who gives a very inadequate history'. The Repatriation Commission Officer-in-Charge of Entitlements regarded him as 'not an easy person to interview as he alternates between laughter, morose silence and periods where he becomes quite garrulous'. George's cause was not helped by his poor opinion of the Department, which had been formed when he was first interviewed in 1945. His appeal was disallowed in October 1966, because the 'present symptoms stated are due to your rejected disability Temporal Lobe Epilepsy'. George made a further declaration, in his own writing, on 12 December 1966, again setting out his case that his life-time symptoms had originated from the head injury of 1941. He also pointed out that from at least 1944 he had attributed symptoms of dizziness, or odd feelings in the head, to malaria.

The report of a further assessment on 8 September 1969 stated that there was no significant deterioration, and that George should continue his anti-convulsant medication. By 1971 his seizures had increased along with headaches. He was not eating regularly and was 'taking alcohol'. The specialist considered that 'much of his current disturbance was self-inflicted'.[13] By April 1975 George had deteriorated further, with complicating conditions of chronic airway obstruction, some deterioration in cognitive and motor function, and dilation of the left ventricle. The detailed report of his assessment was the first comprehensive account to connect his symptoms with an initial war injury. The specialist concluded that he had 'communicating hydrocephalus'.

A ventriculo-atrial shunt was inserted into George's cranium on 2 January 1975, and while this offered some relief, it brought no sustained improvement in his condition. The opinion was that he 'was suffering from normal pressure hydrocephalus which was probably caused originally by his head injury in August 1942 (*sic*)'. (This was when he fell from his courier motorcycle in Syria.) In April 1975

George applied for acceptance of this condition, and in June the acknowledgment he had originally sought in 1966 was granted. The chair of the Repatriation Commission confirmed this, concluding that the history contained in the service documents, and the medical opinions that had been expressed, 'support the veteran's claim that the condition is related to an accident on service'. George then became eligible for treatment, mostly occupational therapy, but by this time, no major improvement could be achieved. He was largely confined to his home until his death in hospital on 23 January 1982, from acute myocardial infarction.

While an organic cause was the fundamental explanation of George's illness, this was denied for ten years. But there is evidence that his problems were not just physical: he suffered intrusions from his war experiences. The disturbances, particularly nightmares, were well known to his wife, who 50 years later still found it too upsetting to talk about at length. It was 'always the same dream of being chased by a Japanese soldier and being unable to get away from him'.

> I never saw him really well – he struggled and achieved a lot. He did achieve but it was really grim. George coped extremely well after the war except for a few epileptic seizures, but as the years passed they seemed more difficult to control until at 59 he had partial paralysis, was operated on and a shunt inserted into his head. After the shunt he was never right. There was so much brain damage the doctor said he had a brain of an 83-year-old man and was never able to work again. He was granted TPI.

Despite his years of struggling for recognition and his apparent irritability and problems with medical staff, at home

> ... he was a wonderful provider, husband and father – a real family man who could turn his hand to so many projects – a very fair man who never asked anyone to do a job he wasn't willing to do himself – and above all a very unselfish man who for the last years of his life spent most of his time either in hospital or sitting in a comfortable chair. For an active man this must have been frustrating, yet not once was there a word of complaint or 'Why me?' He really was an inspiration to us all.

Initially his symptoms were passed off as neurotic, and he was interviewed once by a psychiatrist. His wife and sister knew that the war had deeply affected him and that this had persisted over time, but they were excluded from the therapeutic loop. In the final analysis the psychological aspects of his problems were well and truly suppressed and eventually overtaken by physical illness. His symptoms eventually could be clearly explained by an organic lesion. George's situation mirrored the experience of Alice James, who in the nineteenth century had sought a diagnosis and cure for her recurrent fatigue and strange symptoms. Eventually it was discovered that she had cancer, but in the meantime she was dismissed as hysterical and neurasthenic. Like Alice, George's final diagnosis was a 'palpable malady' that 'lifted him out of the formless vague', but it was discovered too late for cure.[14] George employed a strategy of keeping things to himself, getting on with life, and focusing on the outside world of family and work, and for some time this was successful, but it left his wife with a mixed legacy.

> I really can't say we 'suffered' at all – had a very happy, normal life as a family until the last seven years of George's life. I have no doubts he suffered at times, but he kept this very much to himself. I think the saddest time was after the surgery, to see a man who had made such a success of his life, become virtually a vegetable.

* * * * *

One feature of these case studies is medical history taking. Medical history taking is a stock method employed by doctors to construct a medical narrative of a patient: it is the version of the person's life, usually illness-oriented, that the practitioner has heard, and is recorded predominantly in the words of the medical observer. The resulting clinical history can differ significantly from the personal history. It provides a restricted view of life stories, and does not go far enough to get to the heart of many issues. This is clearly shown in in the cases of the men discussed in this chapter. Many significant medical histories were taken when they were admitted for treatment or assessed for pension eligibility, but specialists never fully addressed the distress that was clearly known by those who shared their private narrative. This is what I call *parallel discourse* – the different narratives do not entwine. The discourse found in the medical files is quite separate and does not incorporate the discourse or narratives in the private lives of veterans.

It is possible that an understanding of traumatic stress could have made a difference to treatment of these veterans. A concept of the trauma and stressful consequences of war would have provided a number of benefits. In the first place, it would have provided a rationale for exploring below the surface of the veterans' symptoms very early in their medical history. The whole culture of veteran health militated against this, in that veteran organisations made sure from the early post-war days that psychological distress was excluded from all post-war discourse, both within veteran organisations and in more public discourse. The active suppression by many men of New Guinea memories was as much an act of conformity to the rules of veteran culture as an act of psychological self-preservation.

However, it may also be the case that men such as William, Lance and George might have been better served if the medical lens had been focused on past understandings rather than on modern views on psychiatric treatment. Whatever the limitations of the concept of neurosis, the specialists of World War One, for example Rivers and Myers, did acknowledge the enduring effects of memory. In this sense the doctors of the second great war had not fully learned the lessons of World War One. In one of standard medical texts of the pre-war years Gordon, Harris and Rees (1936) highlighted the importance of repressed memory.

> The inability of these patients to control and maintain the repression of their fear was illustrated also by the fact that they practically all suffered from war nightmares, and anxiety dreams, due to the emergence of unconscious anxiety in sleep. As soon as the controlling hand was removed from the lid of the box the 'Jack-in-the-box' could emerge, looking more frightening and alarming that it had previously appeared.[15]

The stories of this group of men illustrate a serious level of submerged distress from war, bringing together many of the themes of this study: the interruption of life course by war-related trauma; the struggle for recognition of war-related symptoms; the presentation of symptoms that could be interpreted as either organic or psychologically based; medical and administrative argument about attribution to war service; and the influence of personal bias on administrative decisions.

Most of these men were never recognised as psychologically damaged, and their problems were masked by physical illness. Since physical illness was the primary reason for seeking medical help in the first place, psychological issues were not explored, particularly any relationship between traumatic war experience and their dysfunction. A major consequence of this was that the burden of support fell on their partners, who shouldered responsibility for many domestic and practical matters and the main providers of emotional support:

> I think the wives of returned men are the forgotten ones, as when the men returned home, it was the wives that had to pick up the pieces and be behind them and nurse them when they were ill and depressed. Not just when they are ill and depressed, not just one or two years, but for as many as they are spared.[16]

One final word on these men. Their psychological life was clearly influenced by their war experience, traumatic memory featured in some degree in each case, and their health history was clearly affected by those few years of exposure. In the final analysis these men were poorly served by the ideas and practices in the Department of Veterans' Affairs (DVA) system of the time. Had they been of the Vietnam generation the authorities may have recognised that they were suffering some form of post-trauma syndrome. The Younger Veterans' Program introduced in the 1994–95 Budget accepted Post-Traumatic Stress Disorder (PTSD) as a major focus of its research program for Vietnam veterans, which expanded psychiatric services to include a dedicated PTSD program for older men. However, in the Veterans' Affairs psychiatric programs a distinction is made between World War Two veterans, who are regarded as psycho-geriatric patients, and Vietnam veterans, who are primarily diagnosed with PTSD. Thus a number of historical factors have coincided to prevent these men of Kokoda from receiving effective help, not the least of which was the stigma attaching to mental illness during the period in which they returned to civilian life.

The next chapter explores the psychiatric rehabilitation system then in place, in the context of the administrative and diagnostic frameworks operating within the Department of Veterans' Affairs.

CHAPTER 9

Rehabilitating the 'Neurotic' Casualty

Very little is known about what happened to men who just disappeared from the front line after a breakdown, or about men like Lawrie Howson who described himself as being 'in and out of the bughouse' for years after he stared into the eyes of the Japanese soldier he had been ordered to 'finish off'. This chapter describes the psychiatric rehabilitation system into which men like these were admitted for treatment. It is important to appreciate the conditions in these rehabilitation institutions and the ideas that informed their practices if we are to adequately explain the lives of veterans with mental illness.

An encounter with the system can be seen through the eyes of Tom, who was involved in the early New Guinea battles in 1942. Tom had grown up in an orphanage, and when war was declared he and his brother volunteered for the AIF. In 1942, when he was only 22, he was separated from his section and became lost for several days while on patrol in the New Guinea jungle. The details of this episode are unclear in his mind, but he traces the beginning of his troubles to this time. He experienced some form of breakdown, was assigned to non-combat duties and was eventually evacuated to Australia suffering from chronic dermatitis and what he described as 'nerves'. His brother said he could not really understand why Tom had 'the nerves', because everyone was under the same kind of strain, but he did admit that being lost in the jungle might have made a difference.

Tom could not return to duty and instead spent many months in the psychiatric ward of a repatriation hospital; he was still an outpatient of the same ward 50 years later.

> When I first came back for me nerves they used to give you shock treatment; and they used to tie you down without putting you to sleep; and you know you would scream. Absolutely scream with murder. I was not the only one. And you used to sleep on the floor. There were no beds. For bad cases you had a mattress on the floor. I wasn't getting any better so they turned around and they automatically gave me insulin.
>
> They would give us a good meal the night before – eggs and all – and the next morning they would come around about 4 or 5 o'clock and get us out of bed, and march us down to the toilet. Then back to bed, and they would come along with a great bloody needle and they would shove this needle into you, and away you would go; make sure you had plenty of blankets on you and you started to sweat;

oh, sweat, sweat, sweat and then go into a coma; go out completely. Afterwards they would come around with this big pannikin of glucose and make you drink it.

We used to get up and have breakfast and then we would have a session – what would they call it, group therapy. They'd have all these patients and they would start talking about your life, married life, and all – you'd say something and then someone across the room would say something. I used to say things went wrong with me and then 'Why did you get like this?' and they would go round and round. All the doctors would be taking notes. I was in hospital for a long time. One of the doctors came up and lined us up in the hall instead of having a session and he said, 'I want a volunteer for the truth drug'. Nobody volunteered. I knew I had nothing to hide – what I'd done and what I'd seen. So I said I would do it.

They put me to sleep and they said I talked like a rat. I went on and on. And they got everything out. The next day the doctor called me up and said 'I want to read the statement'. He read it out and said is that true? I said, I didn't say that. Yes it is true, I said. They said they would not put it on the file but I found out afterwards it was on my file. I think I helped them [doctors] a lot – I never refused treatment.[1]

Tom's description of treatment might appear to be the product of the distorted memory of an old man, but in fact the treatments he described are confirmed by Dr W.A. Dibden, who was appointed as a psychiatrist in 1942 at the hospital in which Tom was treated. Dibden, who had expected 'large numbers of psychiatric casualties flooding into civil life' and 'psychiatric casualties returning in continuous streams', argued that the unresolved fears in war did not disappear in civilian life.

The ex-soldier discovers to his cost that the symptoms he sought to escape by severing his association with all things military retain their ability profoundly to affect his peace of mind and his physical health. This projection into civil life of neurotic symptoms that have in many cases become overt during military service forms the basis of repatriation psychiatric practice.[2]

Dibden's own experience of the physical treatments such as those meted out to Tom was not always positive:

The induction of a convulsion by intravenous cardiazol caused me anxiety.[3] Only the satisfaction of seeing depressed patients get better kept me going. Cardiazol was given as a large injection, usually 6–8 ccs depending on the weight of the patient. A large bore needle was used because it had to be injected fast. The speed of the injection often determined whether the patient had a convulsion or not. If the patient convulsed, well and good. If not, then you had to give a second, larger injection as fast as possible to prevent the terrible effects of a mis-convulsion. It was alleged to produce a sense of utter dissolution. The only way to avoid this was to induce a second convulsion. The consequent retrograde amnesia would mask the unpleasant sensations. It was no fun trying to get into a jumping, bobbing vein using a large syringe with a cc more than the first injection, and to push it in as fast as one could. In the end I became as apprehensive giving Cardiazol injections as some of the patients became of taking them. It was a vast improvement and a relief to me when the drug was replaced by electroconvulsive therapy (ECT).

> I must confess that I was rather disappointed with this technique. The reports coming from the combat area gave encouraging accounts of beneficial results obtained. I could only conclude that the disturbances had become more deeply embedded over the intervening months since the onset of symptoms and evacuation across the seas to Australia, and that the repressed traumatic material became less accessible.[4]

The story of Tom's experience with treatment continued throughout his life, but years of extensive treatment did not cure him: 'No it didn't do me any good. I was eventually discharged and went back to work.' He was later granted a TPI pension and had periodic re-admissions to hospital throughout his life. In 1995 he was still anxious and depressed and receiving outpatient psychiatric treatment through the Repatriation Commission, including participating in a trial of Prozac, a modern anti-depressant. By then other conditions like heart disease had complicated his health story. He would still become very distressed whenever he recalled aspects of his New Guinea experience.

Tom had found himself in a rehabilitation system that was virtually in its infancy. Repatriation and rehabilitation were massive undertakings for the 600,000

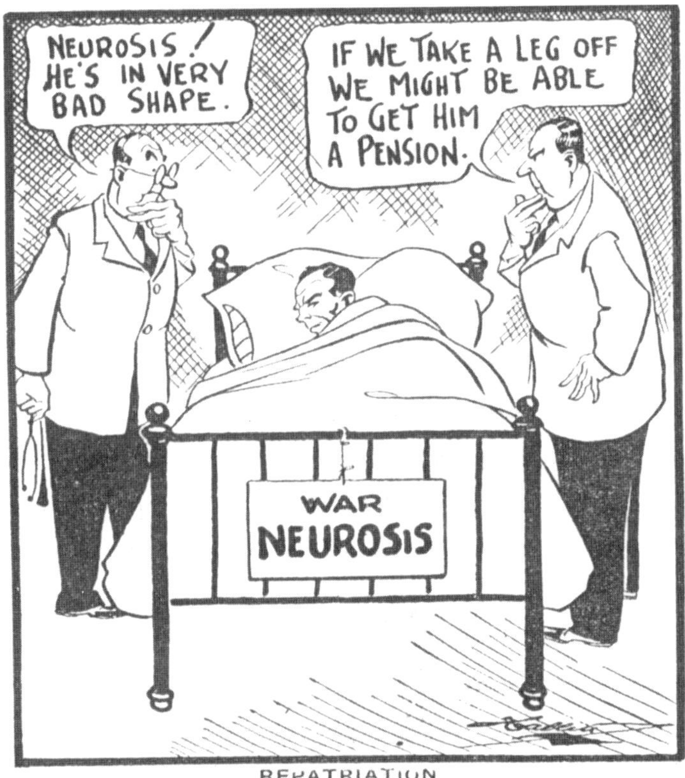

REPATRIATION
News Item: Pensions are not granted in war neurosis cases.

Smith's Weekly, *17 April 1948*

men and women returning to Australia after the war. Psychiatric rehabilitation is an integral component of this broader activity of repatriation which Galbraith (1946) defined as:

> That method by which function, both physiological and psychological, is restored following illness or injury. It thus connotes the restoration of free movement of stiffened limbs, vigour to tired minds, of courage and confidence to quailing spirits; in short, the physical, mental and ethical toning up of the whole individual being.[5]

The foundations for the World War Two veteran psychiatric programs had been partly laid in the aftermath of World War One, when facilities had been established in the larger states by the Australian Red Cross (ARC) to heal the shell-shocked veteran. Even though it had been a leader in the provision of treatment for mentally damaged soldiers (see Chapter 2), by 1939 the Red Cross had reverted to its traditional activities, visiting the sick and wounded in hospitals and convalescent homes, providing activities such as libraries, crafts, and entertainment, and distributing small comforts such as socks and cigarettes. Rehabilitation had to be rebuilt.

To rebuild a psychiatric rehabilitation system, Australian authorities relied heavily on the British policy, and it was not surprising that in 1940, in its search for ideas on dealing with war neurosis the Australian Repatriation Commission turned to a report from the British Minister of Pensions in London. The report had emerged out of a conference held in July 1939 to advise the British government on 'the general principles for dealing with cases of nervous breakdown which may become manifest in wartime'. The British policy was underpinned by a view that any post-war adjustment problems could be largely attributed to a poor pre-war psychological history.

The British conference endorsed the findings of the 1922 Shell Shock Inquiry. It

> [drew] attention to the following factors which tend to increase the incidence and severity of mental and nervous disorders in time of war.
>
> (a) All those factors by which an individual is encouraged to believe that weakening or loss of mental control provide an honourable avenue of escape from duty.
>
> (b) The ignorance of the general community regarding the origin, nature and significance of mental, and especially emotional disorders.
>
> (c) All those preventable conditions which undermine a man's mental and physical health and lower the power of resistance and morale, for example insufficient sleep and rest and recreation and relaxation, bad accommodation, abuse of alcohol, lack of attention to comfort and wellbeing.

The report strongly recommended that 'shell shock, a term that has proved to be a costly misnomer in the last war, should be eliminated from our vocabulary'. Furthermore, the dominant view was 'that war produces no new nervous disorders', and that long-term cases of psychological breakdown could be explained by 'inborn or acquired predisposition'. Furthermore:

> The conference advises that the policy of the Government during the period of the war should aim at dealing with all cases of nervous breakdown by way of treatment and rehabilitation, rather than the endowment by compensation.[6]

These ideas set the scene for developments in rehabilitation, but the contemporary civilian context of the treatment of mental illness was also very relevant. At the outbreak of World War Two civilian mental health facilities and ideas were extremely limited by current standards. There was a long list of shortcomings, such as low medical standards in institutions, a lack of adequately trained psychiatric, medical and nursing staff, and little community focus in any of the mental health facilities. Garton noted overcrowding and inadequate facilities, and estimated that by 1949 there were nearly 3,000 more patients than proper beds in Australian mental hospitals, much of the accommodation was ramshackle and antiquated, and there were too few doctors and nurses.[7] As late as 1955 a report on Australian mental health facilities highlighted the shortcomings in civil psychiatric facilities, and general neglect and inertia in relation to establishing professional world standard resources and facilities. Overcrowding was a major shortcoming, with an estimated shortfall of 10,000 beds throughout Australia.[8] Mental institutions existed to contain 'madness' and treat illnesses, not provide normalisation for return to society.

In the early 1940s there was limited, if any, university-based training in psychiatry, and the neuroses of war were not significant topics in the professional development of psychiatrists and general practitioners. Ideas about war neurosis were discussed periodically at meetings of the British Medical Association in some Australian states, but no professional medical body took them up as a major issue. There was minimal involvement and interest from other professional bodies such as psychologists. The Australasian Society of Psychiatrists, founded in 1946 and the forerunner to the College of Psychiatry in Australia, formed in 1963, did not take up veterans' problems as part of their brief. Psychological societies such as the British Psychological Society, which had Australian members, were not concerned with the mental health of veterans or problems of war, but more with issues of mental measurement and assessment for vocational purposes. The Psychoanalytic Institute, still in the early stages of development, paid little attention to war veterans. The only sites of medical discourse on war-related issues were the *British Medical Journal*, the *Medical Journal of Australia* and the *Lancet*, where a number of articles appeared.

The standard British work on psychiatric training, Henderson and Gillespie's *Textbook on Psychiatry* (Henderson was professor of psychiatry at Edinburgh University), was the most widely used text. The authors did not incorporate any new learning from World War Two into post-war revisions. In the 1962 edition it was even suggested that 'traumatic neurosis and traumatic psychoneurosis should be abandoned' as diagnostic categories. The authors admitted that a terrifying experience would produce a short-term reaction of anxiety and panic and often terrifying dreams, but these symptoms 'usually diminish and ultimately disappear'.

It was as though the war was only a minor interruption to the stream of received knowledge in psychiatry.[9]

The only significant text in analytical psychiatry was Otto Fenichel's *The Psychoanalytic Theory of Neurosis*, first published in 1945. It was recommended to psychiatrists and trainees in the post-World War Two period, but was mainly of interest to those doing psychoanalytic work.[10] Fenichel described trauma as

> a relative concept, in which factors such as mental economy, dependent on constitution as well as on previous experiences, and on the actual conditions before and during the trauma, determine what degree of excitation overtaxes the individual's capacity.[11]

How one coped depended on the capacity to take action at the time – 'foxhole waiting is more dangerous than active warfare'. Fenichel listed the symptoms of traumatic neurosis as: (a) blocking, or decrease of ego functions; (b) spells of uncontrollable emotions; (c) sleep disturbance with dreams in which trauma is re-experienced, including mental repetitions during the day; and (d) secondary psychoneurotic complications. He maintained that if the event was sufficiently severe it could precipitate a neurosis. If the person already had a neurotic disposition, he would react to a minor event 'with a reactivation of his infantile conflicts'. For Fenichel, essentially 'traumatic neuroses represent an insufficiency of the basic function of the ego' to overcome past traumata and avoid future traumata. His psychoanalytic ideas had some influence on the work of psychiatrists in the 1940s and 1950s at the Rockingham treatment centre in Victoria. Another influence was the work of Maxwell Jones and his concept of the therapeutic community. However only a few practitioners, such as Paul Dane, took an active long-term interest in the traumatic neuroses.[12]

In the 1940s not only the psychiatric rehabilitation system but psychiatry itself was in a very early stage of development. In South Australia psychiatric training in the medical school was limited to eight one-hour lectures per year, including a lecture on psychoanalysis and a visit to a psychiatric hospital. The other training that might have occurred was while medical officers were members of the armed forces. To equip them for front-line psychiatry the army initially provided a basic twelve-week training course at Kenmore in New South Wales, run by Alec Sinclair, 'a pleasant chap, a good teacher', according to one participant, William Salter.[13] This was a rudimentary training course with basic topics about therapy and management of psychiatric cases, and training in the use of insulin and coma therapy, ECT and rudimentary psychotherapy. Trainees were also introduced to the ideas of Freud and to how the subconscious expressed itself in symptoms.

For his army psychiatric training Dibden completed a twelve-week course at the School of Neurology and Psychiatry in Melbourne. This enabled him to qualify as an adult psychiatrist in South Australia. The school was run by Drs H. Wadsley and J. Williams and involved most of the senior Victorian psychiatrists from the state mental hospitals. Dibden described his experience:

> We had lectures every day, sometimes in the evening. We read a lot and there were

> visits to hospitals. We had an opportunity to see patients under supervision. Convulsion therapy and full coma insulin therapy were demonstrated and the malaria treatment for syphilitic nervous disorder, GPI, or general paralysis of the insane. The lectures provided us with a grounding in psychopathology. In 12 weeks it was impossible to acquire any but the simplest psychotherapy skills. The course was comprehensive, intensive and very stimulating. After the war about half of those who took part remained in psychiatry.[14]

Given the reasonably extensive body of medical literature emerging out of the World War One Shell Shock debate, the amnesia in psychiatric literature is quite astounding. The notion of enduring psychological impact was virtually lost before World War Two, and the richness of the work of neurologists such as Rivers and Myers was sidelined. As the work of Paul Dane shows, Freudian views on neurosis and hysteria prevailed, without the sexual dimension. Australian writers were very thin on the ground.

In this impoverished context, psychiatric ideas were borrowed from army literature. The only significant psychiatric text written specifically for the Australian armed forces, by Bostock and Jones (1943), was intended for medical personnel in the field, but was not widely known among medical practitioners. These authors believed that soldiers, 'though bludgeoned by the blows of fate, must be prepared to rise above their difficulties', and if they did become mental casualties they were basically considered to be a nuisance. Men with these disorders 'are a source of constant anxiety in the field, undermining morale', and occupy 'beds often urgently needed for casualties'. They would also be a 'recurring expense' to the state after discharge. In another paper Bostock (1943) argued that over-diagnosis of nervous conditions had led people to expect a pension as a right, not a privilege. He argued that specialists too often elevated normal symptoms into unwarranted disease categories, and two decades of military and civil pensioning after World War One had made 'mere prostration or nervous breakdown into a pensionable disease'.[15]

In the 1940s, in medical circles there was some discussion of the needs of the mental casualties of war. These views were aired at the end of the war, but had obviously been around for some time. At a meeting of the New South Wales Branch of the British Medical Association on the rehabilitation of war neurotics in April 1946, McCarthy argued that the 'illness is essentially no different from that occurring in civilians who were not subjected to the emotional stress of service conditions'. Furthermore, 'it is generally medically agreed that the war neurotic does not differ essentially from the civilian neurotic'. Dr Hastings Willis stated that 'in few cases does neurosis arise directly from battle stress or conditions peculiar to warfare. Most neuroses in the services could equally well have arisen in the same way in civilian life'. The general notion that 'pensions or compensation should only be granted in exceptional cases', because they are 'serious obstacles to the recovery of the neurotic', was supported by speakers. However, they did support the need for a comprehensive approach incorporating rehabilitation and vocational adjustment.[16]

Within this context, the Menzies government made a commitment in 1941 to establishing a national rehabilitation system for all Australians, but the Federal legislation confirming the provisions for the mental health of ex-servicemen was not passed until 1950. The Repatriation Commission treated only those with disabilities accepted as war-related, and since psychiatric disabilities were not automatically accepted as war-related, many veterans with psychiatric problems were catered for within the Department of Social Services which established the Commonwealth Rehabilitation Service.[17] In his history of the service, Tipping noted that 'among the people with non-war-caused disabilities who became clients under the scheme, there were a high proportion of people (25 per cent) who had psychological and psychiatric complaints', brought about by the high rate of rejection of claims by ex-servicemen.[18]

The British influence on Australian policy was pervasive. The most significant contributor was Alan Stoller, a British psychiatrist who served with the Australian Army (1940–45), and was later appointed as the specialist in psychological medicine in the Repatriation Commission (1947–53). Stoller could rightly be regarded as the architect of the system. His ideas can be seen in the policy underpinning the comprehensive system of psychiatric rehabilitation detailed in the Commonwealth parliament in June 1950.[19] In his parliamentary speech, the Minister for Repatriation, Walter Cooper, outlined the ideas, practices and policy in the post-World War Two period. Cooper recalled that the beginning of the 1939–45 war found a number of men from World War One still under medical care in a variety of institutions. These mentally disabled men had been certified under state laws, and were housed in separate repatriation blocks in State mental institutions. Cooper was quick to dispel any 'loose thinking' about mental illness, and the legislation would enshrine the widely held belief that 'war neurosis, as such, presents nothing new to medical science':

> The same disorders that are found in our ex-servicemen occur in ordinary civilian general medical practice and the methods of treatment follow well-established patterns. Their mental afflictions ranged from the 'little nervous or over-anxious' to the violently homicidal or suicidal.[20]

The battle to have pensions awarded on psychiatric grounds had been won during World War One. At the end of World War Two, there were two basic types of pension. The first was a full or part allocation of a general rate of pension for disability – a range from 10 per cent to 100 per cent. A greater rate was granted for those who were classified totally and permanently incapacitated (TPI). For very damaged men who could not 'support their families', the granting of TPI was a considerable relief for their anxiety. Even so, Cooper still needed to make the case that 'the national responsibility to the discharged man or woman so far as war service is concerned, is to treat him or her and provide pensions in respect of any disability which is war related'.[21] Meanwhile, medical specialists such as W.A. Dibden in South Australia still argued in World War Two that pensions should not be automatically granted even when the soldier was clearly disturbed. In Dibden's view, a pension 'served no useful purpose', did not encourage a person to 'shrug off his mental demons', and only confirmed in the patient's mind that he was suffering from 'organic lesion resulting from war service'. For the mentally damaged soldier 'compensation was often particularly harmful to the individual'.[22]

The diagnoses bore the familiar labels: hysteria, neurasthenia, anxiety neurosis and obsessional neurosis. Traumatic neurosis applied to only 2.5 per cent of claims and one-third of these were accepted. Traumatic neurosis was a rare classification reserved for those who had experienced some form of commotional shock.[23]

Even if the mental disability experienced by veterans was accepted as due to war service, there were limits to the treatment offered in the army/repatriation hospital. The more severe cases, such as psychotic or seriously disruptive patients, with destructive, aggressive, suicidal or alcoholic tendencies, would be sent to one of the civil institutions, most of which were still operating under the various state lunacy acts.[24] In an institution at Northfield, South Australia, there was a special ward (Ward 7) where eligible ex-servicemen could be segregated and provided with some additional attention. However, these institutions were only for psychiatric treatment or containment, not rehabilitation. As late as 1949, Stoller reported in his annual inspection of services for ex-service personnel that minimum accommodation requirements (e.g. floor coverings in the locker rooms, doctors' rooms, and linen room) that applied in the state system were not being met. In the same report it was noted that of the 191 ex-servicemen and two ex-servicewomen in these facilities, only 51 were Repatriation cases.[25]

Little special attention was given to ex-soldiers admitted to this public system, where there was no specialised treatment. One psychiatrist, Dr Harry Southwood, Deputy Superintendent of Enfield Receiving Home in South Australia during the war years and until 1949, did not see any need for special consideration of veterans, who 'went mad just the same as civilians'.[26] The only concession for war service was support from members of outside groups such as the RSL visitation committees. Treatments, including ECT, coma therapy, early forms of behaviour therapy, and medications such as barbiturates, were the same for veterans as for civil patients. After 1957 the profession had access to the major tranquillizers. In addition, the anti-psychotic drugs Melleril and Largactil were introduced at around this time. These controlled psychotic symptoms, especially those of the delusional. This meant that in institutions effective control could be achieved without keys and physical restraint. It would still have been very easy for a veteran to be lost in these institutions or have his difficulties masked by alcohol abuse and attempted suicide. At this time there was no political will to make a special issue of veterans in public institutions, which were in need of reform and did not serve the needs of many of their general patients well. Reform of these state institutions was not achieved until the 1960s, far too late for early and effective treatment for damaged men of war.

Repatriation psychiatric rehabilitation facilities evolved out of the military establishments, particularly army hospitals, and these functions were transferred gradually to the Repatriation Commission from the army system. For example, in South Australia the Daws Road Military Hospital (105 AGH), which had a psychiatric ward, was transferred to the Repatriation Commission and became known as the Repatriation General Hospital (RGH). While facilities varied in each state, all capital cities had some form of annexe attached to the main hospitals. As former senior psychiatrist W.A. Dibden recalled, these 'were of a temporary wooden construction but were nevertheless satisfactory for the times'.[27] The treatment and methods of disposal within the Repatriation system for those with accepted disabilities followed 'standard psychiatric lines' and reflected contemporary civil practice. Many of these treatments were physical and invasive and included pre-frontal leucotomy, electric shock treatment, convulsive therapy, and full-coma insulin therapy. British military psychiatrists, such as William Sargant, lauded these physical treatments.[28]

Psychotherapy was not completely disregarded and the experience of Tom (pages 119–121 above) indicated that traumatic memory was taken seriously at some stage, but in practice, the pursuit of psychodynamic therapy was largely frowned upon. For example, in July 1951 a ministerial instruction was issued from the Repatriation Commission headquarters advising that psychoanalysis was still experimental in nature and uncertain in its results. It was time-consuming and costly, and it should be provided only with special safeguards, such as approval from a committee consisting of a specialist consultant in psychological medicine and a visiting specialist psychiatrist or psychoanalyst from the state system.

To supplement the work in the psychiatric wards of the repatriation hospitals, re-establishment centres, designed to provide a high level of morale, a 'grand spirit', to enable men to regain their own spirits, were established in Victoria and New South Wales. The re-establishment centres were halfway houses where patients could get 'toned up' before re-entry into the community. The centres, such as the Rockingham Centre in Melbourne, provided a range of social activities, including ballroom dancing, which would help patients overcome feelings of inferiority, and learn to mix again with members of the opposite sex. Various hobbies and trade training were also available.

Rockingham was a former Red Cross Convalescent Home for men with chronic personality disorders and remitted psychosis. The centre was used to introduce Maxwell Jones's concepts of the therapeutic community. Under this regimen patients, through a democratic committee system, had more control over the programs. Group and individual therapy, including hypnosis, and recreational activities were a central part of the program. It was claimed that these ideas improved motivation and general behaviour and reduced the length of stay.[29]

Psychiatric rehabilitation developed into a combination of clinical treatment, re-socialisation and vocational preparation, sometimes referred to as milieu therapy, which provided a supportive environment for psychiatric treatment and vocational readjustment. There was little dynamic exploration of traumatic memory, and the idea was to create a close healing community, rather than focus on war trauma. Psychologists were largely confined to the provision of vocational guidance and placement, and clinical assessments (Rorschach was a popular instrument), but had little to do with policy. Psychiatrists managed treatment, with social workers,

'Repatriation: Pensions not granted in war neurosis cases'. Smith's Weekly; *March 1945*

nurses and psychologists carrying out supportive roles under supervision and medical direction.

Return to suitable employment was a central feature of rehabilitation. A recurring problem for the mentally damaged veteran was securing a sympathetic employer who could make allowances for emotional changes and reduced cognitive functioning. This difficulty was acknowledged by Dr Ken Fry, who had served in New Guinea and later as the chief medical officer with the Local Board of Health in the City of Adelaide:

> Cure depends on the successful re-adaption [*sic*] to employment and social conditions in civilian life. Many will need outpatient oversight during this period of re-adaption. Some will require occasional treatment for the rest of their lives, many will break down, some on repeated occasions, and will require periods of in-patient hospital treatment to rehabilitate them.[30]

In the context of readjustment to work, and emotional readjustment to normal life, it was still argued that a pension would act as a disincentive, because the recipient might not struggle to overcome his problems. In their analysis of the work of the Repatriation Commission in the World War One era, Lloyd and Rees concluded that 'with genuine psychic cases, those who obtained regular work soon after returning usually recovered quickly because they had no time for psychic ailments'.[31]

The developments in the rehabilitation system did not meet the expectations of its principal architect, Allan Stoller. Stoller had been keen to shift the thinking of the Repatriation Commission from what he regarded as the outmoded practice of clinical psychiatry to a more socially oriented environment. He concluded that, whereas before the war there was heterogeneity and variety,

> [t]he war seems to have unified the general outlook, and brought psychiatrists to a common mode of expression and understanding. However, there is still a strong

> psychoanalytical influence. The old concept of the psychiatrist as an asylum doctor has disappeared. His frontiers and outlook have broadened. His interests are extending from medicine into the field of education, sociology, criminology, industry and even political science.[32]

Stoller still argued that wrong or inappropriate treatment and judgemental attitudes could exacerbate and perpetuate any inadequacies in the ex-serviceman. Obviously referring to the World War One experience, he stated:

> Critics again state that one should not bother to deal with individuals who are happy only with the pension and with the regular bottle of medicine. Anyone who has seen these 'happy old chronics' attending the outpatient department, who has followed their life histories, as we are able to do for thirty years or more, and who has received social reports of the family, cannot but deplore such a negative attitude which in the past has produced over the years a miserable inferior male and a family of substandard citizens. Those of us who have the care of the entitled ex-servicemen are endeavouring to stop such developments in the present returnee. We have envisaged a scheme which allows for the very necessary integration of general medicine and psychiatry.

Furthermore, he hoped for a future in which:

> psychiatric problems will not hide behind the cloak of physical disorder for years until eventually the patient has become completely fixed in all his attitudes and obsessionally reaches for the magic symbolism of the medicine bottle.[33]

The thrust of these new ideas was obvious in Stoller's recommendations for reform within the Repatriation Commission. These included establishing advisory consultants at headquarters to take responsibility for maintenance of standards in clinical psychology and psychiatric social work, and the establishment of federal neuropsychiatric hospitals for ex-servicemen. A third recommendation was to establish a comprehensive university-based training scheme for all specialists and psychiatric personnel, including special research fellowship grants from the Repatriation Commission.

In a report on the RGH in February 1949 Stoller pointed out a number of persistent shortcomings, including a deficiency in personnel. There were still only three part-time visiting psychiatrists attending the hospital, Binns, Salter and Dibden, and he recommended the appointment of a full-time psychiatrist as well as a sessional clinical psychologist to provide vocational guidance and personality evaluation of patients. Stoller's report makes it clear that there was no rehabilitation intervention such as educational therapy beyond psychiatric treatment.[34]

Alcoholics were a constant problem at RGH. These patients were particularly troublesome, and if they suffered from *delirium tremens* they would thrash around, requiring confinement to a padded cell.[35] Suicide, at that time officially a criminal act, was not uncommon. If suicide was attempted, the patient was certified and sent to Enfield Receiving Home, a state institution, in a straightjacket. This was mandatory, whoever the patient and whatever the nature of the problem.

One purpose of psychiatric rehabilitation was to prevent the 'contagion' of war neuroses from spreading into the community. Suicide and the high incidence of alcohol abuse, both serious issues in the post-war period, are examples of such 'contagion'. The raw face of suicide can be seen in a patient, CWF, who took his own life on 7 May 1948. He had been admitted to the RGH in South Australia on a Friday evening after his wife had contacted the hospital saying that he had been violent and was choking her. After admission, CWF left the hospital without permission and was later found dead at home after a substance overdose, probably of sodium amytal.[36]

This type of event was not uncommon among patients, as illustrated in a 1959 report and administrative instruction in South Australia on the issue of suicides. An appendix to these records individual suicide attempts made between July 1949 and March 1953. Only 11 of the 140 cases recorded were successful, and the most common method of attempted suicide was the use of some kind of poisoning, including an overdose of phenobarbitone, a drug dispensed by the hospital. The second most popular method was some kind of violent act such as slashing the wrists or slitting the throat. The use of firearms was recorded in only four of these cases.[37] This snapshot of the distress of individuals under treatment in one provincial setting can be assumed to be indicative of a wider problem, and evidence that the control of the neurosis 'disease' was not entirely effective. Many very disturbed men alive more than five years after demobilisation were still distressed enough to attempt suicide. It may be that in many cases these men were making a cry for help, either in response to some intrusive traumatic experience, such as nightmares, or in response to the frustration of not being able to get their lives back in order. Suicides were a reflection of a troubled group of men, as well as an indication of shortcomings in a system designed to help them. However, any criticisms of this system were kept in-house, and not aired in public.

* * * * *

The outcome of the efforts to rehabilitate the World War Two veteran was a more efficient and comprehensive system than had hitherto existed, underpinned by sound legislation. Despite the very limited civil and professional context of psychiatric practice of the era, a few dedicated psychiatrists developed a creditable system. The efforts of such men – women remained the handmaidens as nurses, occupational therapists and social workers – had produced a systematic referral and treatment net for the seriously disturbed that was superior to those in civil facilities. However, these programs were not informed by any new ideas on war neurosis. There was no new body of knowledge, diagnosis or diagnostic technology that would differentiate the mental maladies of war from those of civil life. In fact, it was made clear by all within the system that the war still presented 'nothing new to medical science'.

This meant that in many cases the origins of war-induced suffering were still unrecognised, and as a result the marks of war remained unhealed. The consequences of this for men in the third and most damaged group in my sample is the subject of Chapter 10.

CHAPTER 10

Life in the 'Bughouse'

> One continuous thing right up to this last year [1987] as a matter of fact. I been in the … I call it the bughouse, you call it 'Ward 7' or 'Ward 8' … it was a special place for people when they gone off their rocker (*sic*). I been there a couple of times, been in 'repat' here and there. L. Howson

The final part of this story is the most disturbing. This chapter is about the men who were so affected by their war experience that they were diagnosed with a mental illness and treated within the Repatriation system. In relating their stories I do not attempt to determine just how much of their dysfunction was 'caused' by war experience, but in all cases the war continued inside their minds, and traumatic war memory was at least an explanation, if not a cause, of their continued distress.[1] I have also not in this context attempted to re-diagnose their condition under the rubric of Post-traumatic Stress Disorder.[2]

In this chapter the identities of the informants are protected as far as possible. Some of them have previously made public statements, either in the media or in their Murdoch Sound Archive interviews. In all cases surnames have not been used. The stories have in most cases been compiled from a variety of sources and these are referenced only when appropriate.

There are ten men in this group; only five were diagnosed and treated while on active service. The experience of some of the men is described in detail, but others wanted to remain anonymous and their stories were incorporated into the collective life story. The detailed descriptions provide an insight into what it was like to be labelled mentally ill and to be drawn into the treatment system of the time. They also give some idea of the dilemmas, for both veterans and medical personnel, of trying to make sense of the symptoms and behaviour that persisted for years after the original exposure. These men served in different battalions, but all have stories of struggle over a long period of time, some of which ended tragically.

On the outside, some of the men did achieve both materially and socially, but all continued to have periodic bouts of diagnosed mental illness requiring specialist medical intervention. Even though they kept their worries hidden from most of the outside world, their disturbance spilled over into family life, and their partners and children were also marked. Most men in the group were characterised by long-term psychological instability, chronic drinking behaviour, and disruptive relationships, but there are some success stories. Charles, who was diagnosed with anxiety neurosis and 'couldn't go to work', and 'was very sick', eventually settled and worked consistently until he retired at 65, despite 'plenty of treatment for me nerves'.

> When we came back from New Guinea I was in and out of hospital so often for so long for a couple of years ... I was getting blackouts. You know, just from this war neurosis, this anxiety state thing. I used to black out, you know, completely lose my mind.[3]

Happily, a few of these men did end their days with some peace, having found their own solutions to their problems outside the medical system.

For these veterans, the only arena for exploring ways of relieving distress was within a medical system. There were no counselling or therapeutic groups provided by bodies such as the RSL or veteran organisations outside of the hospital system. There were some attempts at public education for families through organisations like the Red Cross, but most people had to rely on their own limited resources.[4] All of these men had multiple admissions to outpatients' and inpatients' departments because of their mental health problems. All were referred for psychiatric help, either at the request of their wife or by their local medical officer, because of their disruptive behaviour, alcohol abuse, violence, or because they were considered a danger to themselves. When he entered the world of psychiatric medicine, the veteran's experience was translated into a different language and removed to another level of discursive space, which was understood by the expert but was foreign to the veteran, who was a lay person. His distress was subsumed under a label such as 'anxiety state', and if solutions were offered they would come from another foreign medical domain with physical treatments such as insulin and electric shock treatment, psychotherapy and medication. He rarely had the opportunity to explore his life experience using his own language.

Ten men from my sample provide an insight into this experience. Table 1 summarises the group and indicates the problems they experienced, as well as the diagnoses that were applied in the repatriation system.

The treatments applied reflected all the practices of the day. The only physical treatment available that was not used with these men was frontal lobe lobotomy or leucotomy. Seven cases, whose medical files could be accessed, were scrutinised in more detail to explore the nature of their treatment, and this information is summarised in Table 2. This table shows the range of diagnoses, labels and treatments applied to veterans, and these reflect the practices that are outlined in Chapter 9.

The application of diagnoses and treatments is illustrated in the case of a former captain, who will be referred to as Thomas.[5] In his medical assessment and treatment, little importance was placed on his war story. If it had been, this would have recognised his considerable battle experience, such as extended patrols in enemy territory, as a source of trauma. Instead, the 'cause' of his malady was seen to be his poor constitution. In one of his many psychiatric examinations, it was concluded that 'his present breakdown would thus be a neurotic reaction to

Table 1. Problems, outcomes and labels

Rank	War-time	Life problem	Life outcomes	Official diagnosis
Infantry	Detected, not evacuated	Nerves, depression Chronic alcohol abuse	Separation Suicide at 58	Psychopathic personality 1943 Anxiety state 1945 Paranoid personality 1948 Anxiety state 1949 Anxiety state/alcoholism 1950
NCO	Diagnosed, not repatriated	Chronic alcohol abuse	Work disruption Early retirement Accepted by family Early death at 57	Nervous disorder 1945 Anxiety state, alcoholism,depression 1960
NCO	No	Depression	Family distress Psychosomatic problems and illness	Somatic–diarrhoea, headaches, nausea etc. 1941 Mild anxiety state 1944 Nervous debility 1947 Severe psychoneurosis 1965 Depression 1972 Reactive depression 1979 Suicidal tendencies 1986
Ranks	Breakdown evacuated	Anxiety/depression	Work limitations Socially restricted	Not available
Ranks	Detected; not evacuated	Early breakdown	Recovery Late life satisfaction	Not available
NCO	No	Alcohol/depression	Divorce Early retirement Recovery in later life	Not available
Ranks	Detected	Alcohol/ violence	Divorce Early tragic death	Anxiety state connected with war service 1952 Anxiety state, neurasthenic reaction to suppressed trauma, depressed, 1953 Anxiety state, secondary alcoholism 1955
Infantry	No	Alcohol/aggression	Divorce Work disruption	Vaso vagal turns, nerves 1962 Anxiety hysteria;, character disorder, Inadequate personality Inadequate personality complicated by hysterical outbursts and alcohol psychopathic personality 1962 Typical psychopath – anti-social behaviour 1963 Anxiety-depressive symptoms 1988
Ranks	No		Chronic anxiety Restricted relationships Work restrictions	Anxiety hysteria Anxiety state with depression (1972) Reactive depression (family problems) 1972; PTSD (1994)
Infantry	No	'Nerves'	Divorce Social isolation	Not available

irritating, frustrating circumstances, in a man constitutionally predisposed'.[6] This veteran had joined the AIF when he was 38 years old and served for six years before being discharged in October 1945. He had not been referred for treatment nor attracted the attention of senior officers or medical officers, although his diary recorded that he was feeling the strain late in his tour. In 1953 he presented to the

Table 2. Summary of labels and treatments provided [seven cases]

Medical labels applied	Treatments offered
Psychopathic personality; anxiety state; paranoid personality; anxiety state; anxiety /alcoholism 1943–1954	Potassium bromide; occupational therapy, sodium amytal (sedation); vitamin B; psychotherapy
Nervous disorder; anxiety state alcoholism; depression 1945–1960	Sub coma insulin (1945, New Guinea); psychotherapy; amitriptyline (1967)
Somatic–diarrhoea, headaches, nausea etc; Mild anxiety state; nervous debility; Severe psychoneurosis; Depression reactive depression Suicidal tendencies 1945–1986	Explanation. persuasion, suggestion; psychotherapy; Marital counselling, occupational therapy; Pain relievers, temazepam, diazepam
Vaso vagal turns; nerves; anxiety hysteria based on immature character disorder, inadequate personality; inadequate personality with hysterical outbursts and alcohol, psychopathic personality Typical psychopath with anti-social behaviour; anxiety-depressive symptoms 1962–1988	Largactil (long term), pentobarb [*sic*], occupational therapy; group therapy; in-patient and outpatient treatment; advice from GP
Anxiety state connected with war service; anxiety state, neurasthenic reaction to suppressed trauma, depressed, anxiety state, secondary alcoholism	Sub coma insulin, methedrine suggested; inpatient treatment; refused atebrin; persuasion; AA; public mental hospital; phenobarbitone, phenytoin sodium (Dilantin)
Anxiety hysteria; anxiety state with depression; reactive depression; PTSD 1952–1994	Valium; amitriptyline; Mogadon; shock treatment ('well known to unit'); in- and outpatient treatment; variety of anti-depressants.
Anxiety, hysteria, depression, neurasthenia	ECT, insulin therapy; psychotherapy

Repatriation authority complaining of 'stomach pains, loss of confidence and unaccountable tiredness'. He was unable to do his work as a teacher, and his wife was concerned about him. After a psychiatric assessment he was granted compensation of 20 per cent of the full pension for 'Functional Bernhardt's Neuralgia, which is covered by Anxiety State'. Thomas was variously described in the medical notes as 'an hysteric and quite lacking in insight', a 'patient who settled down to work quite well', and a 'patient whose general condition is quite good'. He is always referred to as 'this man' or this 'patient', never by his given or surnames.

In his army role Thomas had developed skills in critical analysis of information, and so during his period of treatment he subjected himself to close analysis, writing profuse letters for his psychiatrist, outlining his symptoms and insights. One of these insights was that his difficulty in concentrating 'must be subjected to some unconscious hindrance'. According to his medical file, at one stage 'abreaction produced 57 pages of material of no particular psychiatric significance', and there was 'not much in the subconscious still to come up'. His diagnoses over time included anxiety state, neurasthenia, hysteric depression and anxiety, neurastheniform reaction, hysteria, and even 'some elements of menopause and melancholia'. Treatments, none of which cured his ailments, ranged from sub-coma insulin, individual and group psychotherapy, abreactive therapy, CO_2 inhalation therapy, to a 'special drug treatment'. Leucotomy was considered as a last resort in 1955, but not carried out.[7] At this time the psychiatrist gave up and Thomas was discharged with a recommendation that he be assessed for a TPI pension, which was eventually granted.

Thomas never returned to his profession but continued to drink and was regularly referred for psychiatric treatment until at least age 60. He was divorced from his wife and separated from his family but described his later life, when he found his own form of healing, as 'satisfactory'. During this time he produced a comprehensive account of his life, which seemed to be cathartic for him. The story of Thomas is relevant in this context in that he provided articulate accounts of his experience, including his war history, which were translated into medical diagnoses. This had the advantage of providing him with a basis for compensation but also served to replace his personal narrative with a medical diagnosis. Late in life Thomas gave up drinking, spontaneously recovered and lived a satisfying life well into his ninetieth year.

The complexity of encounters with treatments shown in Thomas's case can be seen in several other detailed stories.

Beating the system: The case of Lawrie[8]

This story recounts the life experience of Lawrie who was one of those who 'recovered' in later life and no longer depends on the Veterans' Affairs mental health system. The search for mental and physical health was a consistent theme of his narrative in my meetings with him in the 1990s. At the time of the first interview in 1995 he had 'thrown away his pills' and rejected mainstream medicine, exploring alternatives like massage, diet and hypnosis. By then he was pushing himself well beyond the boundaries of the regimens used in his earlier treatment in the repatriation system. Most of his post-war life has been a struggle to maintain mental balance. In the years after discharge he was violent, drunk much of the time, and struggled with his marriage, in which he fathered two children. His relationship was never a settled one and ended in divorce. Lawrie now believes he has discovered the alternative to the psychiatric paradigms and other medical interventions he experienced in 'the bughouse', the Rockingham Psychiatric Centre, where he spent much of 1962.

To explain how he arrived at this point we need to go back to the beginning. As one of 19 children, Lawrie had experienced a poor childhood – 'a lot of hard work and little to eat. We had the arse out of our pants and very little education'. At the age of six he was made to work in his father's market garden every day before going to school. His father drank a lot and 'most of the income from the market garden went on grog and racehorses'. Lawrie left school at 14 and worked in his father's garden. At the age of 18 he applied to join the navy but was rejected. He was too young to volunteer for the AIF but shortly afterwards was conscripted into 52nd Battalion, from which he volunteered for the 39th Battalion, which was sent to New Guinea in 1942. He could have stayed home and grown vegetables for overseas troops but convinced the authorities to accept him for overseas service. 'They said, "If you are that keen to go and get yourself killed, you go". How many times I wished I had stopped home and grown veggies for all you other jokers'.

Lawrie spent his 21st birthday on 15 March 1942 in Port Moresby in an anti-aircraft crew. In mid-1942 he was sent over the Owen Stanley Ranges as a machine gunner. This is a crucial time in understanding the dynamic of the effect of war experience on him. Until then his attitude had been rather blasé and full of bravado, but when his unit was ordered to fix bayonets after they had been fired on at Deniki, 'it really dawned on me at that moment that this is what soldiering is all about. I think that stage was the first time I was really frightened'. In the period from March to December 1942 he was strafed, caught in a Japanese bombing raid, saw his close friend killed, killed an unspecified number of Japanese as a machine gunner, was left behind by his unit in enemy territory, went on night patrols in dense jungle, saw his company commander accidentally shoot himself, and was ordered to kill a Japanese soldier who had been wounded.

This last incident is the most deeply ingrained in his memory and was recounted publicly by Lawrie in his Murdoch Sound Archive interview in November 1988 and in a film by the Training Command of the Australian Army.

> One Japanese bloke had his arse shot away with machine gun fire. The officer at the time didn't have the guts to kill him so he said to me, 'Righto Smoky finish him off'. I have lived with those eyes from that day to this. I shot him in the bloody head. Bloody terrible. But I still done it because I was ordered to do it. His eyes were rolling and looking at you and everything. I dreamed about it for twenty years or so – well. I've been a nut case a couple of times and I was very bad with me nerves at the end of the war.[9]

His version of this is supported by an eyewitness from the same battalion:

> We were attacking Kokoda and we had to go round to the right and we got to this village ... You can't start firing off in the [jungle] because you can't see very much and it all quietened down, we had to move forward and that's when I saw my first enemy soldier. He was laying on the ground beside the track, he had been hit across the buttocks with a burst of Thompson sub-machine gun bullets and they're about half inch round ... you know they're all lead ... and all his feet were laying beside his head and he was nearly dead. His eyes were rolling around ... It turns your stomach to think about it.
>
> Well, one officer there said finish him off, put him out of his misery or something, but nobody would do it. Then one fella did. I think it upset him quite a bit.[10]

Another event that later proved to be significant was being caught in a bombing raid on the retreat from Efogi. Lawrie recounts that 'half the bombs fell close to me and I copped a blast from one of them'. When he was finally back in safety he was admitted to hospital and 'two days later I get a couple of holes bored in my upstairs department to let lots of pressure fluid out'.[11] He does not have a clear memory of the period from then until his discharge in October 1945. It is possible he had amnesia. He claims to have been put on non-combat duties, and as part of this was assigned to hearse driving, and records show that he was assigned to driving duties which meant he was required to collect bodies, some of which had been subject to autopsy. From the end of 1942 until 1945 he had multiple admissions to hospital in Queensland and Victoria with malaria, appendicitis and a number of undiagnosed conditions (NAD). There is no record of a psychiatric diagnosis during service.

Lawrie was discharged in Victoria on 31 October 1945. Initially he returned home to his own family but he did not tell them about his experiences. 'I think they probably summed the situation up a bit themselves and just laid off and didn't ask too many questions'. Readjustment was difficult and 'as time went by things just seemed to boil up inside more'. He recalled that the image of shooting the soldier returned in nightmares and 'flashbacks'. A rehabilitation training program (CRTS) enabled him to qualify as a carpenter. He started work as a builder, married in September 1945 and children arrived in 1947, 1949, 1953 and 1957.

Lawrie's troubled life resulted in a long history of medical involvement. His first recorded contact for medical treatment occurred in November 1945 when he had a bout of malaria, but his first psychiatric treatment came in 1962 when his local medical officer wrote to the Repatriation Commission:

> Herewith Mr ... who states he is entitled to treatment for nerves and headaches under Repat. I treat his wife and family and I am writing to you about Mr ... as he is always belting them up. His wife has left him for a week to try to bring him to his senses about it.
>
> I feel he requires psychiatric treatment before we are faced with a tragedy in the home. He volunteers he has two beers a day. Have given him some amytal to take in the meantime.[12]

The stated purpose on his admission form was to investigate 'vaso vagal turns', which are vascular restrictions through the vagal (neck) area resulting in dizziness, blackouts, and fainting. At the Rockingham Psychiatric Centre he had a number of investigations including EEG, x-ray and psychometry. This psychometry included a Thematic Apperception Test, which led to a conclusion that under his brash exterior he was actually insecure and had 'quite genuine disturbance'. The main outcome of the psychiatric assessment was that there was no organic basis for his symptoms, and the diagnosis of vaso vagal turns was changed to 'inadequate personality'. The examining psychiatrist decided that he had anxiety hysteria, and that his 20 per cent pension entitlement was 'generous'.

He was discharged, but the treatment appeared not to have produced a lasting effect because he was re-admitted in July 1963 in a very aggressive and abusive state. Again his complaints were somatic, with 'headaches and nerves in the stomach', and he was observed as being 'tense and irritable'. He had also been gambling and drinking, and working only spasmodically. On top of this, he had been self-medicating on his wife's sedatives. This time he was prescribed 50 mg Largactil, 100 mg pentobarb and 200 mg sodium amytal (a short-acting barbiturate often used in front-line sedation in World War Two). He had no recollection of his violence, which suggests that he may have been experiencing some type of fugue state. In August he was described as a 'typical psychopath' exhibiting antisocial behaviour 'which will not easily respond to treatment'. Treatment, apart from the drug regimen, consisted of occupational and social therapy. It was observed that he worked 'enthusiastically in the carpentry shop', but was 'boisterous' and that he easily antagonised instructors and other inmates.

It was here that he experienced the control that could be achieved with the new generation of anti-psychotic drugs:

At a medical examination on 5 May 1959, he was noted to be a tense, nervy type. In 1962, a psychiatrist advised that the member's disability should be more correctly described as an anxiety hysteria. A recommendation was made that the member's disability be amended to psychopathic personality and this action was taken on 22 November 1962. It has now been advised that the member's disability should not be described as a psychopathic personality as the condition is a chronic anxiety disorder. It therefore appears that the decision made on 22 November 1962 was based on false evidence and I will review it under Section 31(4) of the Repatriation Act.

The determination of the Repatriation Board of 14 January 1957 as amended by the decision of the Repatriation Board of 22 November 1962, is amended to read "chronic anxiety disorder" in lieu of "psychopathic personality" with effect from 11 February 1986, being the date of my decision. The change in description of the disability will not however affect the rate of pension being paid in respect of the disability.

Mr [redacted] lodged a claim on 18 September 1978 for stress angina and this was diagnosed as coronary insufficiency with angina pectoris. On 9 March 1979 a Repatriation Board determined that it was not related to his service. The member lodged an application to the Veterans' Review Board on 29 July 1985 for review of this decision.

In the case of R.G. [redacted] (AAT June 1980) it was considered that there is a relationship between ischaemic heart disease and anxiety state. In view of this opinion, I will review the decision of 9 March 1979 under the provisions of Section 31(1) of the Repatriation Act.

Incapacity resulting from coronary insufficiency with angina pectoris, now to be described as atherosclerotic heart disease, is accepted under Section 101 of the Repatriation Act from 29 January 1985, being a date six months prior to receipt of the member's application, as provided by Sections 107VZB(1)(b) and 31(1) of the Repatriation Act.

I am now required to determine the extent of the member's service-related incapacity. On 16 September 1985 a Delegate of the Repatriation Commission assessed his incapacity resulting from his nervous condition and his tinea both feet at sixty per cent of the General Rate with effect from 8 January 1985, and I see no reason to alter that assessment.

Section of 'Reasons for Pension Determination' 1986: Lawrie

> Any time if you started to get a bit excited – up goes your dosage ... They used to have a bit of a get-together. They had a bit of a dance amongst the nurses and the family. You get on the dance floor and start skipping around and get a bit excited. After the dance is over you line up for your cocoa and your pills. And you come to so-and-so, and oh, 'Mr H. 250 extra for you tonight. This is Largactil', and all that sort of thing. That fixed you. Quietened you down. You got a bit excited – they really stick it in. They would give you a needle, if the drugs weren't quietening you down.

Lawrie was discharged with the diagnosis of psychopathic personality and took up self-employment in building but continued to return regularly for treatment until 1968. He periodically experienced blackouts, worked irregularly and was still aggressive, although this seemed to moderate, possibly because of the continued prescription of Largactil. By the end of 1968 he was considered to be 'going along fairly well' and had 'no specific problems.[13]

Somatic symptoms continued to emerge, and in October 1978 he was again admitted for investigation of chest pains. His examining physician noted that he had a 'history of nervous state'. No serious abnormality was detected but angina pectoris was diagnosed. This diagnosis of stress angina, according to his examining physician, could not be attributed to his war stress.

> I have examined the service history relating to the member. None of the events which occurred during war service could have caused or contributed to the incapacity claimed by the member.

By 1979 this diagnosis had changed to 'coronary insufficiency', characterised by chest pains. In 1985 he was again examined for 'nerves, anxiety and chest pains'. In this assessment it was noted that he had 'returned from the war in a sorry state'. This was the first time anyone had acknowledged the effect of the war on Lawrie, but it was still not attributed as the cause of his problems. On 16 January 1985 his diagnosis was modified to 'explosive personality, anxiety angina and untreated hypertension'. His blackouts, which had first appeared during wartime, were again noted but not explained. Lawrie was not happy with the psychiatric label and requested to have the psychopathic personality diagnosis removed. A change was made to 'chronic anxiety disorder' in November 1985. The medical report relating to this was lost, but there was a letter from a senior officer stating how stressful the New Guinea campaign had been. This was the only mention of his war experience on any official documentation. In February 1986, just before Lawrie turned 65, his pension entitlement was increased to 100 per cent.

His symptoms and treatments continued to be physically oriented, but there remained an element of mystery. His physical symptoms were not simply passed off as hysterical – he had certainly developed serious illnesses – but he often displayed unusual behaviour. Sometimes diagnostic tests sparked off severe psychological reactions, and in many situations he still experienced anxiety and fainting spells.

At one investigation he panicked when entering an MRI machine:

> Cause when he come in I said, 'Listen, I don't have to go through that MRI scan again do I? I'm not going because I refuse. That was what sent me off. I got all panic attacks and that. Finish up I had to ask them to give me a needle one day [going into the machine]'.
>
> I said, 'I'm not very happy in here'. The first time, I don't feel good, and I said I'd probably be right. I had been in it before a fair while back. Anyhow they stopped the second time and they had to drag me out and put the gas on me.

The heart surgery, although bringing physical relief, did not relieve his psychological disturbance and he remained troubled. Lawrie does not believe that the medical profession has been able to help with his problems:

> I know you have got to have them [doctors]. You have to have someone to sign the death certificates. But they are a closed shop … if I ever write a book I'll be opening up. I don't care a bugger what they do to me because they haven't proved anything at all to me that they know what they are doing.

By 1996 he had a further carotid artery blockage and underwent angioplasty surgery. Psychiatric terminology and investigation was no longer a consideration. At my last contact with him in August 1999 he was not as disturbed by dreams or nightmares as he had been in 1995. He was sleeping well and becoming only mildly upset when relating war experiences. He had decided to 'throw away the pills' and was exploring a range of healthy alternatives, including massage, touch healing, hypnosis and diet. His daughter confirmed this improvement and reported that he had made an almost perfect recovery from what had been diagnosed by his doctor as a stroke. Lawrie mellowed a lot in later life, but despite a very good relationship with him his daughter could still remember some of the scars from her early experiences in the family:

> I remember as a little girl of five being very afraid. He was very violent. He would switch so quickly – I could not second guess him. He treated my mother very badly, he was very cruel and she still has the mental and physical scars. He still has a bit of that switching. Recently he came to stay and was having trouble with the electric blanket. I went in to help him and I saw that *look*, as though you were not there. [14]

Lawrie was keen to demonstrate that he had made a full recovery. He was determined not to be placed in a nursing or rest home and to avoid the fate of many of his mates:

> Better off letting them die as they are. Look how big all these places [aged hostels] are getting now with all the respites and what have you. That's all they are. They are only knacker['s] yards for people, and I could see … I call in from time to time at Rosebud [institution]. They even put fruit out at the table for me. They are that pleased to see me, but all the ones I know there personally you can see them going down, like coming down a stairway, one step at a time. Most of them are at the bottom – I don't know if that's the way to put it or not. Yeah so I'm convinced, maybe I'm a bit hard on a couple of them.

One key question is whether his anxiety, fainting spells, agitation, drinking and aggression can in any way be explained by what happened to him during his war service. Forensically it is impossible to give a definitive answer to this question. In his own story he does make a connection: he clearly accounts for his disturbed life by referring to the order to shoot the Japanese soldier. He also sustained a head injury. There is no record that he used this story or the injury to gain entitlement for pension or argue a case for compensation. His trauma story was firmly a part of his narrative at least as far back as 1982. Clearly he was a man with serious psychic pain and most probably undetected organic injury.

There are a number of assertions that can be made on the basis of evidence: he sustained a head injury that might have accounted for persistent disturbance and experience of pain; he retained a firmly embedded, unresolved traumatic memory that could certainly account for nightmares and most probably for anxiety and guilt; this traumatic memory could also account for his drinking behaviour as a form of self-medication until 1962. The most significant feature of his entire interaction with the psychiatric world was that the effect of war on Lawrie's mental and physical health does not seem to have been seriously addressed. It may have been in some of the group programs at Rockingham, but these are not recorded in his medical history.

Delayed trauma: unlocking traumatic memory [15]

The phenomenon of problems that had not been identified during war service surfacing later is dramatically shown in the case of Reg, who died in 1976. His story has been constructed from two distinct narrative sources; firstly, administrative and medical records held by the Repatriation Commission, and secondly, in the account given by his widow. The medical files contain summaries of his encounters with the medical system from his entry into the army until his death, and contain useful biographical detail and a dramatic record of his deterioration over time. In this medical version he is a recipient of treatment and must conform to the criteria for treatment and receive that treatment in the manner designated by the agency. In this he becomes an object to be examined and treated according to certain requirements. Many different writers contribute to the text – local medical officers, admission officers, administrators, physicians, social workers and psychiatrists. The texts record his medical treatment during wartime and his various contacts with the Repatriation Commission between 1945 and 1975.

The medical story begins when Reg enlisted in June 1940 at the age of 31. At enlistment he stated that he had never had a nervous breakdown, shell shock or neurasthenia. He was physically sound and a strong man of 12 stone (approximately 75 kg), and 5 foot 7 inches in height (170 cm). Reg served in all New Guinea campaigns of the 2/27th Battalion, including the Owen Stanley Ranges and Gona, and was discharged as a sergeant in May 1945, having served 853 days overseas and 771 days in Australia. He was treated on two occasions for malaria, a common complaint, in January and July 1943. The first serious medical intervention was for a gunshot wound in the left calf sustained in October 1943 during the

Ramu Valley campaign. He did 'not receive surgical treatment until about 60 hours later when wound was offensive; discharging pus and bubbles escaping from wound; was in hospital for 17 weeks'. He never regained full mobility and was unable to stand for long periods or march. In the examination for reclassification on 4 November 1944 the RMO noted that he had a 'good record' [i.e. he was a good soldier] and had no abnormality apart from the scarring of his left leg. It was recommended that he be returned to civilian life and do no more marching.

Reg was discharged in May 1945 with a medical classification of B2, meaning he was unsuitable for service as a result of gunshot wounds. He had previously (22 February 1945) been declared by a Medical Board to be unfit for further service because of residual aches and pain in his left leg. He was left with a 'large dog-leg scar' over the upper half of the left calf. He was considered to have a 10 per cent 'incapacity in the general labour market from his disability'. There was no mention of mental strain. He was granted eligibility for treatment for any recurrence of malaria, and was subsequently treated at the Repatriation General Hospital on 1 May 1945 for that condition.

There is a gap in the story between discharge and his marriage in 1949 to his second wife, who is the main informant in this story. He had previously married at the age of 16 before he enlisted, and fathered three children in that marriage. That marriage ended early in the war. There was nothing on his Repatriation file, even though there are indications that he was having difficulties in the early post-war years.

Reg's second wife married again after divorcing Reg, but her story indicated that she still loved him and was sad that they had not been able to work things out. She had known him as a neighbour before the war, so she could make a comparison between his pre-war and post-war condition. She acknowledged, for example, that he did 'like a drink' before she married him, and she later learned that his father, a World War One veteran, was a heavy drinker, but she did not have a concern about his drinking behaviour at the time. He started drinking heavily after 1951, and the struggle with his drinking and unreliability went on for many years.

She was aware from the beginning that he was somewhat disturbed. Her narrative gradually unravels the possible cause of his disturbance:

> He was a nervous wreck when I met him. There were times when he had problems at work and he would get uptight. If he had any problems he would go away for half an hour and forget it all and be himself. Once he had the accident [1951] he could not even talk with me. Only when he went to ANZAC Day and talked with his mates would he come home and talk to me. It was one of these conversations when he felt like talking and he told me about this friend whom he had to shoot. And that was behind it all. This is just what you see afterwards. At the time I did not know where to turn. He would be lovely one day and next day he would be impossible. When he got really bad he would pack up and go away for six months. He had a terrible life and I realised it more later. He was a lovely man and was very well liked but he was … two people. It was disappointing to me the treatment he received in Repat. I battled so hard to get him there [1952].

She maintained that Reg's troubles began after a vehicle accident in 1951. This was not recorded on his repatriation medical file, but his admissions for treatment for non-physical symptoms did occur a few months after this event. She recalled that:

> Three months after T was born we were happy. The weather was good and we'd planned to go ... he was a cricketer you see, and we planned to go on this cricket picnic. Reg went on his own, and he had a flat tray top vehicle at the time and being so wet the water got into the works and they had trouble starting it. So one of the young lads stayed behind to give him a push, which meant they had three in the front instead of two and coming down from ... it was up at National Park ... coming down the hills of Belair they overturned.
>
> Now I don't know how our marriage would have been if it hadn't have been for this incident but for two years afterwards, well for years afterwards, he vomited every time he put his feet to the ground. It was not for two years later that this young lad that stayed behind to give them a push came to stay with us one week-end and it was then that I heard about the accident. I hadn't heard about it before. Reg didn't remember anything about it. He was concussed and he went under the steering wheel and through the windscreen and that injury I'm sure is the cause of all his troubles. It brought the war back to him, and he would get very quiet, and he was able to control it to a point. From that time on Reg was different.

Subsequently, Reg began to drink more, and on the outside, he was just a man who drank too much. His wife recalled that his behaviour changed and believed that this was related to an experience in New Guinea, which had become locked away in his memory and was released by the head injury:

> I reckon we had shares in the pub, and this is where the trouble started. He could control the drink before the accident. He always did like a drink but having had concussion, people can't drink any more, one or two drinks and after that you see the change in them, their eyes and everything, it was definitely a brain injury.
>
> But that seemed to be when his nerves got bad that he had to drink to over-come it; that's what it seemed to me.

It emerged that the memory was of a very distressing incident:

> Well during the war experience – it was in PNG somewhere – the Japanese were right behind them and it must have been a pretty bad period and the men were being shot all around him and this one young fellow was so badly shot that they couldn't take him because he would have died anyway but they couldn't leave him there to be tortured. So it was up to the captain to finish him and he just couldn't do it so Reg did. Only a couple of times he got down to talking about it and he could always see that man's eyes looking at him.

As the alcohol took over, life became very difficult for the new family:

> Yes, [our son] was only 18 months old when we came here, and Reg worked really hard and we were really happy for two years and then probably his nerves got the better of him. And he was working seven days a week, which I was not happy about, to help us, and I think it was too much for him and at that stage he would

> have been fortyish and having the war years which added to his life. He would have breakdowns and he wouldn't give in, he would keep going instead of having a rest – he was very determined. But then he met up with a young fellow and he took him to his home and that is where the trouble started again because they'd have the wine there. Every Sunday he would go there in the morning at about ten o'clock and I wouldn't see him till about eight or nine at night and he wouldn't have any money left in his pocket. They would just get him drunk and take his money and then he would blame me that I'd used his money.

His problems became so bad that Reg's wife sought help from the Repatriation Commission, and he was assessed at the Outpatients Clinic at Keswick on 20 May 1952. The case sheet indicated that he was entitled only to treatment for malaria, since his anxiety state had not been initially accepted as war-related. This changed after his examination by a psychiatrist, who stated:

> Sleeps v. poorly and dreams a lot – has nightmares and wakes up in a sweat. Has frequent headaches. Becomes upset over trifles and work gets him down; has no appetite. This is an anxiety state that he says was present in New Guinea and subsequently, but is becoming worse. I think his condition is connected with war service.[16]

As a result the Deputy Commissioner for Repatriation approved that Reg's anxiety state be accepted as due to war service. He then had three conditions accepted – malaria, gunshot wound and anxiety state. In September he was 'struck off the Out Patients Record' and assigned for treatment from his general practitioner, who was an approved Local Medical Officer. The reason for this was not clear, but it could have been that he did not like the treatment in the hospital setting, which was indicated by his wife in her statement.

This plan for treatment by the general practitioner did not work, and his wife wrote to the Commission after the first contact seeking further help. In her letter to the Repatriation Hospital she stated:

> [He] is the type of man who will not report sick while he is able to get about and he certainly did his share at the war and I feel the only hope for him to get well is to have some treatment. I had an appointment with Dr F last Friday 20 May. He gave me some tablets for him but they didn't agree with him. The following day he was worse than he has ever been and violent; which is not his nature.
>
> We have been very happy together but now I just can't say or do anything to please him and will have to leave him and break up the home if something is not done.[17]

Reg continued to have difficulties and his general practitioner requested that he be admitted for treatment and psychiatric examination again on 15 April 1953. On 17 April the admitting officer at the outpatients' clinic noted that he 'has great difficulty with sleeping – wakes about 3 am and cannot go to sleep again. Also complains of tenseness and fatigue. A carpenter – can manage pretty well'. The same psychiatrist assessed him again, and after noting that 'it is a great effort for him to carry out a day's work,' and 'has very little energy', recommended that he be admitted for sub coma insulin treatment. This was reported to have commenced on 11 May 1953, but his wife maintains that he never received this treatment.

The notes for 13 May 1953 add some biographical material as well as a clinical picture. Reg was described as a 'depressed bald man who began to cry during an interview on discussing war experiences'. At this stage he would have been aged 44 and it was noted he had come from a happy family of eight children and was 'now in a happy marriage'. The notes reinforced the earlier report that for some time he had 'complained of depression with crying fits, inability to concentrate, restlessness, insomnia with nightmares of the war, anorexia and fatigue'.

The psychiatrist was interested to hear of his war experiences, but on 19 May Reg was still 'lachrymose', 'unwilling to discuss his war experiences' and refused to be treated with methedrine.[18] Despite this he was still considered a 'good type', but with a 'neurasthenic type of reaction to some suppressed trauma'. Clearly there was some attempt to understand his dysfunction in terms of previous war experience. By 29 May he had gained half a stone (probably as a result of the sub coma insulin treatment) 'and is symptomatically much better, but still has much repressed material'. His wife's opinion was that the specialist was not competent and did not understand either her or her husband.

> [T]his is something I'd like to tell about. One stage he was really bad and I did talk him into going to Daws Road to the doctor – in fact I think it was our doctor I spoke to – and he sent him to Daws Road. We were unfortunate the doctor in charge of that ward was a Dr L. ... But he was hopeless and he just asked me in to interview him. He interviewed Reg first then called me in on another occasion and all he talked about was sex; I think he must have thought every soldier was a sex maniac, he was terrible.
>
> Yes, he was a psychiatrist, and Reg just wouldn't speak; he wouldn't answer his questions because he was so rude and he got so frustrated in the end and he said 'Right, take your wife out to lunch', and that was our interview.
>
> I only had the one [interview] with him, but Reg wouldn't go back to Daws Road again, and you see this was our problem.[19]

Over the next two years Reg's condition deteriorated and the degree of sympathy offered by medical specialists seemed to diminish. A significant shift in diagnosis and treatment occurred in 1955. After a period of in-patient treatment Reg was discharged to his Local Medical Officer with a diagnosis of chronic alcoholism, which he had 'no desire to give ... up'. The psychiatrist admitted that in his opinion 'chronic alcoholism is secondary to his anxiety and (reluctantly) I recommend payment of sustenance'. He was discharged on 11 August 1955 and did not reappear on record until 1963. During this time Reg worked erratically in the country. He could no longer support his wife and child:

> Yes, he'd be there [in the country] 18 months or two years and come home and he'd be a different man and oh yes we're going to be right ... 12 months sometimes six months ... it was all on again, and then he'd go away again. In the early stages he'd send me money but then when he got really bad they wouldn't have

> him back at **** because he started fighting when he was drunk. So he got a job at Katherine and I didn't hear from him for six months.

The heavy drinking eventually affected Reg's physical health and the next recorded admission to the Repatriation Hospital was for stomach and liver complaints. No psychiatric treatment was offered, but when he was sent home he was not vomiting and was 'less jaundiced'.

A crisis in their marriage led to their separation. His wife had been able to tolerate Reg's behaviour for many years, but the turning point came when he became violent for the first time with their son. She left him in 1965:

> Well we sold the house and I still tried again by taking a flat but then because we had a little bit of money he just wouldn't work and he drank all the time and then he started to abuse my son. They were so fond of each other this was the one reason why I couldn't part earlier and my son was 16 by this time. This particular night Reg had been drinking all day. My son came home from school at about five o'clock that night and heard the way his father was speaking to me and he said 'Look, leave Mum alone,' and Reg just turned around and gave him a terrible smack across the face. Next day my son said, 'Mum we can't live with this'. But I'd lived with it for 16 years.

During the separation, out of desperation his wife arranged for Reg to be admitted to the public mental hospital at Hillcrest. It was then under new management and was beginning to experience the benefit of the reforms to the mental health system introduced by Dr Bill Cramond. At this time the Medical Superintendent was Dr Bill Salter, who had supervised the opening up of the hospital, made possible by the availability of the major tranquillisers.[20] Salter had introduced Alcoholics Anonymous as the primary treatment program in the hospital:

> Bill Salter was a good chap. I interviewed him once and he said that in years to come they'd be able to tell a child of eight or nine if they were going to be an alcoholic but they can only help them if they want to be helped. And we had sold the home by this time and I really thought Reg was going to try.

Reg was admitted to Hillcrest Hospital on 29 July 1965 at the age of 56. Treatment consisted of abstinence, detoxification, supervised care and counselling. His medical record indicates that he was often observed to be 'very confused and tremulous', and Reg stated that he had suffered 'from nerves for years', and that alcohol had helped him with this. He had had a normal childhood, had 'got on well with both parents', there were no alcoholics in his family, and he had 'no neurotic childhood traits'. At this stage he was living in the country by himself. War service was noted as part of his history, but there was no mention of any distressing events. He was still in receipt of a 50 per cent Repatriation pension. He was once happily married but 'drink affected it'. Most of the report is about his drinking behaviour, and his good intentions of changing his life.

His final stay at Hillcrest in 1971 did not produce any positive change. Instead, his health deteriorated, and other medical problems developed. He was admitted to the RGH after a wound from an attack by a dog turned septic. By this time he was working on a pastoral station in the north of the state, and it was noted he had a 'long history of anxiety state, with recent loss of confidence and exacerbation of alcoholism'.

The Repatriation Commission was again involved in December 1974 when Reg was referred to the social worker for assistance after he was evicted from his boarding house. The medical officer stated in his referral that 'medical investigation is now complete and his problems are now mainly social'.

The end came on 27 August 1976 when, at the age of 67, Reg died as a result of burns received in a fire in the workman's cottage he occupied on a property in a small country town. By this time he was subsisting on a pension and was cut off from family and friends. He had been drinking and had fallen against an electric radiator around midday on a Friday afternoon. His former wife recalled the occasion:

> He fell on a radiator that night and about five days later his son found out where I was and contacted me and I had all the wedding arrangements [for her second marriage] for the next week. It was terrible. So he was buried on the Tuesday and I was being married on the Wednesday – it was a terrible time.

Reg's life story is a tragedy that had begun to unfold two years after the war, after he sustained a head injury in a motor vehicle accident. He had been a competent person in many areas of his life until he was wounded. He was a skilled worker and able to manage building projects independently. In the early days of marriage he was a good husband. His wife's narrative about his and their lives is much softer than the medical files. In the latter his symptoms and dysfunction are the sole focus. No psychiatric intervention worked, and his life became progressively worse. There was some early attention to his traumatic experience in New Guinea, but this was never a primary focus of his treatment.

It is important to report on the final outcome of the story. I re-interviewed Reg's wife in 1998. The only change was that she reported, on reflection, that she had known something was not quite right with Reg from the moment she met him. She had learned about war-damaged veterans when she had been nursing in the Repatriation Hospital between 1940 and 1945. She was in a transition ward where all soldiers were placed before allocation to a special treatment ward. A number of these men were psychologically damaged. Even though she was not involved in their treatment, she did observe them and realised that they were different from other patients. She saw the same anxiety, moodiness, nightmares and disturbance in Reg when they were first married. Until the accident this was manageable, but after the head injury he got progressively worse until his tragic death.

Reg's wife had never reconciled herself to the manner of his death. She had worried for years that she did not know the state of his grave or the exact circumstances of his death. A short while before I was in final contact with her, she had accompanied her current husband on a tour to a country town where Reg had been buried. She had never seen his grave, and had imagined that it would be uncared for and overgrown. She had often woken in the night worrying about this. She visited the local cemetery and she was able to find Reg's grave and see that it was in excellent condition with a headstone displaying his name and serial number. This allowed her to close one part of the final chapter on her former husband. Since that time she has not worried about Reg and no longer becomes disturbed at night:

> Whenever I thought of Reg I had that picture of a grave. Now I have hardly worried about it since. Until I knew where he was buried I could not be happy. Now I don't worry. I was so thrilled. All these years I have not been able to shed a tear over Reg dying. But immediately I saw that I just broke down. From then on I have been all right. I wrote to the mayor and sent him a cheque for the rose garden. I was so happy someone was looking after it.

There was one more issue to resolve: the circumstances of Reg's death. The coroner's report of 27 August 1976, which I obtained, revealed that there had been five witnesses to his last days: the local police officer, who confirmed the identify of the body; the owner of the property where Reg was living; an employee who first assisted Reg after the fire; the medical officer who rendered assistance and pronounced him dead; and the ambulance officer who attended him and witnessed his death in transit to hospital. It was important for his wife to know that he had not been alone in his last conscious hours. The medical officer reported that Reg was extensively burned and there was a moderate smell of alcohol on his breath. Intravenous saline was administered in the ambulance but he became restless and died before reaching Adelaide. The police officer confirmed there were 'no suspicious circumstances'.[21] This report allowed the widow to place the final piece in the jigsaw and reconcile herself to his death.

Stories like that of Reg show how the problems of war were transformed into a private individual pathology. This individual pathologising was enhanced by the general culture surrounding war and mental health. Apart from a minor flurry of public concern recorded in Chapter One, which was soon dismissed by the RSL and the Repatriation Department, there was no public discussion on war-related mental health problems. Any individual problems were managed privately by experts within the Repatriation Department. Reg's story had been confined to the medical and administrative files, which were hidden behind the veil of confidentiality until 1998. His wife had nowhere to explore her concerns, or offer her explanations of his problems. She thus became marginalised in the treatment process.

John: You don't know what war is like until you have been there [22]

The story of John's experience at Kokoda has been recorded publicly, but the details of his life after discharge are not generally known. Even in 1995 John became extremely distressed watching a replay of footage of the Damien Parer film

REPATRIATION GENERAL HOSPITAL, SPRINGBANK.

Writer: PJR   R. No. ▇▇▇   C. No. ▇▇▇

REPORT ON DISCHARGE.

Ward: 13/16   Date Admitted: 11.5.53

Entitled to Treatment for: G.S.W. LEFT CALF. MALARIA. ANXIETY STATE.

NAME: ▇▇▇▇▇▇   Reg. No. SX▇▇▇   Unit 2/27 Bn.   Age: 44

11.5.53 ADMIT I.P. : ANXIETY STATE.

Weight on Admission : 12 stone 13½ lbs.

Urine : S.G. 1010
React. Acid
Colour Lemon
Alb. -
Sug. -

RECEIVED

S.C.I. commenced.

13.5.53 This man came from a happy family - the middle of 8 children. Prior to enlistment he was a carpenter and at the age of 16 he married a girl aet 26 who was unfaithful before he left for the Middle East. On return he divorced her.
He saw all the campaigns through except Tarakan as a rifleman.
On return to Australia he married a girl 7 years younger than himself and has one child, a happy marriage.
He is a carpenter and has his own home.
However he has for an indefinite period of years complained of depression with crying fits, inability to concentrate, restlessness insomnia with nightmares of the war, anorexia and fatigue.

O.E. : Depressed bald man who began to cry during the interview on discussing war experiences.
Eyes - N.A.D.
Teeth - N.A.D.
Tongue - N.A.D.
B.P. - 140/90.
Heart - N.A.D.
Lungs - N.A.D.
Abdomen - N.A.D.
Reflexes - N.A.D.
G.S.W. calf left leg.

Summary : Anxiety state. S.C.I. and perhaps methedrine later.

19.5.53 Refused methedrine. Is unwilling to discuss war experiences.
Lachrymose.
A neurasthenic type of reaction to some suppressed trauma.
A good type, I think.

29.5.53 Discharged to O.P.C. To see me at 2.30 p.m. on 1.7.53.
Unfit to Work 2 weeks.
Diagnosis : Anxiety State.
I would continue to assess his disabilities at 50%.
He has gained half a stone and is symptomatically much better, but still has much repressed material.

Sgd. P.S. ▇▇▇▇

Appt. Dr. ▇▇▇ O.P.C. 1.7.53, 2.30 p.m. Form 135 completed.

A.B. ANDERSON
MEDICAL SUPERINTENDENT.

Discharge Report for Reg, Repatriation General Hospital May 1953 of the Kokoda campaign, in which he features struggling up the track. Paradoxically, he does not avoid talking about his war experience. He said he would cooperate in the study if there were some chance of helping someone else. In a break in one of our interviews his wife stated he would have nightmares after I had gone.

At the time of his first interview John had survived two strokes, and had been diagnosed with chronic airflow limitation, gastro-oesophagal reflux, hiatus hernia, coronary, cerebral and abdominal atherosclerosis, and anxiety hysteria with digestive symptoms. He listed 14 different medications that were currently being prescribed, one of which was for depression. None had removed the haunting memories of war. Memories always disturbed: 'If I sit and don't read and do nothing things come creeping back.'

He was on 100 per cent entitlement for a war pension, which was still under review by the Veterans' Affairs department. He had been recently diagnosed with post-traumatic stress disorder according to the DSM-IIIR classification. He was still disturbed by his experiences, which have haunted him since 1943 when he was evacuated from Port Moresby with a B2 health classification (unfit for overseas duty) after severe bouts of malaria.

John was born in Melbourne in 1921. His parents were Greek and his mother was very supporting and loving. His early life was dominated by a number of incidents, including the bombing of an inner city club that his father managed. His father was injured, and with no work struggled through the Depression with four young children. John was about eight years old when his 12-month-old brother died. His other brother died at the age of five from diphtheria.

John was prepared to reveal more detail about his experiences than many other veterans, even though their recollection disturbed him. He was with 37th Militia Battalion in 1941 and when they called for volunteers for the 39th he 'jumped at it', at the age of 20 heading off to Port Morseby, which he thought was somewhere in North Queensland. The Japanese had been bombing Moresby fairly consistently from February 1942, and, having had minimal training, John and his battalion were soon under air attack:

> Some blokes used to go to pieces during air raids. One bloke used to shake like a leaf – he later had his throat cut at Kokoda. His mother wrote to me before we left there. She wanted his scapulars. I wrote back and said all that stuff went back to divisional HQ. After the war a bloke wanted to see the mother but I could not do it. Today I regret it. When we wrote home we would put a little note in each other's letters. Our mothers would get together and share news. Colin got killed and they went to see her and she was all broken up – he was her only son. Those mothers went through hell.

One night in May 1942 in a hastily dug trench John cried himself to sleep in the arms of one of his mates after receiving a letter from home with a clipping of his father's death notice from the *Sun* newspaper. His father had actually died two months earlier but the family had withheld the information. His father had been reading about the war in New Guinea, and after folding the paper, called his wife and died in her arms.

There was little time to reflect on this as over the next few months John was engaged in two major battles – on the Kokoda Trail and at Gona. Memories of that time still haunt him. His narratives are not presented in the order in which the battles happened but are placed somewhere between May 1942 and January 1943. The substance of these recollections can clearly be substantiated from other accounts:

> Bloody Gona [November 1942] was terrible. These cows [Japanese] were dug in and they were making us do frontal assaults. All coconut palms had been blown to pieces. I was never religious but there was a big white cross, it was the only thing that did not have a bullet hole in it.
>
> I heard young blokes crying in the night for their mothers. I saw men losing arms and legs. I knew that we would be killed if we were caught. Our company commander got killed the first day, colonel got killed a few days later. In those days we were not issued with digging implements. Only the padre had a shovel to bury people.
>
> The only thing that would worry me was the chaplain. Nobby Earl would come along and say, there are two blokes down and I've got to go and bury them. He would say 'You will do …'. What could you do – I had to.

In the early part of the New Guinea campaign soldiers were faced with difficult choices. One of John's mates was ordered to shoot a wounded Japanese:

> I was there at the time – I did not see them kill him. Smoky and Ted Morrison were looking at this poor bugger. He was still alive but he wouldn't have lasted as he was puffing out bubbles of blood and he looked to be a young fellow of 18 or 19.[23]

And there were occasions of tension:

> I had to do a very bad patrol behind Japanese lines at Isurava to do a panoramic survey. I would carry a rifle and a pistol. Off we went and we finished up behind Deniki which was in Japanese hands. When we got there we had to wait but the clouds had come in. I drew this stupid thing – it is in the War Memorial now. I could hear the Japanese behind, talking, chopping wood and all this. It was a bit dicey.

The man who had been with him was shot the next day.

The closest call for the battalion was at Isurava when the 39th was severely depleted, almost out of ammunition and supplies and was the only unit confronting the Japanese:

> I remember getting out of Isurava. Phil Gough went down to fill a water bottle and crawled back saying 'They're all gone'. All I could see was boxes of stores scattered all around. So we decided to clear out. The only way we could find our way was hanging on to signal wire. We caught up and found out that the colonel thought he could find a better killing field. We stood there and then the 2/14th came in. That was a shambles. All sorts of blokes. There were something like two

or three hundred wounded there. There was this wounded bloke in the hut and making a hell of a noise. In the morning they carried him up the track.

These buggers would blow a bugle and up they'd come in waves. Before that they would sing this bloody war song. All the hairs on the back of your neck would stand up. We used the bayonet too. You've got to get pretty close to a bloke to stick a bayonet in him.

We were told at Menari by the colonel, 'When you go back there don't talk about it don't tell anyone.' We struck troops coming back and one bloke said 'Don't go back there, it is bloody hell.' You don't know what war is like until you have been there.

With experiences like this in his mind, John returned to Australia but the early years were clouded by drinking and bouts of malaria:

I just couldn't settle down. I was drinking a lot in those days. Any money that would come my way I'd say 'Righto, we'll blow this.' I would find a couple of mates and live it up for a while. Until I met this one – quietened me down a bit.

You were a stranger among people. I was in Swanston Street one day shaking with malaria and no one stopped to ask if I needed help. I think most of them were a bit crackers anyway.

Blokes like Morris – he was in a bad way. When he was getting married he went into town looking for 39 blokes to form a guard of honour.

Most time you would talk about stupid things. You were not interested in your future. I know that there were a few blokes who were smarter than others. Like Vic Austin – he decided to go to university – he had it up here [head]. Most of us blokes, to count up to ten you'd have to take your boots off.

Life went on. On the outside John went about getting married, settling into a job, starting a family and establishing a home. None of these responsibilities made life any easier. John met his wife in 1948. She recalled that 'He seemed quite alright then; then later on he got very sick and got the shakes.' She admitted that he was difficult to live with for most of their marriage. John acknowledged some of this disturbance:

I used to work and support the family the best I could and spent a lot of time working on the house. On Saturday I would say, I'm off. Now my daughter is starting to realise that it was not me that was going bonkers. I got them to read the psychiatrist's report.

His wife was aware of his troubles from the early days of marriage:

He was pretty bad when we got married. I would go into a shop and when I would come out he would be shaking like a leaf. They [the veterans] don't talk to us at all. When he would go to work you were shaking in your shoes because you did not know how they were going to behave when he got home. The children suffer too.

We did not understand them at all. More or less I would be crying all the time. Because they were so nasty. And you don't understand why. I knew he had nerves.

It's been no marriage at all really. You are like strangers in the house. He would

Members of the 2/27th Battalion salute as they pass the City Hall in King George Square, Brisbane. 8 August 1944

Members of the 2/27th Battalion march in King William Street, Adelaide, on ANZAC Day 1993. [Photo: John Raftery]

> be depressed a terrible lot. I thought about leaving many times. You just think of the children and him and forget all about it.

In later life he still remained a closed book to her. She experienced his sickness and withdrawal, and it was clear that she too was withdrawn and felt helpless:

> It's been terrible. He holds everything in. It would last for three or four days. Life's not worth living sometimes. I just sit and listen. I don't know what's troubling him. The war has never, never really stopped. The older they get the worse it gets. We did not get any help as a family. Wives did not count. You just took it. Mostly the mother who cried. In the last five or six years he has really mellowed. He does what the doctor tells him.

Despite many years of treatment, John had no further insight into his trouble. Medical intervention had brought him only monetary compensation.

> I don't know if I was insane or not. I don't know because no one has told me. I knew I was not quite normal. Up here it never goes away [in the mind]. I can't talk to you [his wife] about that stuff. They [the wives] did not understand – I did not understand myself.

John did not avoid reminders of New Guinea. He returned to Gona in 1967 for the 25th anniversary of the battle. His family urged him to go. He described going back to the battle sites as 'unreal'. Everything was so pleasant and peaceful, but there was still the underlying distress, and the grief and memories surfaced. This may have been a catalyst for John's subsequent, more serious breakdown.

> At that time I was alright – I was on a 20 per cent pension for nerves. But I was coping. I wasn't too bad then. They were old men. They more or less said they had to do what they had to do. The widows upset me – every time I went past they would bow.
>
> I wouldn't have missed it [the re-union] for quids. That was good. The saddest part was in the morning before dawn we would go the cemetery at Bomana. I was thinking, what the hell am I doing here? I was looking at my mates across the aisle. The bus stopped and we got out and they made us fall in – and when the light came there was row after row of headstones. My Adjutant Keith Lovett made a speech. These other blokes were crying like girls. I was amazed he could make a speech.

The second opportunity to return to New Guinea was in 1972 for the 30th anniversary but by that time John was in the 'funny farm'. His wife went in his place as part of her attempt to understand his experience. The course of his breakdown seemed to be progressive: 'I used to get moods and depressions and want to keep to myself.' The crunch came on Christmas Day 1970:

> That's what happened Christmas Day. Before Christmas 1970 I didn't think there was anything wrong with me. Some time after 1967 my brother came down one day and said we are going somewhere and he took me to the outpatients. They sent me to Rockingham and I stayed there for two months. I do know I used to cry a lot ...
>
> I took them bloody capsules – everyone was down in the kitchen laughing and

that and I was by myself and it got to me and I said 'Bugger me'. They then sent me to Heidelberg and the young doctor said 'You tried to commit suicide'. And I said 'Go to buggery'.

John was admitted to Veterans' Affairs Heidelberg hospital, then to the 'real muck farm' at Bundoora where he was placed in a security ward:

> Bundoora – by Christ I would not send my worst enemy there – they locked me up in the cage with others. Jack Boland, when they locked me up my wife told him and he was banging on the door. 'I'll smash this bloody door down. My mate's in there.' I remember saying I did not do it on purpose. They kept me there for 24 hours – that was a real education. There were blokes there who did nothing all day but watch children's' programs and then line up for drugs. My wife got me out of there – released in her charge. There was one bloke there he had come back from Tobruk – they'd done a lobotomy on him. He would be crook forever that bloke. But they didn't know. The First World War blokes, they were in a terrible position. There was no such thing as what the Yanks called battle fatigue.

Embedded in this story of struggle is the bonding with mates from wartime. They would be at hand when things went wrong, as in Bundoora, but also when there was some perceived injustice. When John tried to return to work after he was treated for his mental condition he was rejected by his former employer:

> I've had every drug that the bloody psychiatrists use and nothing seemed to work. I had six shocks. Those bloody shock treatments, that is nothing to laugh about. All I know is after you have had that treatment you are like 'glug'. I had to agree to them – I had no choice. When I got the job with the National Bank I said I will do my utmost to keep away from the nerve hospitals because of the drugs and the bloody stigma. Especially when I went back to my employer the manager said 'We can't have you back here – you could get sick again'. I told some of my [war] mates and they were going to kill this bloke [the manager].

These bonds were forged in New Guinea when his battalion was forced to survive together. John reflected that he probably did not commit himself to the war in New Guinea out of loyalty to his country so much as out of loyalty to his mates: 'Once you were in the battalion you did it for the battalion'.

After Bundoora, he was sent as a day patient to Rockingham where he had been admitted on a previous occasion. Rockingham was not as depressing as Bundoora or Heidelberg but there were still moments of breakdown:

> I was having a shower and all of a sudden I started to cry like a girl and when I went back to the ward blokes said, 'What is the matter', and one bloke said 'Leave him alone' – he knew. I sat on his bed and bloody bawled like a girl until I got over it.

None of the treatment resolved any basic issues, and getting back to normal life after treatment was not easy. John has been admitted to many hospitals, and some of the treatment and exposure to other disturbed people was as bad as the original condition:

> Out of the psychiatric hospitals – Kew was probably the best. If a bloke went off his head they would straitjacket him. It wasn't pleasant. I was on drug after drug and nothing was working – even shock treatment. I was discharged – I was in a mess and I did not know what to do. I had no work. Anyway I saw a doctor and he said would you like to go to Rockingham as a day patient until I got a job at the bank – through the Corps of Legionnaires.
>
> I stayed there but I kept getting crook – the bank was carrying me. The doctor said, you would be better off not working at all. Repat put me on a service pension.

One of John's main motivations throughout his life and a key source of security has been his mates. Some form an unlikely alliance, with little in common other than that experience of war in New Guinea for a little over a year in the 1940s. For example Vic, a former university lecturer in linguistics, and John, who left school in grade eight, are still good mates:

> We used to get together every couple of months. Used to be Jack, Ted, Vic and Mick, and now there is only three. Ted was the bravest man I knew. At Gona he got clobbered through the leg – you could hear his voice above the noise of war.

By 1990 John had been diagnosed with post-traumatic stress disorder. He had found his way through the maze of psychiatric labels and treatment interventions. Fortunately he was spared the early treatments of insulin and glucose and the experimentation of the 1940s and early 1950s. When recommended that he seek treatment in a new clinic established for veterans he said he wanted no more pills or anything that would revive the memory of past treatment. The PTSD diagnosis brought him financial security and helped him make a little sense of his troubled life:

> Sometimes I am walking down the street and something comes back and I say 'Where the hell did that come from'. That's what they call it post-traumatic stress. I had never heard of it until my local doctor told me.

John's latter days have been spent in relative comfort in an RSL nursing home complex, where he has been more comfortable and settled.

4. Hank: ' I have got no regrets' [24]

The story here is told from his widow's perspective. His medical files obtained from the Department of Veterans' Affairs show that he was diagnosed with a 'nervous disorder', which was considered a 'persisting disability', when he was discharged on 30 October 1945, but was considered fit to resume work (Form AAFD2(a), Medical Examination Prior to Discharge). As will be seen, he returned to work in the bank, but he soon masked his problems with alcohol. While continuing to work he had multiple encounters with the Repatriation psychiatric system, as well as a stay in the public Hillcrest Hospital to address his alcohol problems. None of these interventions resolved his problems.

The story of what happened to him on the Kokoda Trail never really emerged. In the final analysis he was recognised as a psychiatric casualty and awarded a part pension, but some of this was posthumous when his widow applied to have his death in 1978 recognised as war related. Even though the primary cause of death was strangulated ventral hernia, she argued the case that he was a disturbed man and that this had contributed to his drinking behaviour and secondary cirrhosis. In the Statement of Claim (Form EL7) his widow articulated the two themes of grief and traumatic memory:

> My husband came home from war service an entirely different man, obsessed with war memories and losses of men from his battalion. As time progressed he became worse. His appetite was poor and he slept badly and then began drinking. This resuted in a deterioration of family life, and much unhappiness.

His mental condition was recognised as part contributor, but the conclusion of the expert review was that:

> The member's death was due to factors attributable to war service. He had had a nervous breakdown from recurrent malaria and hookworm in a personality which could not accept the stress for long in conditions of war.

Furthermore, the review stated that:

> This veteran has died at age 57 years, 32 years after discharge from service in the army in World War Two. He has died from the effects of his accepted disabilities, which to the extent that his 'anxiety state with organic dementia' was made manifest on service, induced the development of liver cirrhosis from alcohol over-indulgence. His service records indicate that he had a good deal of stress during his service in the Middle East and New Guinea, with hookworm and malaria undermining his 'nervous' potential. (Form D206312, May 1978)

Hank was born in 1920. Prior to enlistment he was employed in a bank in Adelaide and had joined the militia. His parents would not let him enlist so he waited till he turned 21. He met his future wife in 1939; she believed that he was too good-natured to have been involved in the violence of war:

> he was wonderful, very attentive and very loving, and that, I think, was a lot of the trouble. That's the personality he was and see all the things that he did, they hit him so badly because it just wasn't his nature and yet you couldn't have kept him away.

They were married in 1943 before Hank went back to New Guinea for the Shaggy Ridge and Markham Valley campaigns. While on the Kokoda Trail Hank had his pack shot off his back. He said little about other things that happened:

> He would say they were good soldiers and what they did and how they used to take all these things for malaria, but he still had it seven times. But mainly it was dates: 'We went into action at Buna ...' and 'We went into action at Shaggy Ridge ...', and 'People don't know what life was like on the Kokoda Trail ...' He didn't carry on about the Middle East, that was different entirely. That was more like a tour; they didn't carry on about that at all.

Hank returned to his job in the bank and there was little sign of anything wrong in the first years:

> He seemed to be pretty well OK then [immediate post-war period] although he was very badly affected. He was a very bad war neurosis ... on the Kokoda Trail the man in front of him or the man behind him was killed, and his own haversack on his back was shot ... and I think that seemed to be the end of him and the autopsy when he died said that he should never have gone to the war because he was very emotional and so it affected him very, very badly. He came back and straight back into the bank because that was his job and they took him back into that and that was at the end of war.

Their first daughter was born in 1945. The family then moved to the country and by the end of his country service they had three children. In 1952 they shifted to another country town, by which time Hank was aged 32. His wife enjoyed living there but between 1952 and 1958 Hank seemed to change. He became more obsessed with the war, appeared to be living in the past, and became more involved with the RSL through building the hall. At that time he started drinking heavily. He became unpredictable and moody when drinking:

> It might have been gradual but it came to a head on the West Coast when they built that RSL hall ... the men would get together and drink and from that he started drinking at home, and I didn't have any problems at Barmera, I really didn't, so I think it could have been gradual but it suddenly came to a head. He was just absolutely wrapped up in building the RSL hall and he used to say, men up there all the time with bricks building the hall and they are so proud of it.

Hank kept his job in the bank even though he was drinking heavily. In 1958 he was transferred to a town closer to the capital city. His wife tried to understand Hank, though the family used to get tired of hearing his wartime experiences. By this time he had been referred to a psychiatrist, and by this time his drinking was beginning to upset the family. His wife had nowhere else to go with the children, having no mother. Hank bought the children presents to compensate after upsetting them:

> He would be just be lost in that little world of his with his memories, but he didn't seem to want to be with his mates ... and, well, he began drinking heavily then and he was an alcoholic and that became very difficult for us because you'd know it's another one of those days when he was just going to go out and he's going to drink ... And with the children he would roar hell out of them. He'd be upset and he'd go and buy them twenty dollars' worth of lollies and presents and things because he knew he'd upset them. And you'd try to say to him, you can't buy people, but he felt so guilty because he upset people so much that life really became pretty difficult, and I think in fact the doctor once told me if it hadn't been that I coped so well I don't know that the children would have.

Hank doted on his son but would upset his girls by stating that money was being wasted on their education. By 1963 he was receiving treatment at the

Northfield Hospital, a civilian hospital that had separate wards for veterans. The strain of managing a difficult husband affected his wife's health and during this time she was diagnosed as having multiple sclerosis. Hank had difficulty coping with and accepting this. His wife turned this into a positive experience and helped found a support group for multiple sclerosis sufferers:

> What was I supposed to do? I had my life as well, and it was a way of me coping and I was seeing people so much worse off than I was but he couldn't think of it that way of course.

Alcohol did not overtly affect Hank's work, and he became a manager in the bank and was transferred to the city. He actually hated his job and would have preferred to be outdoors. It was in the city that Hank and his wife were referred for help at the psychiatric unit in the Repatriation Hospital:

> Well, I did a lot of yelling and screaming. In fact he was under a psychiatrist up the Repat and they asked to see me so I went with him, and they spoke to Hank first and I went in and I said 'I will listen sometimes for two hours and he will just go on and on', and he said to me then 'You've got to yell. You've got to shout. And if you don't you are going to end up with a nervous breakdown'. And so I did then ... I just simply yelled and shouted back, which wasn't exactly good for the kids, but they've grown up well in spite of it. But I suppose I'm pretty strong emotionally, and I know a lot of them didn't cope. I did think mainly for the children I couldn't have left – I had nowhere to go.
>
> I suppose when I lost my mother so young and during the war in 1943, the year we were married, in March ... my father died suddenly in the house and I was on my own and I was only 21, and I had that to cope with ... and I think we learned to cope during the war and I think you find most women of my age are survivors, and I hear people say 'Oh terrible thing for a son to go away on a ship', or their boyfriend or something. You understand how they feel but you know you think when you've been through it and you're stronger for coping with it anyway.

Hank was coping with his job but his drink-related illness caused him to be invalided out of the bank at the age of 47 years. His wife thought he improved a bit, and she made no demands on him. However, a life of retirement only exacerbated his behaviour and symptoms. Hank had nightmares in which his traumatic memory experience were reactivated:

> After years went by the war memories became more vivid and they seemed to prompt these things. Certainly over the years he got worse and worse about the war, but he just couldn't watch that ANZAC march... he would go out the back and he would come in to say something to me and his eyes would fill with tears and he would just walk out again, the minute he could see them marching.

Increasingly he isolated himself from the family and he would not sit down and have a meal with them. His family could not understand the changes in him and received little support from other people; they kept the secret to themselves.

I can put on a brave front. I don't think whether you want to call it pride ... I don't know, but I suppose I just didn't believe in taking the problems out with me, I always thought I could cope and I did.

One time [Hank's brother] caught him in one of these moods and he said 'How do you put up with him', and I said 'Well I just do'. No, I never told a soul. I did say to my brother when he was going on about life ... 'Well, you just wouldn't know, if I could tell you the story of what I've been through I could really shock you all'. But I didn't.

The war continued to eat into Hank's mind and he became bitter about some of his war experiences. This all had an effect on the children, who found it increasingly difficult to invite friends home as they did not know how their father would react.

Hank's health deteriorated progressively and he died a relatively young man. The irony was that after his death his wife's health improved, and she was able to walk instead of using a wheelchair:

I really was quite bad. I even had a wheel chair up till the time Hank died, and from that time I improved ... you see the pressure was gone. The worst thing for MS is stress and tension, and I was living on it, I really was living on it. And people say to me, we can't believe how good you are since Hank died, and I feel terrible when they say that. But it's a fact because suddenly the pressure was gone, the tension was gone and I sent the wheelchair back ... I have a walking stick if I walk any distance, but you can see what I'm like.

Despite all his troubles and distress, Hank's wife described him as a good father. He ran his wife down privately, but praised her to his family. Reflecting on her life, she said she would go through it all again. She loved Hank through the bad times and the good:

I can honestly say I have got no regrets and if I had my time over again I would have still married him. I feel quite sure about that, and for all the bad times I really loved him and we were really very much in love and we had the good times, too. So you take the good with the bad don't you, at least I do. I think, well, it's life.

* * * * *

This chapter ends the account of the lives of men who emerged from the jungles of New Guinea, and is the saddest chapter of the book because it documents the lives of those who suffered most intensely. Their suffering was sometimes exacerbated by medical diagnoses and treatment that did not address their core concerns. Their lives were permanently marked, but this was not openly acknowledged. The marks of war extended to their partners and families, who shared in the conspiracy of silence enshrined by medical practice. The final chapter revisits the broader social, political and medical context in which they struggled to manage the legacies of war, and suggests that prevailing ideas and values may well have added to their difficulties.

CHAPTER 11

Hiding the Marks

Marks of War has provided a window on the experience of men who went to war at a critical time in Australia's history. Since the men featured in this book returned to their civilian lives, the global village has been scarred by many more wars and conflicts. Between 1945 and 1999, 160 wars and armed conflicts have been fought, which have led to 22 million deaths, 90 per cent of which have been of civilians. Some of these conflicts have occurred near the sites of the 1942 battles – on the Solomon Islands, Timor, Bougainville, Aceh, and West Papua to name a few.[1] These wars and conflicts have affected many millions more – combatants and civilians – and destroyed families, communities and countries.

Warfare continues as a major world health problem, and as Tony McMichael, an eminent scholar in population and global health, points out:

> Human life expectancy, in the space of a mere century or so, has become much longer that ever before ... We have partially reined in two of the four Biblical Horsemen of the Apocalypse: Famine and Pestilence ... The other two horsemen, War and Conquest, still roam menacingly on their red and white steeds.[2]

The scale of global war and conflict since World War Two and the monumental suffering they have caused might seem to overshadow the experiences of the men in this book. However, the lives of these men are as important as any of those who have been affected by the suffering of war, and much can be learned from their lives and struggles. Their stories have shown how a few moments, hours, or months can have a profound effect on the rest of one's life. They also illustrate what the trauma literature of late twentieth century has been clearly saying, that is, that traumatic experience can have a lifelong but differential effect. Much of this damage remains hidden, unless a public discourse is created.

The lives of these men represent the many possible outcomes of traumatic experience. On the surface most men managed well after returning to civilian life; they demonstrated resilience and strength and had very good lives, despite submerged experience. However, a significant minority of men were more profoundly affected over time and many others were mentally marked with a strong undercurrent of disturbing experience that was never fully acknowledged or dealt with appropriately. These marks extended to the families of veterans as well: they were affected both primarily and vicariously over time, although this has never been adequately recognised.

Among veterans the most common strategy for dealing with their marks of war was to be busy and 'get on with life', but this did not always work as the inner struggles described earlier clearly show. Two themes dominated the inner struggles that the men experienced. The first was unresolved memory of very traumatic times. The second was the grief at losing so many mates, and in some cases, their own youth. Sometimes this grief and post-traumatic memory were fused, as in the case of Maurice Little:

> Reading our history still upsets one at times and why did so many young people have to die, and the country is in such a mess, and politically and morally did they die in vain? I dream of how many of my mates died and the circumstances. I, like so many front-line troops, could never, I believe, eradicate from our minds the loss of our mates. I remember them every day and the terrible circumstances under which many of them died.[3]

The most compelling conclusion from these personal histories is that, even beneath all the success in life, the majority of men had no space to explore what they, like Maurice Little, had kept hidden for so many years. If they had had such a space they would have been less constrained by moral judgements or by the possibility of their self-disclosure leading to the shame of a diagnosis of mental illness. Despite the post-war attempts by some sections of the media to make the mental damage of war a public issue, any exploration of the impact of traumatic memories was generally down-played, and was construed as a medical problem only.

Stored traumatic memories were at the heart if the ongoing problems experienced by veterans, but these memories were carefully contained within social constructs.

> It is through memory that we frame our sense of individual, group and national identities, give meaning to our own life history, and understanding of our social past. Our individual memories, however, are constantly supplemented, altered and mediated by the circulation of representations and articulations of the past that constitutes collective memory. [4]

In the repression of memory, various forms of institutional and social gate-keeping ensure that an individual internalises social and cultural norms. At an individual level, a person can perform individual gate-keeping to protect himself or others from distress associated with traumatic memories. Social gate-keeping operates through restrictive social norms about what is acceptable in public talk. Institutional gate-keeping has been achieved in the veteran arena through organisations like the Department of Veterans' Affairs and ex-servicemen's organisations, which can control the personal narrative. Earlier in the book I described the carefully orchestrated constraint on any public discussion of the 'nervous' soldier by the RSL and other agencies. Such constraint is not new in medical discourse. For example, Arthur Kleinman argues that illness narratives, or narratives of perceived psychiatric illness, are culturally defined by the medical context in which they are elicited. This is a crucial understanding, since treatment centres on dealing with memory, either in eliciting material that can be used in therapy, or in treatment aimed at suppressing memory.[5]

In the search to ameliorate the effect of stored toxic experiences, World War Two veterans might have been served well by men like William Rivers, who maintained that repression was both a process and a state. It was a *process* by which a person tried to 'thrust out of his memory some part of his mental content' and it was the *state* that ensued when 'either through this process or by some other means, part of the mental content becomes inaccessible to manifest consciousness'. Repression was a mechanism necessary to adapt to extreme conditions in war-time, and provided the only effective way of coping with the emotions aroused by these conditions, but problems occured when the soldier tried to banish disturbing memories from his mind after battle. Rivers called this pathological state a form of anxiety neurosis. The soldier 'is encouraged by family and friends and many experts to forget his war experiences but in reality he cannot, and they re-emerge in dreams and nightmares'.[6]

Rivers argued that active repression kept painful thoughts under a 'kind of pressure' during the day, building up energy that 'burst forth in the quiet of night'. The remedy, although not recommended for all patients, was to bring the content of the repressed experience into consciousness and facilitate a cathartic experience. Further re-education, or what might now be called cognitive behavioural therapy, could help the patient re-adjust to reality and release his repressed emotions and thoughts. Rivers was quick to point out however that a 'cure' might not always be attributable to the treatment, and there might be other factors operating such as faith in the physician, and autosuggestion. In practice, Rivers advocated a middle course. Lifting the 'veil of repression' needed to be done carefully, and it was imperative for the therapist to find a balance between encouraging 'morbid and obsessive' concentration on thoughts and memories, and the constructive integration of memory through the release of repressed material.[7]

This advice is just as relevant now as it was in 1917, when Rivers treated Siegfried Sassoon at Craiglockart Army Hospital, but it addresses the issue only at the individual level. In fact Rivers 'persuaded' Sassoon to return to the front and do his duty and not follow his pacifist conscience, which had led him to protest about the senseless slaughter in France and Belgium. Sassoon was dissuaded by both medical and military authorities from questioning a war that he had publicly challenged, and he eventually returned to the Western Front. Rivers earned a reputation as a therapist, and insights such as his inspired a more humane treatment of the neurotic soldier than the regimens of the Faradists with their punitive use of electricity. The more sensitive approach of Rivers reflects that of many medical specialists, who by and large displayed concern and compassion and supported those who did 'genuinely' break down. However, he stopped short of examining the nature of war as a stressor.[8]

Rivers had something to offer the troubled soul of the veteran, but he was still constrained by the restricted medical and political framework of his time. He focused only on unravelling the strands of memory and said nothing about the horror of the place where the memories were laid down, unlike Sassoon, who railed against the war's madness in his war poems. Because the focus was only on the individual pathology, there has been virtually no examination of the war as a major health hazard. This restricted construction of the issues remains characteristic within medical culture.

This brings us to the other story of this book, that is, the way medical ideas and practices have perceived and dealt with the stress of war, which had a profound impact on how men dealt with this stress. The constructions of mental illness adopted in World War Two involved the same labelling as was used in the Great War and in civilian life – hysteria, neurasthenia, anxiety and other forms of neurosis. No radical new explanations emerged and diagnoses and official labels bore no semantic relationship to wartime experience. The labels did not mention the war and thus failed to acknowledge the toxic effect of combat. Instead the focus was on the inability of individuals to either stand the strain, or healthily integrate their experience. The advances made in working with traumatic memory during World War One, which encouraged patient unravelling of war experience, were virtually lost by the end of World War Two, when more credence was given to physical treatments.[9]

The medical specialist of both wars insisted that 'neuroses of war' presented 'nothing new to medical science', and that 'war neurosis does not connote some new nervous disorder which does not have its counterpart in civil life.'[10] Thus the distress of post-war life was confined to the only space in which it could be explored – in the psychiatrist's or doctor's room or in the psychiatric ward – and the traumatic memories of dead mates and dismembered bodies were further exorcised from the public arena. The marks of war were dissociated from the traumatic experience of warfare and confined to the arena of the neuroses, which Freud described as 'flights into illness'.

Along with Rivers, the medical men were occupying part of the high ground that had been taken by mainstream psychiatry in the twentieth century. With minor exceptions the purpose of psychiatry in both world wars was to examine the 'madness' of the men who could not cope with strain, rather than examine the policies and behaviour of those who made decisions to wage war or who gave the orders to subordinates to commit themselves to battle. One major consequence of the medical hegemony in this discourse has been to restrict any scrutiny of the broader health consequences of war. Because the focus has been squarely on the individual pathology, there has been virtually no examination of war and conflict as toxic agents, or sources of 'infection'.

Questioning the madness of war is not without moral and intellectual dilemmas. To re-examine the place of medical ideas that have become firmly entrenched in the Australian Army since World War Two, and in the veterans' administration in the post-war period, would mean questioning national security needs, patriotism, and the Hippocratic imperative to heal the wounded.

In fact the Hippocratic Oath can find itself in mirky waters in war-time. In the pursuit of war, medical and legal principles are applied in a way that reverses their application in civil life. In war-time, killing is sanctioned, and medical and other experts actually assist the cause by studying the psycho-dynamics of withstanding the stressors of war and how men and women can be 'inoculated' against stress. In this sense they are ensuring that the perpetrators are able to carry out their work in the first place. These same experts never ask how it is that what is regarded as abnormal in one situation (civilian murder) is normal in another (killing in wartime).[11] Evil in one arena is construed as goodness in another, and if people experience revulsion or distress when required to conform to this reversal of values, they can be accommodated within a diagnostic category that deems them ill. Medical experts do not examine the sickness in those who make the decision for violence to be perpetrated with military force. In some ways this is similar to what has often occurred in an epidemic or outbreak of disease in society: the history of public health is replete with examples of blaming the victims rather than addressing the underlying causes.

The experience of war veterans is both similar to and different from the experiences of civilians who have their lives interrupted by traumatic events. It is similar in the way personal narratives are appropriated into a psychiatric diagnosis to determine treatment and settle litigious issues. It is different in that the traumatic events they experience are perpetrated under the guise of world order and a pursuit of national goals for the good of the people. When responding to the psychological casualty in war-time, medical specialists have, throughout the twentieth century, in the classic disease triad of host, environment and pathogen, focused on the host. It is hard to find anyone in the Australian psycho-medical field who has challenged the 'madness' of war itself, particularly in the World War Two era.[12] A rare exception was W.E. Mickleburgh in his address to the Third Annual Congress of the Australian and New Zealand College of Psychiatrists in Sydney in October 1966. He argued that 'understanding the genesis and control of wars is among the most urgent and important problems of today', and that 'psychiatrists should have valuable insights to contribute to the subject'. In his view, social psychiatry should expand to 'embrace the study of maladaptive international behaviour of all kinds', and that psychiatrists were well placed to understand the dynamics of war because 'armed conflict lends itself to analysis'. Basing his analysis on a motivational model that explained why seeking social goals could lead either to conflict or harmony, Mickleburgh argued that prevention could be achieved through 'education, international communication and the provision of moral equivalents of war'. He even advocated epidemiological surveys to elucidate the 'warlike or peaceful propensities of populations'.[13]

Mickleburgh was a voice crying in the wilderness. His understanding of the dynamics of war may have been naïve and simplistic, but at least he went further than most of his colleagues in critiquing the evil of war. His reference to the capacity of 'mankind' to destroy itself many times over is still relevant today, and his desire to tip the balance in favour of survival of the human race, is daily more imperative.

The madness decried by Mickleburgh was not far from the thoughts of the many veterans who told their story in *Marks of War*. In the survey of opinions on war, only one of the respondents believed that war was a reasonable way to resolve disputes, despite the fact that they had all served in a bloody conflict. In May 1993 Paul Wright for example, a survivor of both the Kokoda and Gona campaigns, who went on to serve in Bougainville, was asked to speak in the church where the 55th Battalion colours had been laid up in 1953. Of his war experience he noted:

> In the Islands during the war, as only those who experienced it can testify, the nights were very long and lonely. Sleep did not come easily. I am not talking about the times when you slept with one eye open, both ears tuned in and your finger close to the trigger of your rifle; but more the times behind the lines when you had time to reflect and worry about how the family was going back home
>
> I used to ask God. Ask Him why He didn't bring war to an end, but God does not make wars. Only men make wars; only madmen make wars.[14]

Ray Baldwin also asked why atrocity and inhumanity should be part of a civilised society:

> You wonder why these things were allowed to go on. When you have to go around with a sandbag and pick a mess of bones and bury them – young fit men a moment before. The older you get the more vulnerable you get. In each campaign I lost someone I knew pretty well. You don't forget things like finding three of your chaps strapped to a tree and bayoneted by the Japanese.[15]

The persistent claim made by medical experts that there was 'nothing new to medical science' in the neuroses of war was valid, but for reasons other than those that they gave. There was 'nothing new' in that the psychiatric effort in war-time, as in peace-time, focused on treating the individual 'sickness' without addressing the source of the epidemic. In terms of the imperative to address the root cause of disease and disorder there was a persistent failure to recognise that the toxic stressor of deliberately perpetrated mass violence was 'man-made'. While it might seem to some to be an idealistic view, the health of society may have been better served if the same degree of intellectual effort and clinical insight had been applied to critiquing and finding alternatives to the use of violence to achieve social goals, as was applied to identifying, labelling and treating dysfunctional individuals.

The men of New Guinea were caught up, not only in a world conflict not of their own doing, but also in a world of medical practice and ideas about mental health of which they had little understanding and over which they certainly had no control. They were no different from the British soldiers who returned from Dunkirk in a very distressed state who demonstrated that officers and men of good standing, and not just those of poor background, could be profoundly affected by trauma.[16] Some men of sound background did break down, but others survived and prospered without needing any assistance. The story in this book is that many of these men were of sound mind but suffered in silence, and had nowhere to talk about their well hidden marks of war. These marks are not paraded publicly on ANZAC Day, nor are they mentioned as part of the losses sustained in wartime on Remembrance Day, but they are with many until their final hours.

* * * * * * * *

I return finally to my initial reflection on William George Raftery. I now know that he had more than enough material for traumatic memory that might have 'burst forth in the quiet of night', but I do not whether this actually occurred. Perhaps my grandparents heard some of his nocturnal replays of traumatic memory in 1919 after he returned home. I do not know how the anxiety of having him and his brother Jack away fighting a war for years affected the health of my grandparents. Because I was with him in his last hours I know that he did not return to the fields of Flanders in his mind then, but I do not know if he caught a fleeting glance of Blanche. I do know that his life course was radically altered by those few years of 'adventure' in foreign lands, and I know more of this than can be shared in a public arena.

Having listened to the stories of the New Guinea survivors I now know the questions I might have asked when my father was alive so that I could know his life more completely. He thought he was going to a war that would be over in a few months. As we face the prospect of another generation of Australians being involved in a 'short and sharp' war in the Middle East the experience of the men of New Guinea and William George Raftery give a clear warning. Those who go to serve and those who remain behind in anxiety will have their lives marked by the mayhem of war. Trying to heal the marks of war after the event is no cure. While we need to attend closely to the long-term effects of their experience, we need also to question the ideas and practices sustaining such mayhem, and continue to search for more peaceful ways of sharing global space.

Notes to the Chapters

Note: due to the nature of some of the resource material and the need to maintain confidentiality, some of these notes are of a generic nature.

Preface

1 A full account of the Rabaul invasion and Tol massacre can be found in I. Downs (1999) *The New Guinea Volunteer Rifles: 1939-43; A History*. Pacific Press, Broadbeach, Queensland. Sir John Nimmo, Red Cross, interviewed survivors of the massacre and obtained first-hand accounts of the atrocities. See AWM, Murdoch Interview, 16 January 1990, p. 45.

2 *Instrument of Surrender*, 1947, Awani Press, Fredericksburg, Texas.

3 For a more complete historical account of World War Two see Gavin Long (1973) *The Six Years War*, AWM and AG Publishing Service, Sydney, and Allan Walker (1957) *The Islands Campaigns*, AWM, Canberra. For the total period of the war in Papua and New Guinea, 170,000 Japanese and 14,500 Australians died.

4 S. Ashenden, 'War has left its mark on every household.' Private communication

5 Discourse is used to refer to the talk, narratives, stories, writings and other representations surrounding a particular theme, idea or event.

6 For example, Bert Bishop (1991) *The Hell, the Humour and the Heart Break: A Private's View of World War 1*. Kangaroo Press, Kenthurst NSW.

7 They had stopped off at Marseilles on their way from Port Said to 'Blighty'.

8 Birdwood was alleged to have asked a soldier his name after he refused to salute. 'What's yours?' the soldier answered back. 'Don't you know I am General Birdwood?' The soldier retorted 'Why don't you wear feathers on your tail like any other bird would?'

9 William George Raftery, recorded conversations and letter 9 October 1978. During the war, white feathers were sent to men who did not volunteer and were accused of shirking their duty. My father used it here as a symbol of cowardice. The white feather tradition was continued into the Second World War.

Chapter 1

1 A. McMichael (2001) *Human Frontiers, Environments and Disease*, p. xi. Professor McMichael is the Director of the National Centre for Epidemiology and Population Health, Canberra.

2 This may be disputed by some in relation to Aboriginal history. The 1997 Human Rights Commission Inquiry into the Australian government policy on the removal of Aboriginal children concluded that the policy and practice amounted to genocide.

3 A.G. Butler (1940) *The Official History of the Australian Army Medical Services in the War of 1914–18, Volume 2 The Western Front* Australian War Memorial, Canberra, pp. 864–875.

4 G. Long (1976) points out that it is very difficult to give accurate estimates of participation and casualties in both wars. My estimates were compiled from a number of sources: A.G. Butler (ed.) (1943) *The Official History of the Australian Army Medical Services in the War of 1914–18, Volume 3 Problems and Services*; A. Morrison, Repatriation, in H. Heseltine (1989) *The Shock of Battle*, ADFA; A. Walker (1952) *Clinical Problems of War*. The Australian War Memorial Archives record that 300,000 enlisted in World War One and over 60,000 died. In World War Two the estimate is 30,000 prisoners, 39,000 deaths. The *Australia Remembers* Campaign of 1995 rounded out the deaths in World War Two

to 50,000. One person could have been wounded and/or injured more than once. The higher survival rate of World War Two reflects the improvement in evacuation and treatment, especially the availability of antibiotics.

[5] I acknowledge that the invasion of Aboriginal lands and the destruction of their culture has been a significant event and a major component in our traumatic past but is the subject of a separate discussion. See H. Reynolds (1995) *Fate of a Free People*. Penguin, Ringwood.

[6] M. Creamer, P. Burgess, W. Buckingham and P. Pattison, P. (1993) Post-trauma reactions following a multiple shooting, in J. Wilson and B. Raphael (1993) *International Handbook of Traumatic Stress Syndromes*, Plenum Press, New York, pp. 201–212; Beverley Raphael (1984) *Anatomy of Bereavement*, Century Hutchinson, London.

[7] A.. McFarlane PTSD Synthesis of Research and Clinical Studies, in J. Wilson & B. Raphael, pp. 421–429.

[8] B. Gammage (1974) *The Broken Years*, Penguin, Harmondsworth, p. 272.

[9] See A. Thomson, (1994) *ANZAC Memories: Living with the Legend*, Oxford University Press, Melbourne.

[10] P. Adam-Smith (1992) *Prisoners of War: From Gallipoli to Korea*, Viking, Melbourne.

[11] J. Damousi & M. Lane, (1995) *Gender and War*, Cambridge University Press, Cambridge. In New Zealand the long silence has been broken by the publication of *Silent Casualties* (1995) in which Alison Parr makes public the lives of seven men who had experienced war neurosis. The personal impact of war is also explored in the dramatic portrayal of the lives of women affected by war in the film by Gayle Preston and later in book form by J. Fyfe (1995) *War Stories Our Mother Never Told Us*.

[12] See J. Barrett (1987) *We Were There*. Penguin, Sydney.

[13] S. Garton (1996) *The Cost of War: Australians Return*, Oxford University Press, Melbourne.

[14] Peter Brune (1991) *Those Ragged Bloody Heroes. From the Kokoda Trail to Gona Beach 1942*, Allen & Unwin, Sydney, and Margaret Barter, (1994) *Far Above Battle: The Experience and Memory of Australian Soldiers at War*, Allen & Unwin, Sydney.

[15] M. Johnston (1995) *At the Front Line: Experiences of Australian Soldiers in World War 2*. Cambridge University Press, Cambridge.

[16] J. McCalman (1993) *Journeyings: The Biography of a Middle Class Generation 1920–1990*, Melbourne University Press, Melbourne, p. 202.

[17] A.S. Walker (1957) *Australia in the War 1939–45: The Island Campaigns*. Australian War Memorial, Canberra, ACT; A.S. Walker (1952) *Medical Services of the RAN and RAAF*, Australian War Memorial, Canberra, ACT.

[18] J. Burns (1960) *The Brown and Blue Diamond at War*, Griffin Press, Adelaide (2/27 Battalion) and V. Austin, (1988) *To Kokoda and Beyond. The Story of the 39th Battalion 1941-43*, Melbourne University Press, Melbourne.

[19] See M. Bowman (1997) *Individual Differences in Post-traumatic Response*, Lawrence Erlbaum Ass., London. Bowman advances the argument that the effects of traumatic experience, particularly as it is formulated in the PTSD literature, have been under-examined. She argues that the shift in the PTSD diagnosis to focus on the traumatic event resulted in a distortion in thinking. In effect she shifts the emphasis back to the contribution of the individual – 'toxic life events have different power depending on the way in which they are construed.' (p. 144).

[20] See J. Wilson (1989). Diagnostic criteria for Post-traumatic Stress Disorder are stated in the American Psychiatric Society Diagnostic and Statistical Manual Version IV: 1994, APA, Washington.

[21] At this point I am only presenting the dominant paradigm. I am aware of the critique on at least two fronts. The first is the challenge to post-traumatic stress disorder PTSD as a medical construction of experience. Bracken (1998), for example, challenges the western construction of PTSD as context bound. The other front is the assumed linear relationship between event and consequence as a form of dose-response modelling (see Bowman 1997).

[22] A. Spiro, P. Schnurr and C. Aldwin (1994) Combat-related post-traumatic stress disorder symptoms in older men, *Psychology and Aging*, Vol. 9, No. 1, pp. 17–26.

[23] G. Vaillant (1977) *Adaptation to Life*, Little Brown, Boston; and Kimberly, L. Vaillant, G., Torrey, W. & Elder, G. (1995) A 50-year prospective study of the psychological sequelae of World War II combat, *American Journal of Psychiatry*, Vol. 152, No. 4 516–522.

[24] G.H. Elder & E.C. Clipp War Experiences and Social Ties: Influences Across 40 years in Men's Lives, in M. Riley (ed.) (1988) *Social Change and the Life Course: Volume 1, Social Structures and Human Lives*, Sage Publications, Newbury Park California, p. 30.

[25] B. Kahana, Late-Life adaptation in the aftermath of extreme stress, in M. Wykle, E. Kahana & J. Kowal (1992) (eds) *Stress and Health Among the Elderly*, Springer Publishing Company, New York, p. 168.

[26] Kidson M., Douglas J., & Holwill B. (1993) Post-traumatic Stress Disorder in Australian World War II Veterans attending a Psychiatric Outpatient Clinic, *Medical Journal of Australia, 158*, 563–566.

[27] In his summary of World War One pension disabilities, Butler (1943) did use 'war neurosis' as a general category, but the actual diagnoses were neurosis, shell shock, hysteria, neurasthenia, psychasthenia, pycho-neuroses, and various neuroses (e.g. cardiac).

[28] For an extended treatise of the nature of neurosis and traumatic neurosis see O. Fenichel (1945) *The Psychoanalytic Theory of Neurosis*, WW Norton & Co., New York.

[29] The book is based on an intensive study completed as part of a Doctor of Philosophy in Psychological Medicine completed in the Department of Public Health, Adelaide University. G.J. Raftery Nothing New to Medical Science: Constructions of War Neurosis and the Life Course Outcomes of WW2 Veterans. PhD thesis. Adelaide University, December 2000.

[30] M. Horowitz (1986) *Stress Response Syndromes*, Jason Aronson, New York,

[31] R. Josselson (1993) *The Narrative Study of Lives, Vol. 1.* Sage, Newberry Park, p. ix.

[32] See P. Armstrong (1991) *Qualitative Strategies in Social and Educational Research: The Life History Method in Theory & Practice.* University of Hull School of Adult and Continuing Education. Newland paper No. 7; and D. McAdams, Narrating the self in adulthood, in J. Birren (1996) (ed.) *Ageing and Biography*, Springer, New York. for in-depth reviews of the use of narrative and life history methods.

[33] Telephone interview June 1997.

Chapter 2

[1] A.G. Butler (1943) *The Official History of the Australian Army Medical Services in the War of 1914–18: Vol. III: Problems and Services.* Canberra: Australian War Memorial, pp. 79 and 142. Arthur Graham Butler (1872–1949) served as a Regimental Medical Officer with the AIF and had a distinguished career in Egypt, at Gallipoli and in France. He was awarded the Distinguished Service Order at Anzac, and commanded the 3rd AGH until

1918. After a period in medical records he returned to Australia to private practice. When he agreed to write the official history he moved to Canberra, where he died in 1949 (*ADB*, 1891–1939).

2 An extensive treatment of hysteria can be found in A. Roy (1982) *Hysteria,* John Wiley and Son, New York.

3 See P. Ellis (1984) The origins of war neurosis: Part 1. *Journal of the Royal Naval and Medical Service*, 70, pp. 168–177, and E. Shorter (1992) *From Paralysis to Fatigue*. The Free Press, New York.

4 See E. Dean (1997) *Shook Over Hell: Post-traumatic Stress, Vietnam and the Civil War,* Harvard University Press, Cambridge, Massachusetts.

5 H. Binneveld (1997) *From Shell Shock to Combat Stress: A Comparative History of Military Psychiatry,* Amsterdam University Press, Amsterdam, p. 4.

6 P. Ellis (1984) op. cit. pp. 168–177. Ellis argues that at the time of the Civil War (1861–1865), Mitchell's patients were either diagnosed with 'irritable heart' or nostalgia. Mitchell did not use the term neurasthenia until Beard and Page influenced his own theory on a form of post-traumatic neurosis brought on by gunshot wounds.

7 P. Ellis (1984), ibid., pp. 168–177.

8 See P. Lerner (1996) for an extensive analysis of the German experience and war neurosis. Hysterial Men: War, Neurosis and German Mental Medicine, 1914-1918. PhD thesis, Columbia University.

9 A.G. Butler (1943) *The Official History of the Australian Army Medical Services in the War of 1914–18: Vol. III, Problems and Services.* Australian War Memorial, Canberra, Chapter 2; C. Lloyd and J. Rees (1994) *The Last Shilling: A history of repatriation in Australia.* Melbourne University Press, Melbourne.

10 Letter from Sgt A.G. Carey, 2nd Infantry Brigade, AIF, AWM Archives. The complete letter contains more detail of the landing and the battle experience.

11 C.E.W. Bean (1939) *Official History of Australia in the War 1914–18 .Vol. 5; The AIF in France, 1918.* Sixth edition. Angus and Robertson, Sydney; and A. Butler (1940) *Official History of Australia in the War 1914–18: Photographic Record.* Angus and Robertson, Sydney.

12 See A.G. Butler (1940) *The Official History of the Australian Army Medical Services in the War of 1914–1918, Vol. II, The Western Front.* Canberra, Australian War Memorial.

13 See A.G. Butler (1943) op. cit. Butler devotes Chapter Two to an extensive discussion of the 'moral and mental disorders'.

14 S. Freud, Introduction to psychoanalysis and war neurosis. In J. Strachey (ed.) (1955) *The Complete Psychological Works of Sigmund Freud*, Volume XVII, (1917–1919) Hogarth Press, London.

15 A.G. Butler (1943) op. cit., p. 106.

16 A.W. Campbell (1916) Remarks on some neuroses and psychoses in war. *Medical Journal of Australia.* 1, pp. 319–323.

17 A.G. Butler (1940) *The Australian Army Medical Services in the War of 1914–18*, Volume II, Australian War Museum, Canberra, pp. 462–463

18 A.W. Campbell (1916) op. cit., p. 323.

19 A.W. Campbell (1916), ibid.

20 A.G. Butler (1943) op. cit.

21 From Ferenczi, Simmel and Jones, *Introduction to Psycho-Analysis and the War Neuroses,* quoted in A.G. Butler Vol. II (1943) op. cit., p. 92.

[22] 'Treatment of neurasthenia in soldiers', Medical Journal of Australia, December7, pp. 480–481.

[23] From 1917 to 1939, an average of 32 ex-soldiers committed suicide in New South Wales per year. The number peaked in 1930, a time of high unemployment and poverty, and suicide rates among World War One ex-soldiers exceeded those in the general population in all years. In 1930 there were 4.005 veteran deaths per 10,000, compared with 3.5 per 10,000 in the civilian population. Social isolation and alcoholism were identified as veteran problems. In 1933 there were 226,438 surviving veterans in Australia. If the NSW rates are extrapolated nationally, this represented a major health problem (see S.J. Minogue (1945) Suicides among returned soldiers of the 1914–18 War. *Medical Journal of Australia*, 24 February; pp. 195–200.

[24] See J.W. Springthorpe (1903) Our Metropolitan Asylums, *Intercolonial Medical Journal of Australasia, 8,3:* 109–124. In South Australia for example, at the end of World War One, the only legislation dealing with the mentally ill was the Mental Defectives Act of 1913 and the Inebriates Act of 1908.

[25] *Annual Report of the Inspector General of Hospitals on the Mental Hospital, Parkside,* p. 15, and *The Certified Mental Defectives*, 1918. Government Printer, Adelaide.

[26] J.W. Springthorpe (1919) War neuroses and civil practice. *Medical Journal of Australia*, 11, 14, pp. 279–284.

[27] W.E. Jones (1916) A case of shell shock, *Medical Journal of Australia,* 1, pp. 203–204. He is not Professor Ernest Jones of London, who later became the President of both the International Psychoanalytic Society and the British Psychoanalytic Association and was editor of the *International Journal of Psychoanalysis.* For reference to W. Ernest Jones, see C. Brothers (1957) *Early Victorian Psychiatry, 1835–1905.* AC Brooks, Melbourne.

[28] W.E. Jones (1916) ibid., p. 203.

[29] F.W. Mott (1918) War psycho-neurosis (I) Neurasthenia: the disorders and disabilities of fear. *Lancet. 1;* 127–129, and Sarbo (1915) *British Medical Journal*, July 11 [quoted in Jones without further detail].

[30] Editorial *Medical Journal of Australia*, 1, 1916, p. 205.

[31] Review section *Medical Journal of Australia*, 1, 1919, p. 173.

[32] W.R. Regnell (1919) The psycho-neuroses of war. *Medical Journal of Australia,* 1, 23, pp. 455–460.

[33] W.R. Regnell (1919) ibid., p. 456.

[34] Reported in *Medical Journal of Australia,* 7 June 1919, pp. 472–473.

[35] See *Medical Journal of Australia*, 2, 1920, pp. 324–325.

[36] Godfrey and a number of others including W. Ernest Jones were at a Medical Congress Meeting in 1920. This was reported in the *Medical Journal of Australia* in September 1920.

[37] See C.S. Trahair (1984) *The Humanist Temper: The life and work of Elton Mayo.* New Brunswick: Transaction Books.

[38] This is a brief outline of a very complex story. For much more detail, see Lloyd and Rees (1994) op. cit. A brief yet detailed account is found in Galbraith (1946) *Medical Journal of Australia*, 2, pp. 1–8.

[39] The first organisation was the Returned Soldiers' Association (RSA), which was changed in 1940 to the Returned Soldiers, Sailors & Airmens' Imperial League of Australia. This became the Returned Services League (RSL) in 1965, which was renamed the Returned and Services league in 1990. All have been national organisations with state branches.

[40] A.G. Butler (1943), op. cit.

[41] Lloyd and Rees (1994) op. cit., p. 142.

[42] Sir James Joynton Smith was a champion of veterans' causes. See for example S. Garton (1996), 88–89.

[43] Department of Veterans' Affairs internal document, 1999. See Lloyd and Rees (1994) op. cit. for an extensive history of the Repatriation Department, although the mental health aspect of this receives cursory treatment.

[44] *Medical Journal of Australia*, 2, 1918, pp. 480–481.

[45] The information on the work of the Red Cross is from the Annual Reports of the New South Wales Red Cross Society Archives from 1914. In the period June 1917–June 1918, the numbers treated in the NSW homes doubled on the previous year. In 1918, 10,168 passed through the No.4 Convalescent Room, and in 1919, 17,194.

[46] Australian Red Cross Chairman's Report, 1921–22, p. 12.

[47] Callan Park later became the training hospital for army psychiatrists in World War Two.

[48] One example of this support was a 'nerve case' who was out of work and very depressed (1938 report) and unable to pay his rent. He was given food and rent relief, 'We probably staved off another nervous breakdown by this prompt assistance'.

[49] A.G. Butler (1943) op. cit., pp. 831–835.

[50] R. Graves (1995) *Goodbye to All That*, Berghahn, Oxford. (First published 1929.)

[51] For an extended discussion of eugenics in Australia, see S. Garton (1994) Sound Minds and Healthy Bodies: Reconsidering eugenics in Australia, 1914–1940, *Australian Historical Studies*, 26(103) pp. 163–181.

[52] Details of his life were gathered from an obituary written by R.C. Winn in the *Medical Journal of Australia*, 23 December 1950 and from an interview with the psychiatrist Dr Howard Whitaker, who trained under Dane in the late 1940s.

[53] P. Dane (1925) The Psychoneuroses of Soldiers and Their Treatment, *Medical Journal of Australia*, 25 April, pp. 427–431.

[54] P. Dane (1949) Traumatic Psychoneuroses, *Medical Journal of Australia*, 25 February, pp. 266–267.

[55] P. Dane (1949) Shell Shock or Traumatic Neuroses, *Psychoanalytic Review*, 36, 3. Reproduced in Australian Archives D2048/0, G1220. Page numbers not given

Chapter 3

[1] C.C. Minty (1940) War Neuroses, *Medical Journal of Australia*, October, pp. 386–387.

[2] A.G. Butler (1943) *The Official History of the Australian Army Medical Services in the War of 1914–18: Vol. III: Problems and Services*. Australian War Memorial, Canberra.

[3] Southborough, Lord (1922) *Report on the Committee of Inquiry into 'Shell-shock'*. Wyman & Sons, London.

[4] A.S. Walker (1952) *Clinical Problems of War* Australian War Memorial, Canberra, p. 465.

[5] J. Hurt and E. Nettle (1962) *A Survey of Psychiatric Services to Veterans in Australia and Overseas*, Repatriation Commission, Melbourne, p. 2.

[6] Arthur Tucker's story was derived from a number of sources, including an interview conducted in February 1999, subsequent telephone contact on several occasions, letters and a questionnaire, as well as the text of the original Murdoch Sound Archive interview conducted in June 1989 by E. Stokes.

[7] Arthur Tucker, Murdoch Sound Archive interview transcript, p. 95.

[8] A. Walker (1952) *Medical Services of RAN and RAAF.* Australian War Memorial, Canberra, p. 272.

[9] G. Beard (1880) *A Practical Treatise on Nervous Exhaustion* William Wood, New York. See E. Shorter (1992) *From Paralysis to Fatigue* The Free Press, New York.

[10] D. Forsyth (1915) Functional Nerve Disease and the Shock of Battle, *Lancet*, 25 December, pp. 1399–1403.

[11] E. Miller & H. Crichton-Miller (1940) *The Neuroses of War.* London, MacMillan. Ernest White (1918) Observations on shell shock and neurasthenia in the hospitals in the Western Command. *British Medical Journal,* 13 April; 421–442.

[12] J. Bostock and E. Jones, (1943) *The Nervous Soldier* University of Queensland Press, Brisbane, p. 27.

[13] General headquarters, Middle East Forces (1942) *Psychiatric Casualties: Hints to Medical Officers in the Middle East Forces.* Canberra, Australian War Memorial.

[14] Ibid.

[15] Lord Southborough (1922), op. cit.

[16] J. Bostock and E. Jones (1943), 46–47

[17] H. Love (1942) Neurotic casualties in the field, *Medical Journal of Australia*, August 22, 137–143.

[18] A. Walker (1952), op. cit., p. xxiii

[19] A. Walker (1952), op. cit., p. 685

[20] A. Walker (1952) op. cit., p. 685

[21] E. Cooper and A. Sinclair (1942) War Neurosis at Tobruk. Internal Report, Australian Infantry Forces. AWM54 48/12/120.

[22] E. Cooper and A. Sinclair, ibid., p. 505

[23] A. Sinclair (1943) Psychiatric casualties in an operational zone in New Guinea, *Medical Journal of Australia*, 2, 4 December, 453-460.

[24] A. Sinclair (1944) Psychiatric aspects of the present war, *Medical Journal of Australia,* 1, 28, 501–514.

[25] A. Sinclair (1944), ibid., p. 514.

[26] A. Sinclair (1945) The psychological reactions of soldiers, *Medical Journal of Australia*, 2, 229–234.

[27] A. Sinclair does not reference Grinker and Spiegel but he is probably referring to R. Grinker and J. Spiegel (1945) *Men Under Stress* Blakiston, Philadelphia.

[28] R. Grinker & J. Spiegel (1943) *War Neuroses in North Africa: The Tunisian Campaign.* Washington: United States Army Air Forces.

[29] A. Walker (1952) op. cit.

[30] A. Walker (1952), 675.

[31] A. Sinclair (1944) Psychiatric aspects of the present war. *Medical Journal of Australia,* 1; 28; 501–514.

Chapter 4

[1] Interview Jack Reddin, 2/27th Battalion, November 1994.

[2] Joanna Bourke (1999) *An Intimate History of Killing: Face-to-face Killing in Twentieth Century Warfare*, Granta Books, London.

[3] Diary of Fred Burr, 1969.

[4] This description is mostly based on information from Lt Col O.C. Isaachsen, former company commander, 2/27th Battalion, and Commanding Officer, 36th Battalion.

[5] V. Austin (1988) *To Kokoda and Beyond. The story of the 39th Battalion 1941-43.* Melbourne University Press, Melbourne.

[6] Dr Jim Fairley, RMO 2/27th Battalion, Interview 1994.

[7] See V. Austin (1998) op. cit., pp. 91, 97.

[8] P. Morris, B. Raphael and A. Bordujenko (eds) (1999) *Stress and Challenge: Health and Disease.* Repatriation Medical Authority, Brisbane, p.10.

[9] Interview, 5 June 1995, D. Simonson, L. Suckling.

[10] Seventh Division Medical Diary. AWM Archives.

[11] J. Barrett (1988) *We Were There,* Penguin Books, Ringwood, p. 230. Burns also has a detailed description of their survival in his 2/27th unit history.

[12] A. Walker (1952), op. cit., p. 32

[13] See P. Brune (1991) *Those Ragged Bloody Heroes.* Allen & Unwin, Sydney, Chapter 13.

[14] P. Brune (1991), op. cit.

[15] John Burns (1960) *The Brown and Blue Diamond at War.* Adelaide: Griffin Press, p. 153.

[16] John Manol, interview 1995.

[17] Peter Brune (1991) op. cit.

[18] A. Walker (1957) *The Island Campaigns*, p. 99. See also B. O'Keefe (1994) *Medicine at War*, Allen and Unwin, Sydney.

[19] Dr Jim Fairley, RMO 2/27th Battalion.

[20] Interview, T. Kimber, 2/27th Battalion, 1992.

[21] M. Uren (1959), *A Thousand Men at War: Story of the 2/20 Battalion.* Allen & Unwin, Melbourne.

[22] Interview, Horrie Savage, April 1992.

[23] Interview, Bert Ward 2/27th Battalion, November 1992.

[24] Interview, Robert Johns, 1995.

[25] Paul Hope, Murdoch Sound Archive interview.

[26] Murdoch Sound Archive interview S 752, Bishop J. Morgan, 29 January 1990, pp.144-148.

[27] W. Refshauge, Australian Army Medical Corps; Murdoch Sound Archive interview 2 August 1991, pp.30-32.

[28] Interview Don Simonson, 5 June 1995.

[29] Australian War Memorial Murdoch Sound Archive interview 541/74.

[30] Interview, Jim Ashton, August 1993.

[31] Interview, Harold Norris, 31 March 1999.

[32] John Burns, personal communication 1994.

[33] S. Solomon (1992), p. 290.

[34] Interview 1993 – name withheld.

[35] 'Messed their pants' seems to be a code phrase for men going to pieces as well as what literally happened under extreme duress. One senior officer was reported to have messed his pants in his first action in Syria. He was later repatriated to Australia. Most men wet their pants in fear, but the term was also used colloquially to describe those who could not take it. Interview J. Burns, 1997.

[36] Murdoch Sound Archive interview 13 June 1989, AWM.

[37] Questionnaire response, PW.

[38] A.S. Walker (1952), op. cit., p.69.

[39] A.J. Sinclair (1943) Psychiatric casualties in an operational zone in New Guinea. *Medical Journal of Australia, II,* 4 December; 453-460.

[40] D. Ross (1946) Psychotic casualties in New Guinea, with special reference to the use of convulsive therapy in forward areas. *Medical Journal of Australia,* 15 June; 830-833.

[41] A.S. Walker *Clinical Problems of War,* (1952) Canberra, ACT: Australian War Memorial. p. 692

[42] A.J. Sinclair (1944), op. cit., p.

[43] K. Norris (1945) The New Guinea campaign. *Medical Journal of Australia,* 15 December, p. 431.

[44] See also K. Norris (1945) op. cit.

[45] Medical Report 7th Division January 1943, Australian War Museum, Canberra.

[46] H.D. Steward (1983) *Recollections of a Regimental Medical Officer,* Melbourne University Press, Melbourne.

[47] 53rd Battalion Diary, Australian War Museum.

[48] ibid.

[49] 39th Battalion Diary, Australian War Museum.

[50] Interview K. Viner-Smith, RMO, 15 April 1991. Alan Cameron, RMO, Murdoch Sound Archive tapes, 1990.

[51] Interview, Jim Fairley, 2/27th Battalion, 1991.

[52] Ibid.

[53] Letter from J.A. Mc. Shera, RMO.

[54] Letter from Douglas Leslie, 15 September 1993.

[55] A. Bentley, interview and questionnaire 1995.

[56] Dr Don Duffy, questionnaire response and letter, December 1994.

[57] Letter and questionnaire 12/10/93. The unit referred to is the 53rd/55th Militia

[58] Questionnaire response, J. Reddin, 1994.

[59] Questionnaire response, Clive Edwards, 2/27th Battalion.

[60] Stirling Ashenden 'My Love, My Wife, My Own', poem, unpublished.

[61] Questionnaire, J. Reddin: May 1994.

[62] Glen Williss, interview, February 1993.

[63] Interview, John Burns, 1994.

[64] Questionnaire and telephone interview, Jim Moir, 1994.

[65] Interview, Hugh Dalby, 1993.

Chapter 5

[1] A.N. Ward, questionnaire response, 13 June 1995. A survey of 28 veterans in this study supported the view that they talk only about amusing incidents.

[2] Letter, Maurice Little, May 1992.

[3] This is the current name. The previous titles were the Returned Servicemen's League (RSL) and the Returned Sailors, Soldiers & Airmen's Imperial League of Australia (RSSAILA).

[4] Questionnaire response, Jim Moir, 19 July 1990.

[5] L. Stuart and J. Arnold (1987) *Letters Home 1939–45*. Collins, Sydney, p. 212.

[6] Ibid.

[7] Letter from informant in Port Moresby to his fiancée, 15 November 1942, given to me by his wife. Subsequent investigation indicated that he had elaborated on details of his war story.

[8] J. Burns (1960), op. cit.

[9] The diary is kept in the archives of the Australian War Memorial.

[10] See for example, Burns (1960), op. cit.; Austin (1988), op. cit.

[11] Interview, John Burns, 2 December 1998.

[12] Note attached to questionnaire, Clive Edwards, November 1994.

[13] Brown and blue is the colour patch of the 2/27th. A reproduction is displayed in all association material and some members have it displayed on their car number plate and even on their houses.

[14] *Brown and Blue Diamond*, 79, September 1987.

[15] *Brown and Blue Diamond*, 85, 1995.

[16] J. Burns (1960), op. cit., p. 231.

[17] Maurice Little, letter May 1992

[18] Copies of the original Murdoch recordings and transcripts are kept in the Australian War Memorial archives.

[19] Australian Broadcasting Commission Archives Document *Blue Hills*; and *ABC Weekly*, 29 January 1949.

[20] The *Sun*, 1945.

[21] These articles also showed a general lack of sophistication in understanding psychological issues, which was reflected in the way 'nerves' was portrayed in the press. It was implied that these problems could be addressed with simple prophylactics such as analgesics. In the same publications that contained the references to war neurosis there were advertisements for Aspros, which would 'speedily relieve these depression effects'. Another in May 1943 advocated a new hormone treatment for nerves that would relieve fatigue, restlessness, irritability and disinclination to work. It would 'soothe nerves that had not lost their tension'. In the same issue Dr William's Pink Pills were promoted as a cure for the 'anaemic and nervy'.

[22] *Smith's Weekly*, 10 June 1944, p. 3

[23] *Smith's Weekly*, 17 April 1948, name published at the time.

[24] *Sunday Mail*, 17 April 1948. I interviewed this man in the early stages of my research. He had a lifetime of periodic admission for treatment to the psychiatric ward at the repatriation hospital.

[25] Copy of letter forwarded to the Minister for Repatriation, 29 September 1949. Australian Archives SA: D2048/0 G1220.

[26] Australian Archives SA: D2048/0 G1220.

Chapter 6

1 J. Burns (1960) op. cit., p.231.

2 G.J. Raftery (2000) Nothing New to Medical Science: Constructions of War Neurosis and the Lives of World War 2 Veterans.

3 Questionnaire response, Jack Reddin.

4 This incident is on the public record and is verified from a number of other sources. Records include an ABC *Four Corners* program, an Australian Army film of the Kokoda campaign, and an interview for the *Australian* newspaper Saturday Magazine.

5 AA Form D1 Medical History Sheet, Australian Military Forces, revised May 1939.

6 There were five possible classifications: A1, fit for all duties; A2, fit for all where the disability is not a bar; B, fit for restricted duties; C, temporarily unfit for duty; D, unfit for military service. See Walker (1953) pp. 435–436.

7 In this last case the young man returned home to find his fiancée no longer considered him a man and rejected him. He went bush for a few years until he eventually found a new partner and settled down. Questionnaire, identity withheld.

8 In the most recent pension provisions there are four disability pension rates: Special Rate (Totally and Permanently Incapacitated); an Intermediate Rate; an Extended Disablement Adjustment; and a General Rate (ranging from 10–100 per cent). The TPI and EDA provide the best security for veterans. A Service Pension is paid purely on the grounds of having served and carries no entitlement for disability.

9 Personal communication, Rosslyn Russell, August 1990.

10 Interview, Harry Katekar, November 1996.

11 Interview from Murdoch Sound Archive April 1989. SS63.

12 Interview, Robert Johns, 1995.

13 Interview, Hugh Dalby, 1995.

14 Letter from Faye Johns, February 1992.

15 Interview, Bill Russell, 1991.

16 The effect on families is explored in more detail in J. Raftery and S. Schubert (1995), *A Very Changed Man,* University of South Australia, Adelaide.

17 Interview, Robert Johns, 1995.

18 Questionnaire, MKB, 39th Battalion.

19 There was no term in the Australian Army for what the US Army later called Combat Stress Reaction (CSR), which causes the soldier to become dysfunctional in the field.

20 Interview PW, 1995, 39th Battalion.

21 Interview with EG, 1995, whose husband survived the battles of Milne Bay and Sanananda, returned home to eventually become a senior public official and repressed his war memories.

22 The Memory Intrusion Scale is a modified form of the Impact of Events Scale (Horowitz). It was included as part of the Life History Questionnaire.

23 Interview, Jim Ashton, 1994.

24 For an extended discussion of the soldier settlement schemes see S. Garton (1996), op. cit.

25 Interview, 1991, Bill Russell.

26 Many veterans reported that during a recurrence of fever bad dreams reappeared. The

irony is that malaria was actually used as a cure for syphilitic-induced psychosis from as early as 1917 and was used in South Australia in the 1940s. In the procedure, attributed to Wagner-Jauregg, blood was transferred from a patient with malaria to the infected patient, which produced high temperatures that were then reduced with quinine. The fevers cured the psychosis. Information from Dr H. Southwood, former superintendent, Enfield Receiving House; also see Shorter (1997) *A History of Psychiatry*, p. 193.

27 Interview, Ray Baldwin, 1991.

Chapter 7

1 Final moments can reveal previously unrecognised remnants of traumatic experience. Experience with other veterans and a study of families (Raftery & Schubert 1995) has shown that the weakness of illness and debility can remove defences built up in earlier life.

2 PW, questionnaire 1994.

3 The account has been formulated from a number of interviews with the veteran. One interview was conducted jointly with his partner. A number of other texts were incorporated, including his short stories and a novel based on his own career, and a letter from his partner.

4 Letter from Faye Johns, February 1992.

5 V. Austin (1988) *To Kokoda and Beyond*. Melbourne University Press, Melbourne, p. 206.

6 Interview, Mick, 15 November 1994.

Chapter 8

1 Actual names are not used and as far as possible, identifying details are excluded, except where the veteran or surviving family were prepared for the subject to be identified.

2 His story was compiled from a number of sources, including his Veterans' Affairs medical file.

3 Extracts from an interview recorded by ABC Field Unit on location in New Guinea circa December 1942.

4 Interview November 1991.

5 Interview by a journalist in an Australian Army Documentary, *Kokoda – The Bloody Track*, 1990.

6 Testimony of fellow officer.

7 Partner's input to interview November 1990.

8 William's story was constructed from questionnaire responses from his son and widow, and an interview with his widow. These were all gathered over a period of months in 1994.

9 Lance completed a questionnaire in 1995, and was interviewed by telephone on two occasions.

10 When he told me this, I suggested to him that he might benefit from some form of counselling and offered him the option of contacting a psychiatrist colleague of mine or the National Centre for Post Traumatic Stress Disorder which has a program catering for older adults. He did not take up the suggestion and it would appear that his knowledge of what had happened to other men who had given in to the difficulties was a major influence in this decision.

[11] George, who in fact was a cousin previously unknown to me, died before the study was completed. His story was compiled from interviews with his widow, sister and Department of Veterans' Affairs Medical and Hospital files.

[12] Wife's testimony.

[13] All the details of his medical treatment were taken from the medical and hospital files. Family information was compiled from interviews and correspondence from his surviving partner and sister.

[14] Letter, Repatriation Commission, 28 July 1966.

[15] Letter, A. Fisher, 2 July 1971.

[16] See J. Strouse (1980) *Alice James: A Biography.* Boston: Houghton Mifflin.

[17] Gordon, Harris and Rees (1936) p. 157.

[18] Questionnaire response from partner of Reg.

Chapter 9

[1] Name withheld, personal interview, 1994.

[2] W.A. Dibden (1945) Psychiatric casualties as a repatriation problem. *Medical Journal of Australia.* 1, 3; p. 49.

[3] The purpose of coma-inducing treatments was to induce a short-term coma or state of shock. The recovery from shock was facilitated by ingestion of glucose to re-establish the levels of supply to the brain. Two substances used to induce this shock were insulin and cardiazol, the latter (experimented with originally by a Dr Meduna in Budapest) having similar effects without the risk of complications with camphor. Electro shock treatment was another development that was first experimented with in Italy by Drs Cerletti and Bini. Details supplied by W. Salter.

[4] Interview, W.A. Dibden, 1991.

[5] D. Galbraith (1946) The responsibility of the doctor in regard to rehabilitation and hospital practice. *Medical Journal of Australia*, 6 July, 1-8, p. 1.

[6] Australian Archives D2048/0, G1220, memorandum circulated to senior medical personnel in each state in 1940. A document that accompanied the original report, *Neuroses in Wartime*, was to be made available to the Deputy Commissioner but was not in the archival material.

[7] S. Garton, Changing Minds, in A. Curthoys, A.W. Martin and Tim Rowse (eds) (1987) *Australians from 1939*, Fairfax, Syme and Weldon Associates, Broadway, NSW. p. 343.

[8] A. Stoller and K. Arscott (1955), *Report on Mental Health Agency Facilities and Needs of Australia*, Department of Health of the Commonwealth of Australia. Report commissioned by the Minister for Health in Australia, Sir Earl Page.

[9] D. Henderson and R. Gillespie, (1992) *Textbook on Psychiatry*, Oxford University Press, New York.

[10] O. Fenichel (1945) *The Psychoanalytic Theory of Neurosis*, W.W Norton & Co., New York. This was a standard text used by trainee psychiatrists, particularly those training in psychotherapy: testimony of Howard Whitaker, a psychiatrist who trained in Melbourne and worked at Rockingham Centre 1949–54.

[11] O. Fenichel (1945) ibid., p. 117.

[12] See H. Whitaker (1954) Group therapy: a review and report on its use in a therapeutic community. *Medical Journal of Australia.* 2, pp. 899–904.

[13] Interview, William Salter, 26 June 1997.

[14] Interview, W.A. Dibden, 1991. Dibden's biographical details are recorded in his unpublished autobiography held at the University of Adelaide Barr Smith Library.

[15] J. Bostock (1943) The Problem of Returned Soldier Organisations, *Medical Journal of Australia*, 12 June, pp.534-536.

[16] Report on meeting of the British Medical Association in NSW, April 1946, *Medical Journal of Australia*, 1946, 25 May, pp. 738–739.

[17] It is too complex to convey all the history of the work of the Repatriation Commission here, and I will concentrate only on aspects of psychiatric rehabilitation. See C. Lloyd and J. Rees (1994) *The Last Shilling: A History of Repatriation in Australia*. Melbourne University Press, Melbourne.

[18] J. Tipping (1992) op. cit., pp. 18, 35. Those veterans not accepted for war pension and medical benefits were to be accepted under Part IV of the *Re-establishment and Employment Act, 1945*. The Rehabilitation Plan was authorised to be implemented by the Department of Social Services in June 1946.

[19] Commonwealth of Australia, *Parliamentary Debates*, 22 June 1950, Appropriation Bill No. 2, 1949/50 (Psychiatric Disorders in Members of the Forces). Australian Archives SA D2048/0, item G1220.

[20] Australian Archives SA: D2048/0, Item G1220.

[21] ibid.

[22] W.A. Dibden (1945) Psychiatric Casualties as a Repatriation Problem, *Medical Journal of Australia*, 1, 3, pp. 49–57.

[23] Australian Archives SA: D2048/0, Item G1220.

[24] Australian Archives SA: D2048/0, Item G1220. File No. G 1869/1/8.

[25] Australian Archives SA: D2048/0, Item G1220. 'Report of a specialist in psychological medicine: Visit to Adelaide, February 1949,' A. Stoller.

[26] Interview, H. Southwood, 20 September 1999. Southwood was more interested in psychoanalysis. He undertook training during the war years, and was one of the founders of the Australian Association of Psychiatry after 1945.

[27] Interview, W.A. Dibden, 15 January 1991.

[28] W. Sargant and E. Slater (1940) Acute War Neuroses. *Lancet*, 6 July; 1

[29] See H. Whitaker (1954) 'Group therapy: a review and report on its use in a therapeutic community'. *Medical Journal of Australia*. 2; 899–904.

[30] Letter, K. Fry to City of Adelaide. Australian Archives SA: D2048/0, Item G1220.

[31] Lloyd and Rees (1994) op.cit., p.

[32] A. Stoller (1947) Modern Trends in British Psychiatry, *Medical Journal of Australia* 2, 26, p. 771.

[33] A. Stoller (1947) ibid.

[34] Australian Archives SA: D 2048/0, Item G1220. Stoller, report, Visit to Adelaide, February 1949.

[35] Bill Salter took a special interest in alcohol problems. He noted a breakthrough when Antabuse, a chemical that acted as an aversive stimulus when administered with a bottle of beer or stout, became available as a treatment for alcohol abuse in the late 1940s. The patient would subsequently experience severe headaches and hot flushes, thus establishing a conditioned aversion to alcohol.

[36] Repatriation General Hospital Memorandum, RGH.91, 28 May 1948.

[37] Administrative Instruction No. 60/76; G.8/4/122. Because attempted suicide was a misdemeanour, not a felony, under common law in South Australia suicide among patients raised serious legal issues for repatriation staff. The Commission decided that when a patient was admitted to an institution for treatment, and their condition might reasonably suggest that a crime had been committed, it was the duty of the officer in charge to report the matter to local police. Not mentioned in the official reports was the suicide of a senior psychiatrist and how this might have affected the morale of the unit. This was verified by a number of interviewees, including Sister Henderson who was in charge of the ward, and Dr Keith Le Page who worked as an intern and the partner of the Senior Medical Officer of the time.

Chapter 10

[1] See A. Young (1990) 'Moral conflict in a psychiatric hospital treating combat-related post-traumatic stress disorder (PTSD)' in G. Weisz (ed.), *Social Science Perspectives on Medical Ethics* Kluwer Academic Publishers, Boston; he makes a distinction between cause and explanation.

[2] See G. Mellsop, V. Duraiappah & J. Priest (1995) Psychiatric casualties in the Pacific during World War II: servicemen hospitalised in Brisbane mental hospital. *Medical Journal of Australia,* 163, 619-621.

[3] Charles, Murdoch Sound Archive Interview, April 1989.

[4] An example is the lectures by W.A. Dibden delivered at Red Cross House, Adelaide, March and June 1945.

[5] The information on 'Thomas' was derived from an interview, a questionnaire, his personal diary and his Repatriation medical file.

[6] Repatriation General Hospital assessment, 25 June 1948.

[7] Information from medical and hospital file. The 'special drug treatment' may have been what he referred to in a questionnaire as the 'Repat' taking all his nightmares away.

[8] The life story was compiled from a number of contacts and sources: several telephone contacts and interviews; a questionnaire; exchanges of letters; an interview with his daughter in August 1999; the Murdoch Sound Archive transcripts; the text of a television interview; and the medical and hospital files from the Department of Veterans Affairs. It was left to me to draw on each source and weave the information into his story.

[9] This piece of his narrative does not differ significantly over time. In the *Australian* Magazine of 1993 he described it again.

[10] Interview Jack Boland, 39th Battalion; Murdoch Sound Archive, November 1988.

[11] There is no record of this operation on Lance's medical file, but his subsequent behaviour would suggest that he had some form of brain damage.

[12] Repatriation medical file, 1962.

[13] All psychiatric treatments took place in the Repatriation facilities. Some later physical treatments were undertaken in public and private facilities.

[14] Interview with Lawrie's daughter.

[15] This story was compiled from the veteran's widow, whom he married in 1949, several interviews and letters. He and his wife separated in 1967 but had contact from then until he died. His medical file was also examined.

[16] Form 83B, 10 May 1952.

[17] Letter from Reg's wife to Repatriation Hospital, medical file, May 1952.

[18] Before the introduction of antidepressants, the stimulant methedrine was used to treat depression.

[19] Dr L. was known to have a drinking problem and his wife had a breakdown under the strain. Dr L. eventually took his own life. (Interviews with former nurse and intern.)

[20] Salter was a very religious man. He was familiar with the origins of the AA philosophy and its links with the Oxford Group and the Moral Rearmament Movement. He was listening to a radio program in Adelaide one Sunday afternoon in which Lilian Roth was interviewed and talked about AA. He believed that this was 'the Lord telling me to use the program', and soon after that he introduced the AA program into Hillcrest (personal interview, 26 June 1997).

[21] South Australian Coroner's Report H2/28145.

[22] Story compiled from two interviews, a questionnaire and telephone conversations.

[23] This event was described in the earlier account of Lawrie's life.

[24] Series of interviews with Hank's widow, 1994–95, and his Repatriation medical file.

Chapter 11

1 See D. Summerfield, The social experience of war and some issues for the humanitarian field, in P. Bracken and C. Bracken (1998) *Rethinking the Trauma of War*, Save the Children Fund, London.

2 A. McMichael (2001) *Human Frontiers, Environments and Disease*, p. xi. Professor McMichael is the Director of the National Centre for Epidemiology and Population Health, Canberra.

3 Maurice Little, questionnaire response July 1995 and letter, May 1992.

4 K. Darian-Smith, War Stories: Australian Home Front during the Second World War, in K. Darian-Smith and P. Hamilton (1993), *Memory and History in Twentieth Century Australia*, p. 137.

5 A. Kleinman (1988) *The Illness Narratives: Suffering, Healing and the Human Condition*. Basic Books, New York.

6 W.H.R. Rivers (1918) 'The repression of war experience', *Lancet*. February, 173–177.

7 Ibid.

8 Faradists used electric shock as a tool – if not a weapon – to change the behaviour of hysterical men. See R. Slobodin (1978) *W.H.R. Rivers*. New York: Columbia University Press. Rivers's role as a British psychiatrist has been popularised in the work of Booker Prize winner Pat Barker, and in the 1997 Gillies MacKinnon film *Regeneration*.

9 This was actually against the trend of psychiatry, particularly in the United States, where there was a strong revival of psychoanalytical practice in psychiatry in the civil field. This development seemed to have little influence on thinking about traumatic stress, which remained marginalised in psychiatry – see Kandel (1998) A new intellectual framework for psychiatry, *American Journal of Psychiatry*, 155, 4; 457–469.

10 C.C. Minty (1940) War Neuroses, *Medical Journal of Australia*, October, pp. 386-387. Minty was the Senior Medical Officer, Dept of Repatriation, Brisbane.

11 This contradiction was acknowledged circa World War Two by D.K. Henderson (1945) *Journal of Mental Science*, 389, XCII, pp. 667-681; and J. Bostock (1942) The place of history in war and post-war problems, *Medical Journal of Australia*, 2, 23, pp. 493–499.

[12] Sigmund Freud, 23 February 1920, Introduction to *Psychoanalysis and the War Neuroses*, pp. 214–215

[13] Even now, relatively recent movements such as Physicians for Peace and Psychologists for the Promotion of World Peace tend to function at the fringe of professional groups.

[14] W.E. Mickleburgh (1966) Psychopathology and war, *Medical Journal of Australia*, 24 December, pp. 1247–1251.

[15] Text of talk at St John's Bishopthorpe, Glebe, NSW, 2 May 1993.

[16] Ray Baldwin, interview, 1991.

[17] W. Sargant and E. Slater (1940) Acute war neuroses, *Lancet*, 6 July, pp. 1–2.

Bibliography

PRIMARY SOURCES

Archives

Australian Archives: South Australia:
Series D2048/0, Item G1516; Item G1220; Item G1353; Item G1223; Item G1550; Item G1445; Item G1002; Item G1353.
Series G2250/0, Item: SG62/4/57.

Australian Broadcasting Corporation Document Archives, *Blue Hills*, A2734.

Australian Red Cross Archives, Annual Reports, Sydney, NSW.

State Archives, South Australia: GRG 78/1; No. 2 1/1/18, *Mental Health Treatment (War) Act – 1917*, and associated correspondence.

Sgt A. Carey, 7th Battalion, 2nd Infantry Brigade, 1st AIF. Letter to Mother, Anzac Cove, Gallipoli Peninsula, 29 June 1915. Private collection.

Letter from 'Fred' to his Father, 6 September 1916, Belgium. Australian War Memorial Archives, 1DRL/582.

Primary Informants

S. Ashenden, J. Ashton, V. Austin, R. Baldwin, K. Brown, M.K. Brown, J. Burns, F. Burr, D. Cambridge, L. Clark, J. Cooper, K. Crisp, H. Dalby, C. Edwards, R. Francis, J. Hardie, A. Harrigan, L. Howson, A. Hurrell, S. Innes, O. Isaachsen, L. Jameson, R. Johns, H. Katekar, T. Kimber, P. Langsford, A. Lee, A. Little, M. Little, J. Lloyd, J. Manol, J. Mason, J. McAndrew, J. McKinna, J. Moir, R. Plater, J. Reddin, W. Russell, F. Scanlon, V. Sharrard, D. Sheppard, P. Sherwin, D. Simonson, C. Sims, A. Smith, R. Suckling, W. Tapscott, A. Thomson, T. Todd, A. Ward, N. White, C. Wilkins, C. Williams, G. Williss, P. Wright, A. Zanker.

Interviews with Family Members of Deceased Veterans

A.J. Atkinson, L. Bond, A.M. Aston, F. Burr, D. Cambridge, F. Colyer, K. Crisp, H. Dalby, R. Green, P. Langsford, H. Mattsson, W. McPherson, H. Opperman, G. Raftery, F. Scanlon, W. Tapscott, R. Underwood.

Supplementary Interviews

O. Ashenden, 2/27th Battalion; A. Bastian, 2/27th Battalion; J. Dowie, 2/43rd Battalion; D. Leech, 2/27th Battalion; C. Lofberg, 2/27th Battalion; D. Murdoch, Z Force; H. Savage, 2/27th Battalion; A. Tucker, 75th Squadron, RAAF; C. Wiseman, 2/27th Battalion; R. Wilks, 2/27th Battalion.

Medical Officers Consulted

Regimental Medical Officers:
J. Shera, J. Fairley, D. Leslie, K. Viner-Smith, D. Duffy, D. Beard.
A. Bentley, Medical Orderly, 2/6th Field Ambulance.

Psychiatrists:
H. Whitaker, A. Stoller, W.A. Dibden, W. Salter, K. Le Page, H. Southwood, W. Cramond.

Chaplains:
H. Norris; F. Dryden.

Murdoch Sound Archive Transcripts, Australian War Memorial
J. Boland, 39th Battalion; November 1988.
H. Blundell, 55th/53rd Battalion; 26 May 1989.
J. Burns, 2/27th Battalion; 29 March 1990.
H. Flannagan, 39th Battalion; 29 November 1988.
L. Howson, 39th Battalion; 5 November 1988.
H. Katekar, 2/27th Battalion; 6 March 1990.
T. King, 55th/53rd Battalion; 13 June 1989.
J. Linton, AAMWS; April 1989.
A. Lochhead, 39th Battalion; 7 December 1989.
F. McLean, 2/27th Battalion; 7 April 1990.
Bishop J. Morgan, Army Chaplain; 29 December 1989.
J. Nimmo, Red Cross; 12 December 1990.
J. Reddin, 2/27th Battalion; 31 January, 1990.
Sir W. Refshauge, Australian Army Medical Corps; 2 August 1991.
C. Sims, 2/27th Battalion; 31 January 1990.
A. Tucker, 75th Squadron RAAF; June 1989.
C. Wilkins, 55th/53rd Battalion; April 1989.

SECONDARY SOURCES

Newspapers and Journals
Smith's Weekly
Advertiser
Sunday Mail
Age (Melbourne)
Sun (Melbourne)
The Australian
The Brown and Blue Diamond; the official journal of the 2/27th Battalion AIF Ex-servicemen's Association.
The Good Guts; newsletter of the 39th Australian Infantry Battalion (1941-43) Association Incorporated.
Barbed Wire and Bamboo; Official organ of the Ex-prisoners of War Association of Australia.

Unpublished Work

Annual Report of the Inspector General of Hospitals on the Mental Hospital, Parkside; The Certified Mental Defectives. Adelaide, Government Printer.

Ambrose, B. (1987) The Plight of the POW, Hobart, self-published.

Ambrose, B. (1987) One Family's War, Hobart, self-published.

Ambrose, B. (1989) The Story Behind the Stories, Hobart, self-published.

Ashenden, Stirling, collections of poems.

Cooper, E.L. and Sinclair, J. (1942) War Neurosis at Tobruk. Internal report, Australian Infantry Forces. AWM54 48/12/120.

Dibden, A.W. (1945) The Psychological Aspects of Release and Repatriation of Prisoners of War. Address to Red Cross Society, Adelaide, June 1945.

Dibden, A.W. (1945) Psychiatric Aspects of Relief. Lecture, Red Cross House, 3 March 1945.

Edwards, Clive, Letters to parents, 1941-45; Personal collection of 230 letters.

Johns, Robert, (1990-1996) Under pseudonym John Zee; The Old Lieutenant, and a collection of unpublished short stories.

Lerner, P.F. (1996) Hysterical Men: War, Neurosis and German Mental Medicine, 1914-21. PhD thesis, Columbia University.

Raftery, G.J. (2000) Nothing New to Medical Science: the construction of war neurosis and the life course outcomes of WW2 veterans. PhD thesis, Department of Public Health, University of Adelaide.

Stoller, A. & Arscott, K. (1955) Report on The Mental Health Facilities and Needs of Australia. Melbourne, Commonwealth Department of Health.

Willis, Glen. Victory on the Kokoda Trail. Private collection, G. Willis, 2/27th Battalion.

Published Work

Audiovisual Material

Australian Army, (1990) *Kokoda – The Bloody Track.* Balmoral, NSW: Headquarters Training Command.

Department of Veterans Affairs (1990) Every Inch of the Way, Film Australia, Sydney.

Books

Adam-Smith, P. (1992) *Prisoners of War: From Gallipoli to Korea.* Viking, Melbourne.

Ahrenfeldt, R. (1958) *Psychiatry in the British Army in the Second World War.* Routledge & Kegan Paul, London.

Arieti, S. (1959) *American Handbook of Psychiatry.* Vol. 1. Basic Books, New York.

Armstrong, P. (1991) *Qualitative Strategies in Social and Educational Research: The Life History Method in Theory and Practice.* University of Hull School of Adult and Continuing Education. Newland paper No. 7

Austin, Victor (1988) *To Kokoda and Beyond. The Story of the 39th Battalion 1941–43.* Melbourne University Press, Melbourne.

Babington, A. (1997) *Shell-Shock, A History of the Changing Attitudes to War Neurosis.* Leo Cooper, London.

Barker, P. (1995) *The Ghost Road.* Viking, London. (This is the third of the trilogy with *Regeneration,* (1991) and *The Eye in the Door,* (1993).

Barrett, J. (1987) *We Were There: Australian Soldiers of World War II.* Penguin Books, Sydney.

Barter, Margaret (1994) *Far Above Battle: The Experience and Memory of Australian Soldiers at War.* Allen & Unwin, Sydney.

Bean, C.E.W. (1939) *Official History of Australia in the War 1914-18. Vol. 5; The AIF in France, 1918.* Sixth edition. Angus and Robertson, Sydney.

Bean, C.E.W. (1940) *Official History of Australia in the War 1914-18: Photographic Record.* Angus and Robertson, Sydney.

Beard, G. (1880) *A Practical Treatise on Nervous Exhaustion.* William Wood, New York.

Beaumont, Joan (1988) *Gull Force: Survival and Leadership in Captivity 1941-1945.* Allen & Unwin, Sydney.

Beaumont, J. (1996) (ed.) *Australia's War 1939-45.* Allen and Unwin, Sydney.

Bell, Peter (1996) *If Anything too Safe: The Mt Mulligan Coalmining Disaster.* James Cook University, Brisbane.

Berg, M. & Cocks, C. (1997) (eds) *Medicine and Modernity.* Cambridge University Press, Cambridge.

Berrios, G.E. Obsessional disorders during the nineteenth century: terminological and classificatory issues. In W. Bynum, R. Porter & M. Shepherd (eds) (1985) *The Anatomy of Madness.* Tavistock Publications, London.

Binneveld, H. (1997) *From Shell Shock to Combat Stress: A Comparative History of Military Psychiatry.* Amsterdam University Press, Amsterdam.

Bishop, Bert (1991) *The Hell, the Humour and the Heart Break: A Private's View of World War 1.* Kangaroo Press, Kenthurst NSW.

Bostock, J. & Jones, E. (1943) *The Nervous Soldier.* University of Queensland Press, Brisbane.

Bourke, Joanna (1999) *An Intimate History of Killing: Face-to-Face Killing in Twentieth Century Warfare.* Granta Books, London.

Bowman, M. (1997) *Individual Differences in Post-traumatic Response.* Lawrence Erlbaum Assoc., London.

Boyd, Martin (1984) *When Blackbirds Sing.* Penguin edition (First published 1962), Sydney.

Bracken, P. & Petty, C. (1998) *Rethinking the Trauma of War.* Free Association Books, London.

Brook, R. (1999) *The Stress of Combat: The Combat of Stress.* The Alpha Press, Brighton.

Brothers, C. (1957) *Early Victorian Psychiatry.* A.C. Brooks. Melbourne.

Brune, Peter (1991) *Those Ragged Bloody Heroes. From the Kokoda Trail to Gona Beach 1942.* Allen & Unwin, Sydney.

Brune, Peter (1994) *Gona's Gone! The Battle for the Beach-head 1942.* Sydney: Allen & Unwin.

Burns, John (1960) *The Brown and Blue Diamond at War.* Griffin Press, Adelaide.

Butler, A.G. (1940) *The Official History of the Australian Army Medical Services in the War of 1914-18: Vol. II: The Western Front.* Australian War Memorial, Canberra.

Butler, A.G. (1943) *The Official History of the Australian Army Medical Services in the War of 1914-18: Vol. III: Problems and Services.* Australian War Memorial, Canberra.

Bynum, W.F., Porter, R. & Shepherd, M. (eds) (1985) *The Anatomy of Madness.* Tavistock Publications, London.

Cawte, J. (1998) *The Last of the Lunatics.* Melbourne University Press, Melbourne.

Cocks, G. (1998) *Treating Mind and Body: Essays in the History of Science, Professions, and Society under Extreme Conditions.* Transaction Publications, New Brunswick.

Colp, R., Psychiatry: past and future. In H. Kaplan & B. Sadock (1995) *Comprehensive Textbook of Psychiatry/VI.* Volume 2, Sixth edition. Williams and Wilkins, Baltimore.

Craig, Arthur (1989) Battle shock, an overview, in H. Heseltine, *The Shock of Battle.* Australian Defence Force Academy, Canberra.

Creamer, M., Burgess, P., Buckingham, W. & Pattison, P. Post-trauma reactions following a multiple shooting. In J. Wilson & B. Raphael (1993), *International Handbook of Traumatic Stress Syndromes,* Plenum Press, New York.

Crocq, M., Macher, J., Barros-Beck, J., Rosenberg, S. & Duval, F. (1993) Post-traumatic stress disorder in World War II prisoners of war from Alsace-Lorraine who survived captivity in USSR. in J. Wilson & B. Raphael (eds) *International Handbook of Traumatic Stress Syndromes,* Plenum Press, New York.

Culpin, M. (1931) *Recent Advances in the Study of Neuroses.* J.A. Churchill, London.

Cushing, H. (1925) *The Life of Sir William Osler.* Clarendon Press, Oxford.

Damousi, J. (1999) *The Labour of Loss: Mourning, Memory and Wartime Bereavement in Australia.* Cambridge University Press, Cambridge.

Darian-Smith, K. & Hamilton, P. (1994) *Memory and History in Twentieth Century Australia.* Oxford University Press, Melbourne.

Dean, E.R. (1997) *Shook over Hell: Post-traumatic Stress, Vietnam, and the Civil War.* Harvard University Press,Cambridge, Massachusetts.

Dewhurst K. (1982) *Hughlings Jackson on Psychiatry.* Sandford Publications, Oxford.

Downes, I. (1999) *The New Guinea Volunteer Rifles NGVR 1939-43; A History.* Pacific Press, Broadbeach Waters.

Downing, W.H. (1998) *To the Last Ridge: The First World War Memoirs of W.H. Downing.* Duffy & Snellgrove, Sydney

Drinka, D. (1984) *The Birth of Neurosis.* Simon & Schuster, New York.

Eissler, K. (1986) *Freud as an Expert Witness: The Discussion of War Neuroses between Freud and Wagner-Jauregg.* International Universities Press, Connecticut.

Elder, G.H. & Clipp, E.C. (1988) War experiences and social ties: influences across 40 years in men's lives, in Riley, M. (ed.) *Social Change and the Life Course: Vol. 1, Social Structures and Human Lives.* Sage Publications, London.

Elder, Glen (1983) History and the life course. In D. Bertaux (ed.) *Biography and Society: The Life History Approach in the Social Sciences.* Sage publications, London.

Facey, Albert, (1981) *A Fortunate Life.* Penguin, Sydney.

Fenichel, O. (1945) *The Psychoanalytic Theory of Neurosis.* W.W. Norton, New York.

Figley, C.R. & Hamilton, H.I. (eds) (1983) *Stress and the Family. Vol. II: Coping with Catastrophe.* Brunner/Mazel, New York.

Freeman, H. & Berrios, G. (1996) *150 years of British Psychiatry.* Attica, London.

Freeman, R.R. (1991) *Hurcombe's Hungry Half Hundred.* Peacock Publications, Norwood, South Australia.

Freud, S. (1955) Introduction to psycho-analysis and the war neuroses (1919). In *The Standard Edition of the Complete Psychological Works of Sigmund Freud: Vol. XVII.* Translated and edited by J. Strachey, The Hogarth Press, London.

Frey-Wouters, E. & Laufer, R.S. (1986) *Legacy of a War.* M.E. Sharpe, New York.

Gabriel, R. (1987) *No More Heroes: Madness and Psychiatry in War.* Hill and Wang, New York.

Gammage, Bill (1974) *The Broken Years.* Penguin, Harmondsworth.

Garton, Stephen (1987) Changing minds. In A. Curthoys, A. Martin & T. Rowse (eds) *Australians from 1939.* Fairfax, Syme and Weldon Associates, Broadway, NSW.

Garton, Stephen (1996) *The Cost of War: Australians Return.* Oxford University Press, Melbourne.

Gordon, R.G., Harris N.G. & Rees, J.R. (1936) *An Introduction to Psychological Medicine.* Oxford University Press, London.

Graves, R. (1929) *Goodbye to All That.* Jonathon Cape, London.

Graves, R. (1995) *Goodbye to All That.* Ed. Richard Percival Graves. Berghahn Books, Oxford.

Grinker, R. & Spiegel, J. (1943) *War Neuroses in North Africa: The Tunisian Campaign.* United State Army Air Forces, Washington.

Grinker, R. & Spiegel, J. (1945) *Men Under Stress.* Blakiston, Philadelphia.

Guttman, E. & Thomas, E. (1946) *A Report on the Readjustment in Civilian Life of Soldiers Discharged from the Army on account of Neurosis.* HMSO, London.

Hacking, I. (1995) *Rewriting the Soul: Multiple Personality and the Sciences of Memory.* Princeton University Press, Princeton.

Hacking, I. (1998) *Mad Travellers: Reflections on the Reality of Transient Mental Illness.* University of Virginia Press, Charlottsville.

Haller, J & Haller, R. (1974) *The Physician and Sexuality in Victorian America.* University of Illinois Press, Chicago.

Hart-Davis, R. (ed.) (1999) *Siegfried Sassoon: The War Poems,* Faber and Faber, London.

Healy, D. (1993) *Images of Trauma.* Faber & Faber, London.

Henderson, D. & Gillespie, R. (1962) *Textbook on Psychiatry.* 10th edition revised by I.R. Batchelor, Oxford University, New York.

Heseltine, H. (1989) *The Shock of Battle,* Occasional Paper No. 16, Australian Defence Force Academy, Campbell, ACT.

Hill, R. (1949) *Families Under Stress: Adjustment to the Crises of War Separation and Reunion.* Greenwood Press, Connecticut.

Horowitz, M. (1986) *Stress Response Syndromes.* Jason Aronson, New York.

Horowitz, M. (1999) *Essential Papers on Post-traumatic Stress Disorder.* New York University Press, New York.

Hungerford, T. (1992) *The Ridge and the River.* Third edition, Penguin, Ringwood, Victoria.

Hurt, J. & Nettle, C. (1962) *A Survey of Psychiatric Services to Veterans in Australia and Overseas.* Repatriation Commission, Melbourne.

Hurst, A. (1940) *Medical Diseases of War.* Edward Arnold & Co., London.

Ilton, Ian H. (1995) *Australia Remembers: The Shire of Campaspe Recalls.* The Shire of Campese, Victoria.

Inglis, K.B. (1999) *Sacred Places: War Memorials in the Australian Landscape.* Melbourne University Press, Carlton.

Johnston, M. (1995) *At the Front Line: Experiences of Australian Soldiers in WW2.* Cambridge University Press, Cambridge.

Jones, Ernest (1938) *Papers on Psycho-analysis.* Bailliere, Tindall & Cox, London.

Jones, M. (1968) *Beyond the Therapeutic Community.* Yale University Press, New Haven.

Jones, M. (1968) *Social Psychiatry in Practice.* Penguin Books, Harmondsworth.

Joseph, S., Williams, R. & Yule, W. (1997) *Understanding Post-traumatic Stress: A Psychosocial Perspective on PTSD and Treatment.* John Wiley and Sons, New York.

Josselson, R. & Lieblich, A. (ed.) (1993) *The Narrative Study of Lives.* Vol. 1. Sage Publications, Newbury Park, California.

Kahana, B. (1992) Late-Life adaptation in the aftermath of extreme stress, in M. Wykle, E. Kahana & J. Kowal (eds) *Stress and Health Among the Elderly,* Springer Publishing Company, New York.

Kaplan, H.I. & Sadock, B.J. (1995) *Comprehensive Book of Psychiatry VI: Vol. 2,* 6th Edition. Williams & Wilkins, Baltimore.

Kardiner, A. (1945) *The Psychological Frontiers of Society.* Columbia University Press, New York.

Kardiner, A. & Spiegel, H. (1947) *War Stress and Neurotic Illness.* Paul Boeber, London.

King, D. & Ranck, S. (1980) *Papua New Guinea Atlas.* Robert Brown Associates & University of Papua New Guinea.

Kleber, R. & Brom, D. (1992) *Coping with Trauma: Theory, Prevention and Treatment,* Swets & Zeitlinger, Amsterdam/Lisse.

Kleber, R. Figley, C. & Gersons, B. (1995) *Beyond Trauma: Cultural and Social Dynamics.* Plenum Press, New York.

Kleinman, A. (1988) *The Illness Narratives: Suffering, Healing and the Human Condition.* Basic Books, New York.

Kleinman, A. (1995) *Writing at the Margin: Discourse between Anthropology and Medicine.* University of California Press, Berkeley.

Klerman, G.L. (1987) Psychiatric epidemiology and mental health policy. In S. Levine & A. Lilienfield (eds) *Epidemiology and Health Policy.* Tavistock Publications, London.

Kolb, L. (1943) Post-war psychiatric perspectives. In Sladen, F. (ed.) *Psychiatry and War.* Erlbaum, New York.

Kulka, R. et al. (1988) *Contractual Report of Findings from the National Vietnam Veterans Readjustment Study.* Vol. 1. Research Triangle Institute, North Carolina.

Kulka, R., Schlenger, W., Fairbank, J., Hough, R., Jordan, B., Marmar, C. & Weiss, D. (1990) *Trauma and the Vietnam War Generation: Report of findings from the National Vietnam Veterans Adjustment Study,* Brunner/Mazel, New York.

Last, P. (1994) *The Repat.* Repatriation General Hospital, Adelaide.

Laughlin, H.P. (1967) *The Neuroses.* Butterworths, Washington.

Lembcke, J. (1998) *The Spitting Image: Myth, Memory, and the Legacy of Vietnam.* New York University Press, New York.

Lerner P.F. (1997) Rationalising the therapeutic arsenal, in M. Berg & G. Cocks (eds) *Medicine and Modernity.* Cambridge University Press, Cambridge.

Levine, S. & Lilienfield, A. (1987) (eds) *Epidemiology and Health Policy.* Tavistock Publications, London.

Lifton, R.J. (1993) *The Protean Self: Human resilience in an age of fragmentation.* New York: Basic Books.

Lloyd, C. & Rees J. (1994) *The Last Shilling: A History of Repatriation in Australia.* Melbourne University Press, Melbourne.

Long, Gavin (1973) *The Six Years War.* Australian War Memorial, Canberra, ACT.

Lyons, M. (1978) *Legacy: The First Fifty Years.* Lothian, Melbourne.

McAdams, D. (1988) *Power, Intimacy and the Life Story.* Guildford Press, New York.

McAdams, D. (1996) Narrating the self in adulthood. In J. Birren (ed.) *Ageing and Biography.* Springer, New York.

McAulay, L. (1992) *To the Bitter End. The Japanese Defeat at Buna and Gona 1942–3.* Random House, Sydney.

McAulay, L. (1991) *Blood and Iron: The Battle for Kokoda 1942.* Arrow Books, Sydney.

McCalman, J. (1993) *Journeyings: The Biography of a Middle Class Generation 1920-1990,* Melbourne University Press, Melbourne.

McFarlane, A. PTSD. Synthesis of Research and Clinical Studies: The Australia Bushfire Disaster, in J. Wilson and B. Raphael (eds) (1993) *International Handbook of Traumatic Stress Syndromes,* Plenum Press, New York.

McManners, H. (1994) *The Scars of War.* Harper Collins, London.

McMichael, Tony (A.J.) (2001) *Human Frontiers, Environments and Disease,* Cambridge University Press, Cambridg, 2001.

Mann, L. (1932) *Flesh in Armour.* Reprinted 1985, Unwin Paperbacks, Sydney.

Maudsley, H. (1895) *The Pathology of Mind: A Study of its Distempers, Deformities, and Disorders.* MacMillan, London.

Merskey, H. (1996) After Shell-Shock: Aspects of Hysteria since 1922. In Freeman, H. & Berrios, E. *150 years of British Psychiatry.* Attica, London.

Miller, E. & Crichton-Miller, H. (1940) *The Neuroses of War.* MacMillan, London.

Ministry for Post-War Reconstruction (1945) *Return to Civil Life. A Handbook of*

Information for Members of the Forces on the Road Back to Civil Life. Thomas Henry Tennant, Sydney.

Minichiello, V., Aroni, R., Timewell, E. & Alexander, L. (1991) *In-depth Interviewing: Researching People*. Longman Cheshire, Melbourne.

Morris, P., Raphael, B. & Bordujenko, A. (1999) (eds) *Stress and Challenge: Health and Disease*. Repatriation Medical Authority, Brisbane.

Myers, Charles S. (1940) *Shell Shock in France, 1914-18 based on a war diary*. Cambridge University Press, Cambridge.

Nelson, H. (1985) *Prisoners of War; Australians under Nippon*. Australian Broadcasting Corporation, Sydney, Australia.

O'Keefe, Brendan (1994) *Medicine at War: Medical Aspects of Australia's Involvement in Southeast Asian Conflicts 1950 – 1972*. Allen & Unwin, Sydney.

Op den Velde, W., Flager, P., Hovens, J., de Groen, J., Lasschuit, L., Van Duijn, H. & Schouten, E. (1993) Post Traumatic Stress Disorder in Dutch Resistance Veterans from World War II, in J. Wilson & B. Raphael (eds) *International Handbook of Traumatic Stress Syndromes*, Plenum Press, New York.

Page, W.F. (ed.) (1991) *Epidemiology in Military and Veteran Populations: Proceedings of the Second Biennial Conference, March 7, 1990*. National Academy Press, Washington.

Parr, A. (1995) *Silent Casualties*. Tandem Press, Birkenhead, Wellington.

Paull, Raymond (1958) *Retreat from Kokoda*. Heineman, Melbourne.

Porter, Roy (1991) *The Faber Book of Madness*. Faber and Faber, London.

Raftery, J. & Schubert, S. (1995) *A Very Changed Man: Families of WW2 Veterans Fifty Years after War*. University of South Australia, Adelaide.

Raphael, Beverley (1984) *Anatomy of Bereavement*. Hutchinson, London.

Raphael, Beverley (1986) *When Disaster Strikes*. Century Hutchinson, Melbourne.

Read, P. (1996) *Returning to Nothing*. Cambridge University Press, Cambridge.

Rees, J.R. (1945) *The Shaping of Psychiatry by War*. W.W. Norton & Co., New York.

Reich, W.T. (ed.) (1995) *Encyclopedia of Bioethics*. Vol. 3. Revised edition. Simon & Schuster MacMillan, New York.

Reynolds, H. (1995) *Fate of a Free People*. Penguin, Ringwood.

Richardson, B. (1936*) Snow on Cholera: Being a Reprint of Two Papers by John Snow MD together with a Biographical Memoir*. The Commonwealth Fund, New York.

Richardson, F. (1978) *Fighting Spirit: A Study of Psychological Factors in War*. Leo Cooper, London.

Riley, M.W. (1988) *Social Change and the Life Course, Vol. 1. Social Structures and Human Lives*. Sage Publications, Newbury Park, California.

Rogers, K., Leydesdorff, S. & Dawson, G. (1999) *Trauma and Life Stories: International Perspectives*. Routledge, London.

Rose, N. (1989) *Governing the Soul: The Shaping of the Private Self*. Routledge, London.

Rosenwald, G.C. & Ochberg, R.L. (1992) *Storied Lives: The Cultural Politics of Self-understanding*. Yale University Press, New Haven.

Ross, T.A. (1941) *Lectures on War Neurosis.* Edward Arnold & Co., London.

Roth, S., & Friedman, M. (1997) *Childhood Trauma Remembered: A Report on the Current Scientific Knowledge Base and its Application.* International Society for Traumatic Stress Studies, Chicago.

Roy, Alec (1982) (ed.) *Hysteria.* John Wiley and Son, New York.

Salmon, Thomas. (1918) *Care and Treatment of the Mental Diseases of War Neuroses (Shell Shock) in the British army.* Report of the War Office Committee, New York.

Salmon, T. & Fenton, N. (1929) *Combat Stress Control Historical Experience Booklet 1.* The Medical Department of the United States Army, Washington, DC.

Salmond, G. & Geddes M. (1977) *The Health of Former Servicemen.* New Zealand Pensions Board, Wellington.

Sarbin, T. (1986) *Narrative Psychology: The Storied Nature of Human Conduct.* Praeger Scientific, New York.

Sargant, W. (1952) *Battle for the Mind: A Physiology of Conversion and Brainwashing.* Heinemann, London.

Sargant, W. (1984) *The Unquiet Mind.* Headingly Bros., London. Reprint of earlier edition of 1967.

Sekuless, P. & Rees, J. (1986) *Lest We Forget.* Rigby, Sydney.

Shaw, P. (1989) *Brother Digger: The Sullivans and the AIF.* Esplanade Books, Elwood, Victoria.

Shorter, E. (1992) *From Paralysis to Fatigue.* The Free Press, New York.

Shorter, E. (1997) *A History of Psychiatry.* John Wiley & Son, New York.

Showalter, E. (1985) *The Female Malady.* Virago Press, London.

Showalter, E. (1987) Rivers and Sassoon: Inscriptions of male gender anxieties, in *Behind the Lines.* In M. Higonnet, J. Jenson, S. Michel & M. Weitz (eds) Yale University Press, London.

Showalter, E. (1996) *Hystories: Hysterical Epidemics and Modern Media.* Columbia University Press, New York.

Simpson, K. (1996) Sir James Dunn and Shell Shock. In H. Cecil & P. Liddle, *Facing Armageddon: The First World War Experience.* Leo Cooper, London.

Slobodin, R. (1978) *W.H.R. Rivers.* Columbia University Press, New York.

Solomon, H. & Yakovlev, P. (1945) *Manual of Military Neuropsychiatry.* W.B. Saunders, Philadelphia.

Southborough, Lord (1922) *Report on the Committee of Inquiry into "Shell-shock".* Wyman & Sons, London.

Stone, Martin (1985) Shell shock and the psychologists. In W.F. Bynum, R. Porter & M. Shepherd, *The Anatomy of Madness.* Tavistock Publications, London.

Strouse, J. (1980) *Alice James: A Biography.* Houghton Mifflin, Boston.

Stouffer, S., Lumsdaine, A., Lumsdaine, M., Willaims, R., Smith, M.B., Janis, I., Star, S. & Cottrell, L. (1949) *The American Soldier: Combat and its aftermath Vol. II.* Princeton University Press, Princeton.

Strecker, E. & Appel, K. (1945) *Psychiatry in Modern Warfare.* MacMillan & Co., New York.

Stuart, L. & Arnold, J. (1987) *Letters Home 1939-45*. Collins, Sydney.

Summerfield, D. Addressing human response to war and atrocity: major challenges in research and practices and the limitations of western psychiatric models. In Kleber et al. (eds) (1997) *Beyond Trauma*. Plenum Press, New York.

Thomson, A. (1994) *Anzac Memories: Living with the Legend*. Oxford University Press, Melbourne.

Tipping, J. (1992) *Back on Their Feet: A History of the Commonwealth Rehabilitation Service 1941-1991*. Australian Government Publishing Service.

Trahair, R.C. (1984) *The Humanist Temper: The Life and Work of Elton Mayo*. Transaction Books, New Brunswick.

Trimble, M. (1981) *Post-traumatic Neurosis: From Railway Spine to Whiplash*. John Wiley & Sons, New York.

United States Army (1994) *Combat Stress Control in a Theatre of Operations*. Field Manual 8-51. Washington DC.

Uren, M. (1959) *A Thousand Men at War: Story of the 2/20 Battalion*. Melbourne, Allen and Unwin.

Vaillant, G. (1977) *Adaptation to Life*. Little Brown, Boston.

van der Kolk, Bessel A., McFarlane, A. & Weisarth, L. (1996) *Traumatic Stress: The Effects of Overwhelming Experience on Mind, Body and Society*. The Guildford Press, New York.

Walker, A.S. (1952) *Clinical Problems of War*. Australian War Memorial, Canberra, ACT.

Walker, A.S. (1957) *Australia in the War 1939–45: The Island Campaigns*. Australian War Memorial, Canberra, ACT.

Walker, A.S (1952) *Medical Services of the RAN and RAAF*. Australian War Memorial, Canberra, ACT.

Wilson, J.P. & Raphael, B. (eds) (1993) *International Handbook of Traumatic Stress Syndromes*. Plenum Press, New York & London.

Wilson, J.P. (1989) *Trauma, Transformation, and Healing: An Integrative Approach to Theory, Research and Post-traumatic Therapy*. Brunner/Mazel, New York.

Wilson, J.P., Harel, Z. & Kahana, B. (1988) *Human Adaptation to Extreme Stress: From Holocaust to Vietnam*. Plenum Press, New York.

World Health Organisation (1993) *The ICD-10 Classification of Mental and Behavioural Disorders: Diagnostic Criteria for Research*. World Health Organisation, Geneva.

Wykle, M., Kahana, E. & Kowal, J. (1992) (eds) *Stress and Health Among the Elderly*. Springer Publishing Company, New York.

Young, A. (1990) Moral conflict in a psychiatric hospital treating combat-related post-traumatic stress disorder (PTSD) in G. Weisz (ed.) *Social Science Perspectives on Medical Ethics*. Kluwer Academic Publishers, Boston.

Young, Allan (1995) *The Harmony of Illusions. Inventing Post Traumatic Stress Disorder*. Princeton University Press, Princeton.

ARTICLES:

Adair, M. (1997) Plato's lost theory of hysteria. *Psychoanalytic Quarterly, LXVI;* 98–106.

Archibald, H. & Tuddenham, R. (1965) Persistent stress reaction after combat. *Archives of General Psychiatry, 12,* 475–481.

Ashburner J. (1946) Psychology in the Australian Army. *Medical Journal of Australia,* 20 July; 86–92.

Askevold, F. (1976) War Sailor Syndrome. *Psychotherapy and Psychosomatics, 27,* 133–138.

Bartemeier, L.H., Kubie, L.S., Menninger, K.A., Romano, J. & Whitehorn, J.C. (1946) Combat exhaustion. *Journal of Nervous and Mental Disorders, 104;* 358–389, & 489–525.

Beal, L.B. (1995) Post-traumatic stress disorder in prisoners of war and combat veterans of the Dieppe Raid: A 50-year follow-up. *Canadian Journal of Psychiatry, 40;* 177–184.

Beaumont, Joan. (1989) Gull Force comes home: the aftermath of captivity, *Journal of the Australian War Memorial.* 43–52.

Beebe, G.W. (1975) Follow-up studies of World War II and Korean War Prisoners: II. Morbidity, disability, and maladjustments. *American Journal of Epidemiology, 101*; 400–422.

Bostock, J. (1942) Nervousness: a negligible and not pensionable disability. *Medical Journal of Australia,* 31 January; 133–135.

Bostock, J. (1942) The place of history in war and post-war problems. *Medical Journal of Australia, 2, 23;* 493–499.

Bostock, J. (1943) The problem of returned soldier organizations. *Medical Journal of Australia,* 12 June; 534–536.

Bostock, J. (1949) A psychiatric centenary. *Medical Journal of Australia,* 11 June; 763–769.

British Ministry of Pensions (1939) Neuroses in war time: memorandum for the medical profession. *British Medical Journal,* 16 December; 1199–1201.

Brooks-Gunn, J., Elder, G.H. & Phelps, E. (1991) Studying lives through time: secondary data analyses in developmental psychology. *Developmental Psychology. 27,6;* 899–910.

Burgess, I.P. (1987) Post-traumatic stress disorder in Japanese prisoners of war, *Australian and New Zealand Journal of Psychiatry, 21,2*; 248.

Campbell, A.W. (1916) Remarks on some neuroses and psychoses in war. *Medical Journal of Australia, 1*; 319–323.

Curtis, W. (1946) Pages from a military psychiatric notebook. *Medical Journal of Australia,* 20 July; 76–80.

Dane P.G. (1925) The psycho-neuroses of soldiers and their treatment. *Medical Journal of Australia,* 25 April; 427–430.

Dane, P.G. (1949) Shell shock or traumatic neurosis. *The Psychoanalytic Review, 36.* Reproduced in Australian Archives D2048/0, G1220.

Dane, P. (1949) Observations on group therapy, *Medical Journal of Australia, 2;* 127–129.

Dane, P.G. (1949) Traumatic psychoneurosis. *Medical Journal of Australia, 1*; 266–267.

Davies, S. (1997) *The long-term psychological* effects of World War Two. *The Psychologist, 10,8*; 364–367.

Davis, D. & Whitten, R. (1988) Medical and popular traditions of nerves. *Social Science and Medicine, 26, 12;* 1200–1221.

Dawson, W. (1941) Prevention of war neuroses. *Medical Journal of Australia, 2, 14;* 376–378.

Dent, O.F., Tennant, C.C. & Goulston, K.J. (1987) Precursors of depression in world war II Veterans 40 years after the war. *Journal of Nervous and Mental Disease, 175; 8*, 486–490.

Dibden, W.A. (1945) Psychiatric casualties as a repatriation problem. *Medical Journal of Australia, 1,3;* 49–57.

Eaton, W. (1946) Research on veteran's adjustment, *American Journal of Sociology, 51;* 483–487.

Editorial (1942) War Neuroses. *British Medical Journal,* 7 March; 330–331.

Elder, G.H. & Clipp, E.C. (1989) Combat experience and emotional health: impairment and resilience in later life, *Journal of Personality, 57, 2*, 311–341.

Elder, G., Gimbel, C. & Ivie, R. (1991) Turning points in military life: the case of military service and war. *Military Psychology, 3, 4;* 215–231.

Elder, G. (1997) Linking combat and physical health: the legacy of World War II in men's lives. *American Journal of Psychiatry, 154, 3;* 330–336.

Ellis, P. (1984) The origins of war neurosis: Part 1. *Journal of the Royal Naval and Medical Service, 70:* 168–177.

Ellis, P. (1985) The origins of war neurosis: Part 2. *Journal of the Royal Naval and Medical Service, 71:* 32–44.

Engdahl, B. & Eberly, R. (1994) Assessing PTSD among veterans exposed to war trauma 40–50 years ago, *NCP Clinical Quarterly, 4, 1;* 13–14.

Engdahl, B.E., Harkness, A.R., Eberly, R.E. Page, W.F. & Blielinski, J. (1993) Structural models of captivity trauma, resilience, and trauma response among former prisoners of war 20 to 40 years after release. *Social Psychiatry and Psychiatric Epidemiology, 28;* 109–115.

Fairbairn, W. (1943) The war neuroses: their nature and significance. *British Medical Journal,* 13 February; 183–186.

Fitts, C. (1942) The Effort Syndrome. *Medical Journal of Australia,* 18 July; 41–43.

Flager, P., Op den Velde, W., Hovens, J., Schouten, E., De Groen, J., & Van Duijn, H. (1992) Current Post-traumatic Stress Disorder and Cardiovascular Disease Risk Factors in Dutch Resistance Veterans from World War II, *Psychother Psychosom, 57*; 164–171.

Forsyth, D. (1915) Functional nerve disease and the shock of battle. *Lancet,* 15 December, 1399–1402.

Futterman S. & Pumpian-Mindlin E. (1951) Traumatic war neuroses five years later. *American Journal of Psychiatry. December, 108;* 401–408.

Gade, P. (1991) Military service and the life course perspective: A turning point for military personnel research. *Military Psychology, 3, 4;* 187–200.

Galbraith, D. (1946) The responsibility of the doctor in regard to rehabilitation in private and hospital practice. *Medical Journal of Australia.* 6 July; 1–8.

Galbraith, D. (1949) Rehabilitation of the disabled in Australia. *Medical Journal of Australia,* 27 August; 306–309.

Garton, S. (1994) Sound minds and healthy bodies: re-considering eugenics in Australia, 1914–1940. *Australian Historical Studies, 26, 103;* 163–181.

Gersons, B.P.R. & Carlier, I.V.R. (1992) Post-traumatic stress disorder: history of a recent concept. *British Journal of Psychiatry, 161;* 742–748.

Gillespie, R.D. (1945) War neuroses after psychological trauma. *British Medical Journal,* 12 May; 653–656.

Goldstein, G., van Kammen, W., Shelly, C., Miller, D. & van Kammen, D. (1987) Survivors of imprisonment in the Pacific theater during World War II *American Journal of Psychiatry, 144, 9;* 1210–1213.

Grinker, R.R. (1945) Psychiatric and social problems of war neuroses. *Cincinnati Journal of Medicine. 26, 6;* 241–259.

Henderson D.K. (1947) 'Experientia Docet' *Journal of Mental Science, 92, 389;* 667–681.

Hilton, C. (1997) Media triggers of post-traumatic stress disorder 50 years after the second war. *International Journal of Geriatric Psychiatry, 12;* 862–867.

Hovens, J., Falger, P., Op de Velde, W., Meijer, P., De Groen, J. & Van Duijn, H. A (1993) Self-rating scale for the assessment of post-traumatic stress disorder in Dutch Resistance veterans of World War II. *Journal of Clinical Psychology, 49,* 2; 196–203.

Hovens, J., Op den Velde, W., Falger, P., Schouten, E., De Groen, J. & Van Duijn, H. (1992) Anxiety, depression and anger in Dutch resistance veterans from World War II. *Psychother Psychosom, 57,* 172–179.

Hovens, J., Flager, P., Op den Velde, W., De Groen, J. & Van Duijn, H. (1994) Post-traumatic Stress Disorder in male and female Dutch resistance veterans of World War II in relation to trait anxiety and depression. *Psychological Reports, 74,* 275–285.

Hunt, N. (1997) Trauma of war. *The Psychologist, 10, 8;* 357–363.

Hurst, A. (1919) Hysteria in the light of the experience of war. *Lancet,* 1 November; 771–775.

Ivie, R.L., Gimbel, C. & Elder G.H. (1991) Military experience and attitudes in later life contextual influences across forty years. *Journal of Political and Military Sociology, 19,* 101–117.

Jones, M. (1942) Group psychotherapy. *British Medical Journal,* 5 September; 276–278.

Jones, M. (1946) Rehabilitation of forces neurosis patients to civilian life. *British Medical Journal,* 6 April; 533–535.

Kandel, E.R. (1998) A new intellectual framework for psychiatry. *American Journal of Psychiatry, 155,4;* 457–469.

Kidson M., Douglas J., & Holwill B. (1993) Post-traumatic stress disorder in Australian World War II veterans attending a psychiatric outpatient clinic, *Medical Journal of Australia, 158,* 563–566.

Killer, G. (1996) The health of veterans. *Medical Journal of Australia, 165,* 21 October; 413–414.

Kimberly, L., Vaillant, G., Torrey, W. & Elder, G. (1995) A 50-year prospective study of the psychological sequelae of World War II combat. *American Journal of Psychiatry, 152, 4;* 516–522.

Leslie, D. (1991) A surgeon on the Kokoda Trail, *Medical Journal of Australia, 155,* 16, 828–30.

Lewis, T. (1918) Observations on prognosis with special reference to 'irritable heart of soldiers'. *Lancet,* February 2; 181.

Love, H. (1942) Neurotic casualties in the field. *Medical Journal of Australia, August 22;* 137–143.

Macleod, A.D. (1991) Post-traumatic stress disorder in World War Two veterans. *New Zealand Medical Journal, 104,* 285–288.

Macleod, A.D. (1994) The reactivation of post-traumatic stress in later life. *Australian and New Zealand Journal of Psychiatry, 28*; 625–634.

McCarthy, C. (1946) The rehabilitation of war neurotics. *Medical Journal of Australia,* 29 June; 910–916.

McFarlane, A.C. (1988c) The aetiology of post-traumatic disorder following a natural disaster. *British Journal of Psychiatry, 152;* 116–121.

McFarlane, A.C. (1988) The longitudinal course of post-traumatic morbidity. *Journal of Nervous and Mental Disease, 176,1*; 30–39.

McFarlane, A.C. (1988) The phenomenology of post-traumatic stress disorders following a natural disaster. *Journal of Nervous and Mental Disease, 176,1;* 22–29.

Mellsop, G. Duraiappah, V. & Priest, J. (1995) Psychiatric casualties in the Pacific during World War II: servicemen hospitalised in Brisbane mental hospital. *Medical Journal of Australia, 163,4;* 619–621.

Mickleburgh, W. (1966) Psychopathology and war. *Medical Journal of Australia,* 24 December; 1247–1251.

Miller, T., Martin, W. & Spiro, K. (1989) Post-traumatic stress disorder: diagnostic and clinical issues in former prisoners of war. *Comprehensive Psychiatry, 30, 2;* 139–48.

Minogue, S.J. (1945) Suicides among returned soldiers of the 1914–18 War. *Medical Journal of Australia,* 24 February; 195–200.

Mott, F.W. (1918) War psycho-neurosis (I) Neurasthenia: the disorders and disabilities of fear. *Lancet, 1;* 127–129.

Mott, F.W. (1918) War psycho-neurosis. (II) The psychology of soldiers' dreams. *Lancet, 1;* 169–172.

Mulinder, E. (1945) Psychotic battle casualties. *British Medical Journal,* 26 May; 733.

Myers, C. (1915) A contribution to the study of shell shock. *Lancet,* 13 February; 316–320.

Myers, C. (1919) The study of shell shock: being a consideration of unsettled points needing investigation. *Lancet,* 11 January; 51–54.

Nefzger, M.D. (1970) Follow-up studies of World War II and Korean War prisoners: study plan and mortality findings. *American Journal of Epidemiology, 91,2:* 123–138.

Norris, K. (1945) the New Guinea campaign. *Medical Journal of Australia*, 15 December; 425–431.

Olfson, M. (1984). The Weir Mitchell rest cure. *The Pharos, 51;* 30–32.

Orner, R. & de Loos, W. (1997) Second World War veterans with chronic post-traumatic stress disorder. *Advances in Psychiatric Treatment, 4,* 211–218.

Parker, N. (1972) Malingering. The rehabilitation of war neurotics. *Medical Journal of Australia,* 2 December; 1308–1311.

Potts, W. (1919) Psycho-therapy in ordinary practice. *Lancet,* December 20; 1123–1128.

Rees, J.R. (1943) Three years of military psychiatry in the United Kingdom. *British Medical Journal, 1;* 1–6.

Regnell, W.R. (1919) The psycho-neuroses of war. *Medical Journal of Australia, 1, 23;* 455–460.

Rivers, W.H.R. (1918) The repression of war experience. *Lancet,* February, 173–177.

Rosenheck, R. (1886) Impact of post-traumatic stress disorder of WW II on the next generation. *The Journal of Nervous and Mental Disease, 174* June; 319–327.

Ross, D. (1946) Psychotic casualties in New Guinea, with special reference to the use of convulsive therapy in forward areas. *Medical Journal of Australia,* 15 June; 830–833.

Sargant, W. & Slater, E. (1940) Acute war neuroses. *Lancet,* 6 July; 1–2.

Sargant, W. (1942) Physical treatment of acute war neuroses: some clinical observations. *British Medical Journal,* 14 November; 574–576.

Schnurr, P. (1994) The long-term course of PTSD. *NCP Clinical Quarterly, 4,1;* 15–16.

Segal, J., Hunter, E.J. & Segal, Z. (1976) Universal consequences of captivity; stress reactions among divergent populations of prisoners of war and their families. *International Social Science Journal, 28*; 593–609.

Sinclair, A.J. (1943) Psychiatric casualties in an operational zone in New Guinea. *Medical Journal of Australia, II,* 4 December; 453–460.

Sinclair, A.J. (1944) Psychiatric aspects of the present war. *Medical Journal of Australia, 1; 28*; 501–514.

Sinclair, A.J. (1945) The psychological problems of soldiers. *Medical Journal of Australia, 2, 8;* 229–234.

Solomon, Zahava (1988) The effect of combat-related post-traumatic stress disorder on the family. *Psychiatry, 51,* 323–329.

Solomon, Z., Waysman, M., Levy, G., Fried, B., Mikulincer, M., Benbenishty, R., Florian, V. & Bleich, A. (1992) From front line to home front: A study of secondary traumatization. *Family Process. 31;* 289–302.

Speed, N., Engdahl, B., Schwartz, J. & Eberly, R. (1989) Post-traumatic stress disorder as a consequence of POW experience. *The Journal of Nervous and Mental Disease. 177, 3;* 147–153.

Springthorpe, J.W. (1903) Our metropolitan asylums. *Intercolonial Medical Journal of Australia, VIII, 3;* 109–125.

Springthorpe, J.W. (1919) War neuroses and civil practice. *Medical Journal of Australia, II, 14;* 279–284.

Stephens, H. (1946) Observations of psychoses occurring in service personnel in forward areas. *Medical Journal of Australia,* 2 February; 145–147.

Stoller, A (1947) Modern trends in British Psychiatry. *Medical Journal of Australia,* 2, 26, 965–772.

Stoller, A (1949) Social work and the ex-serviceman: The psychiatric problem, 14, May, *Medical Journal of Australia,* 639–646.

Summerfield, D. (1996) The psychological legacy of war and atrocity: The long-term and transgenerational effects and the need for a broad view. *Journal of Nervous and Mental Disease, 184, 6;* 375–377.

Summerfield, D. (1997) Legacy of war: beyond 'trauma' to the social fabric. *Lancet, 349:* 31 May; 1568.

Swank, R. & Marchant, W. (1946) Combat neuroses: development of combat exhaustion. *Archives of General Psychiatry, 55:3;* 236–247.

Tennant, C. (1987) Post-traumatic stress disorder in Japanese Prisoners of war: Reply. *Australian and New Zealand Journal of Psychiatry, 21,* 2; 249–50.

Tennant, C., Streimer, J. & Temperly, H. (1990) Memories of Vietnam: post-traumatic stress disorders in Australian veterans. *Australian and New Zealand Journal of Psychiatry, 24;* 29–36.

Thompson, S. (1997) War experience and post-traumatic stress disorder. *Psychologist, 10, 8;* 349–355.

Tredgold, R. (1948) The mental health of British Troops in the Far East. *Journal of Mental Science, April;* 351–391.

Vaillant, G. & Vaillant, C. (1990) Natural history of male psychological health, XII: A 45-year study of predictors of successful aging at 65. *American Journal of Psychiatry, 147,* 31–37.

Van Dyke, C., Zilberg, N.J. & McKinnon J.A. (1985) Post-traumatic stress disorder: A thirty-year delay in a World War II Veteran. *American Journal of Psychiatry, 14, 9;* 1070–1073.

Vincent, C., Chamberlain, K. & Long, N. (1994) Mental and physical health status in a community sample of New Zealand Vietnam war veterans. *Australian Journal of Public Health, 18*; 49–70.

Watson, P. (1987) Post-traumatic stress disorder in Australia and New Zealand: a clinical review of the consequences of inescapable horror. *Medical Journal of Australia, 147,*2 November; 443–446.

Weintraub, M. & Ruskin, P. (1999) Post-traumatic stress disorder in the elderly: a review. *Harvard Review of Psychiatry, 7, 3;* 144–152.

Whitaker, H. (1954) Group therapy: a review and report on its use in a therapeutic community. *Medical Journal of Australia, 2;* 899–904.

Whitaker, H. (1956) The management of resistance in psychotherapy. *Medical Journal of Australia, 1;* 48–50

White, Ernest (1918) Observations on shell shock and neurasthenia in the hospitals in the Western Command. *British Medical Journal,* 13 April; 421–442.

Zeiss, R. & Dickman, H. (1989) PTSD 40 years later: incidence and person-situation correlates in former POWs. *Journal of Clinical Psychology, 45,1;* 80–87.

Index

All battalions, brigades and other military units are listed under the entry 'Battalions and other military units'. Battle campaigns are listed under the individual battle names, e.g. Kokoda Trail, Gona, Sananända. Servicemen are listed under their surname, without their rank, which may have changed during the period covered by this book.

Lythrum Press Pty Ltd
1st floor, 128 Hindley Street
Adelaide
South Australia 5000

Telephone: (08) 8415 5150

www.lythrumpress.com.au